S0-BSZ-963

Tie Breaker

Jimmy Van Alen and Tennis
in the 20th Century

By
Eleanor Dwight

for George
who loved to win

The author wishes to thank all those who helped her at
the Redwood Library and Athenaeum in Newport,
particularly Lisa Long and Aimee Saunders.
She also wishes to thank Mark Stenning and Joanie Agler at
the International Tennis Hall of Fame, and the many others
who gave their time helping to find information on the subject
of Jimmy Van Alen and tennis history.

Cover and book design and layout by:
Natasha Tibbott
Our Designs, Inc., Nashville, TN

Drawing, previous spread:
Adam J. Grodin, Jimmy Van Alen VASSS cartoon, 1966
James Henry and Candace Van Alen Papers,
Redwood Library and Athenaeum, Newport, Rhode Island

Published and packaged by M.T.Train/Scala Books
Distributed by ACC Distribution, New York, NY, USA
Printed and bound in Italy by ZoneS

ISBN 978-1-905377-40-4

© Copyright 2010
The James H. and Candace Van Alen Foundation and Eleanor Dwight.
No part of this book may be reproduced without written permission.

Table of Contents

Jimmy playing court tennis

Chapter One:

The Newport Bolshevik

The stands are packed for a semi-final tennis match at Wimbledon, or maybe at Arthur Ashe Stadium at Flushing Meadows. The two players have each held service through twelve games. Suspense mounts. Spectators know that the moment of reckoning is near. At six-all—it's time for the tie breaker! The players change their playing style—the fans perk up and feel a new tenseness, now every point counts more than ever and maybe this close match will produce an upset—like when Serbian Novak Djokovic upset the invincible Swiss champion Roger Federer in Montreal in the summer of 2007, or when Spanish star Rafael Nadal couldn't clinch the tie breaker playing against Federer in the 2008 Wimbledon final but went on to win the fifth set. Or maybe it will turn out to be like that most exciting and lengthy tie breaker of all time, the twenty-two minute battle between past greats Björn Borg and John McEnroe at Wimbledon in 1980.

The tie breaker has revolutionized tennis—most notably in the form of shortened, more entertaining matches. But even when the match isn't shortened it has an effect. In the finals of Wimbledon 2008 Rafael Nadal won the first two sets, but Roger Federer captured the third and fourth sets, each in a tie breaker. Nadal could not win these tie breakers because of Federer's superior serve. But the fifth set, which by Wimbledon's rules never goes to a tie breaker, was Nadal's.

There was a time, in fact, when no set in a tennis match went to a tie breaker. Tennis scoring had been set in stone for the longest time, from the 1880s, when the fledgling racquet game was first played on green croquet lawns until the 1960s, when the sport began to change radically. With such radical social changes taking place during the sixties—from students storming and occupying the university buildings in New York, Berkeley, and Paris, the civil rights movement, and the women's movement—we rarely think about what happened to the game of tennis. But even tennis reflected the changing world. Things were being shaken up. New tennis was replacing the old, and it would take a traditional yet revolutionary man to bring some of these changes about.

Jimmy Van Alen, an activist agitating for reforms in the game of tennis, was an eccentric personality and a somewhat surprising man for the job, given his old-guard patrician background. Called the "Newport Bolshevik" by tennis writer Bud Collins for being both conservative and revolutionary, he was a tennis player himself who mixed with the top players, but later changed his focus to court tennis, Shakespeare's sport of kings, where he excelled and became a national champion three times. Court tennis, or real tennis, is the original indoor racquet sport from which modern day tennis is descended, played with competitors hitting shots off the wall. Eventually he would found the Tennis Hall of Fame at the Casino in Newport, Rhode Island—the site of the first national tennis championships—at the Gilded Age resort where his family had been prominent for generations. In Newport he was known, quite simply, as "Mr. Tennis." It is an apt title for a man who managed to live the entire tennis century, so to speak, from its American beginnings in the 1880s right through its evolution in the 1970s and onwards to the professional, high-paying celebrity sport it is today.

For Jimmy, tennis's white-shoe and wooden-racquet beginnings centered around the lawn tennis matches of Newport, Rhode Island, starting in the prosperous years before the First World War. Spending summers living his young life in the Wakehurst mansion in Newport, built by his grandfather James John Van Alen in the 1880s, Jimmy was privy to the early world of lawn tennis, a world where the well-to-do and famous families of the day would watch the games in the pleasant ambience of Newport's Casino, parasols in tow. These were the days of the "gentleman sportsman," the well-educated, wealthy player dressed in white, who played for love of the game and had no need to earn his wage. Newport, with its social milieu and prominent families—among them, the Goelets, Astors, and Vanderbilts—was the perfect setting for leisure-time activities—and so the world of amateur American lawn tennis was born.

But Jimmy had many satellite interests that orbited around his dedication to reforming the game of tennis—all characteristic parts of his eccentric personality. Robert H. Boyle, in his *Sports Illustrated* profile of Jimmy written in 1972, describes him as "driven by an almost manic spirit of *noblesse oblige*," a man who set out to "make the world a better place than he found it" by taking up not just tennis reform but "the cause of Santa Claus." Jimmy would also "put up the money to rescue the journals of James Boswell from Malahide Castle in Ireland, edit the *North American Review*, rejuvenate the Soldiers', Sailors'

and Airmen's Club in New York…collect the greater bustard and other rare Iberian birds for the American Museum of Natural History," and compose original songs and poems and play his ukulele or mandolin at formal parties. He would later try to introduce the English Robin to North America, for the simple reason that he thought the American Robin a less attractive bird. This was the meat of Jimmy Van Alen's unique personality—his unrelenting zeal for sport, his constant need for action and accomplishment, and his unstoppable creative drive. Once he identified a project, nothing would stop him from pursuing it.

Although a lifelong lover of the game of tennis, Jimmy felt the sport needed a new approach—he wanted to leave the game "better than he had found it." He recognized the need for tennis to go open—that is, to abolish the distinction between amateur and professional tournaments. He wanted to reform the traditional scoring rules, which he found to be unnecessarily confusing and alienating to spectators, fans, and even potential players. He was an early advocate for broadcasting tennis matches live on television. Jimmy Van Alen had many ideas about how to change the game, and his motive was, quite simply, what he cared most about: *fun*—as much fun for as many people as possible.

He felt the traditional rules were confusing and took the fun out of the game. From the beginning tennis players needed to win a game or a set by a margin of two points. Games are played to four points—love (zero), 15, 30, 40, and game. If the score is tied at 40-all, or "deuce," the first player to get ahead by two points wins the game. If, however, the set reaches a score of five-all, or six-five, players were forced to continue until

Mr. and Mrs. James Laurens Van Alen, on their way to tennis at the Casino (1912)

one of them won by at least a margin of two games. Before the tie breaker, matches could go on forever. Nowadays when each player has won six games, they play a tie breaker. In Jimmy's tie breaker plan at six games all players begin to play a nine point mini-game and the first to five would win the game and set.

Jimmy felt that a lead of two points to win the game and two games to win the set "is the same as requiring two runners in a mile race, if tied at the finish, to keep going until one leads by five yards." After years of dissatisfaction with the long matches and complicated scoring system, he was determined to show both the players and the spectators alike that his new scoring system was the answer. It was a subject he was knowledgeable about, as Jimmy had encountered many frustrations in regards to the traditional scoring throughout his life. From the time he was captain of the lawn tennis team at Cambridge University in the 1920s and he had to make sure his team's matches were completed at Fenners—the grass courts of Cambridge—on rainy English afternoons, to his days as president of the Casino in the 1950s, the length of tennis games was always a problem.

A revelation came to him in 1954. At the Newport Casino Invitational tournament he had watched Ham Richardson play Straight Clark in the singles final. Richardson, then an undergraduate at Tulane, was ranked third in the world and was expected to beat Clark, who was ranked thirteenth, comfortably. But the day before the Invitational, Richardson, a diabetic, had fainted from low blood sugar on the way to a party; Clark, on the other hand, was playing exceptionally well. Instead of a clean, surgical victory for Richardson, spectators suffered

through an endlessly dragged out five-set, four-hour battle. Richardson ultimately won 6–3, 9–7, 12–14, 6–8, 10–8. But meanwhile, spectators were looking forward to the doubles finals that would come next, the four best-known players in the world: Australian superstars Lew Hoad and Ken Rosewall playing against Vic Seixas and Tony Trabert, the first- and second-ranked American players. But the singles final went on and on, and the doubles match had to be moved to an outside court and played before the singles finished. Van Alen, in charge, was fuming: "I came up with the tie breaker after that match," he said. "I was determined not to deal with anything like that again." After the fiasco at Newport—the long Richardson-Clark match that exhausted the players and fans—he went to work. "Any fat head can improve on this," he told a reporter.

Jimmy dreamed up a complicated brainchild he called VASSS (Van Alen Simplified Scoring System) to change the scoring system. And the tie breaker was part of its revolutionary system. His VASSS would change the scoring of points, change the scoring of games, it would enable handicapping, it would harness the power serve, and it would shorten the length of matches by introducing the tie breaker system.

In the mid-1960s Jimmy was president of the Casino and could use it as a laboratory for his experiments, and so he staged a tournament to try out his famous VASSS at the historic tennis complex. It was years after the wonderful sports center had been the social heart of Newport. But it was still a venue suggesting historical and aesthetic grandeur and the conservative, traditional, and stylish attitudes of the old game.

A Marathon Match: Schloss/Mozur lose 3–6, 49–47, 22–20 to Leach/Dell (August 1967)

For his VASSS tournament Jimmy drew in the celebrity players and the greats who had turned pro and had not played on the likes of the Casino's grass courts for some time. At this time, the 1960s, Newport's amateur tournaments excluded pros. He sent out teasing invitations and bulletins. An announcement for the tournament declares: "The PRO VASSS Medal Play Championship to be held at the Casino will produce the greatest concentration of super-tennis ever to be presented to the public."

Jimmy's format was carefully thought out. Ten players would compete and it was great for the fans, because they would see thirty half-hour matches in a round robin form instead of only watching a handful of players compete in long matches. In the first three days each player would play four singles and four doubles matches. Like a golf tournament, the best action would be on the weekend, the four high scores in the singles and the three high-scoring doubles teams would survive the "cut" and qualify to play on the weekend.

Instead of the traditional fifteen, thirty, forty, deuce, ad scoring, the points would run from one to thirty-one—like ping-pong, but with ten more points. As he teased people to come to compete, he coaxed: "No tennis lover or junior tennis hopeful can afford to miss it. Further to this, it will demonstrate conclusively the value of the simple and accurate handicap formula, which only VASSS makes possible. It is more accurate than that of golf." Since Jimmy was "Mr. Newport" and "Mr. Tennis," everyone knew that the VASSS tournament would be an event not to miss.

After years of trying to shake things up and hounding clubs to use his scoring system, Jimmy was finally masterminding his own production, his VASSS tourney. It was pure theatre. His creativity and playfulness took over and even nature and the elements added to the show. Players and fans got to see the many aspects of Jimmy Van Alen. There was the party-loving Jimmy. There was Jimmy the intense organizer. There was the Old Newport Jimmy, the musical Jimmy, and the poet Jimmy.

"Old Newport"—the setting of the mon-eyed Newport of the Gilded Age and the Roaring Twenties—provided the glittering backdrop for Jimmy's Invitational. Matches were played at the Casino, the enormous, or-nately shingled building with tripartite Palladian windows, a large bell-shaped clock tower furnished with Tiffany & Co. works, and a grand Romanesque arched entryway. Entering the Casino, the visitor found himself in a large interior courtyard recalling a Roman Circus in its rectangular-oval shape— the famous Horseshoe Piazza. Beginning in the 1880s, players in white clothes and shoes had been batting balls with wooden racquets across the freshly manicured, white-chalked grass courts. Spectators sat under parasols in boxes and bleachers around the courts, fanning themselves from the summer heat as they turned their eyes from one player to the other. In such a setting, the iconoclastic rules of Jimmy's 1965 Newport Invitational seemed all the more enigmatic.

All involved got to enjoy Jimmy's flamboyance. On one evening of his tournament he staged a dinner on the Horseshoe Piazza where he introduced speakers, played his ukulele, and recited his own poems. The next evening everyone got to enjoy the hospitality of Newport's grand dame and Jimmy's mother, Margaret Bruguiere, at her Tudor mansion, Wakehurst, built by Jimmy's grandfather in 1884. According to Mrs. Bruguiere, Wakehurst was the only house left in Newport that was running "properly" at the time of the VASSS tournament—and by "properly," she meant with "23 servants, a greenhouse across the way providing fresh flowers daily, and 146 candles to light the dining room, since she will not tolerate electric bulbs there." Master works of painters like Rembrandt and Franz Hals were on display. A monument of Gilded Age lifestyle was opened to the public. Mrs. Bruguiere was also a tennis fan, and each summer she would show up at the Casino in her glimmering black Rolls Royce parked at courtside in its special place.

At the VASSS tournament the Newport summer fog swirled over the courts most of the time. Foghorns bellowed and the buoys on Narragansett Bay whistled. Jimmy had arranged for banks of lights so the players could play at night, which was unusual for those days, considering it wasn't until 1975 that the U.S. Open had its first night match. Jimmy had also arranged an electric scoreboard, which displayed the money won for each point.

The prize money was $10,000, no small sum in those days, and each point won earned the player five dollars, which was registered on the electric scoreboard. As a reporter covering the VASSS tourney wrote, "The pro players with their Midwest, West Coast, Australian and Latin American accents may be indifferent to the significance of the

Van Alen name and social position and call him a kook if they wish, but VASSS might eventually earn them a great deal of money. Any parvenu understands this; as Jimmy Van Alen points out, even the Newport Rotary Club knew there was a tennis tournament in town." But players weren't the only ones who could pad their pockets under VASSS rules. The profit potential from adopting Jimmy's scoring system had become even more apparent as television increased in popularity during the 1950s—shortened matches meant more predictable schedules, which would soon allow broadcasting companies to begin integrating tennis into their weekly sports lineups, and paying the players a lot more.

A sportswriter reported that "at the stroke of ten on Saturday night when the crowd was enjoying itself immensely, Chilean champion Luis Ayala lifted his racquet to serve, innocent of the knowledge that at that very moment the weekly Newport fireworks display was to start at the nearby town beach." Just as Ayala threw up the ball, the first skyrocket of the night swooped into the sky overhead. "Ayala watched it, fascinated. As it exploded with a wild crackle, he dropped racquet and balls in the Casino turf and gracefully followed them in a ballerina's swoon, as if drilled through the heart by one of Jimmy's partridge guns." Did Jimmy plan this too? The "once-staid Casino on sacred soil where this whole tennis bit got started in America eighty-four years before transformed into a mad avant-garde arena for the most revolutionary weekend in the history of tennis."

There was Jimmy, standing out as usual with his big brimmed planter's hat, Casino striped tie, beige slacks, and suede shoes, and even accompanied by his dog, a spaniel

An early match on The Casino lawn

puppy named—what else—VASSS, the only man who could "commercialize the old institution with such a radical format and get away with it." The fans loved it, and the experience of tennis became charged with a new intensity.

Jimmy's VASSS scoring system, and the addition of the tie breaker in particular, significantly altered the landscape of the matches at his Invitational. Also, because players were serving three feet behind the baseline, games no longer consisted of a series of short, protracted, serve-rush-volley games. Instead, matches tested the pros' groundstrokes, agility, and cross-court playing skills. As one player commented, "In this game, now, now you have to think a little."

Who was in this all-star group that Van Alen recruited to play in the tournament, which Bud Collins called "a giant step for tennis kind"? An international collection of greats participated. Rod Laver came to play: one of the greatest men's singles players of all time, and the only person to have twice won all four major titles in the same year. Besides Laver there was Pancho Gonzalez,

Casino Clock Tower

NEXT PAGE: *Jimmy confronting Pancho Gonzalez at 1965 VASSS Tournament*

the self-taught Los Angeles player who utterly dominated tennis during the 1950s, and Ken Rosewall from Australia, nicknamed the Doomsday Stroking Machine for his resiliency in outlasting his opponents.

The competitors had different reactions to the VASSS innovations. Laver was first doubtful, but by the time he had won his way through to the finals he was becoming more receptive to the new system: "It was tough coming onto grass after playing on hard courts, then trying to cope with the new service line and a 31-point match. It took a while to learn. The system needs a longer trial before you can make up your mind."

Although the players were critical of the scoring innovations, the fans seemed to be happy with VASSS. According to Van Alen, Newport fans are generally quiet, but they got excited during these matches. As he said,

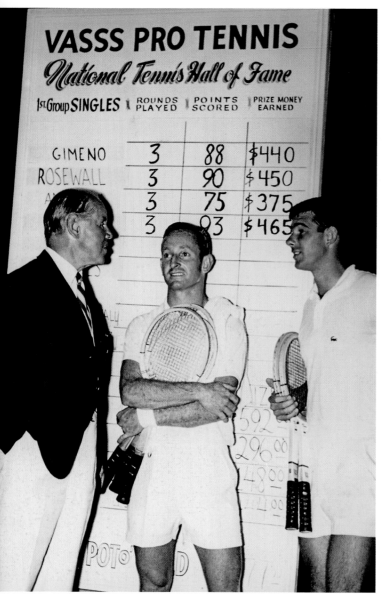

VASSS PRO TENNIS			
National Tennis Hall of Fame			
1st Group SINGLES	ROUNDS PLAYED	POINTS SCORED	PRIZE MONEY EARNED
GIMENO	3	88	$440
ROSEWALL	3	90	$450
A	3	75	$375
	3	93	$465

VASSS Pro Tennis — Jimmy with Rod Laver and Butch Buchholz

tennis player and commentator Barry MacKay said. "This might be what the forward pass was to football when it was first introduced—the game of the future."

It wasn't just for tournaments and the fans that Jimmy was doing this. He also wanted more people to play tennis. As he said, "There are 8 million people who play tennis," and he would like 80 million to play. "My ambition is to promote a healthful game that keeps people on their toes and alert." Jimmy himself confessed to running a mile every day, playing a round of golf, playing a tennis match, and swimming 200 yards— all this at the age of 62. He realized that everyone couldn't do that, but if matches were scored better, people might at least play tennis more.

Jimmy was not the only one sensing that tennis had to change. By lobbying for his VASSS innovations he was in the spirit of rebellion and reform. The professionals—most of the best players in the country—wanted to change the two-tiered system: one set of matches for pros and one set for amateurs, a big purse for pros and a small one or none for amateurs. Jimmy wanted to improve tennis, to bring it along with changing times, make it a viable vocation for players, and allow all the best players to play against one another—what the fans also wanted.

"This system is good for the spectators. For one thing, there are no marathon matches that last two or three hours. Each of our matches lasted about thirty minutes, give a few minutes more or less, and in three or four hours the onlooker could see all 10 of the world's finest players. And they see them playing all out for every point." "We might use the system in some of our tournaments next year,"

In any event he had started something that would become controversial at a time when tennis was looking for changes. Arthur Ashe, the first African American to win a title at Wimbledon, would later speak out to reporters on Jimmy's "sudden-death" tie breaker and its drama in 1970, after losing a match to John Newcombe: "They say that on Broadway it's easy to make people laugh, but much harder to make them silent. Well, in the middle of that last tie breaker game, the only sound I could hear was your typewriters. Nobody in the stands was even breathing." So Jimmy had brought a new drama and intensity to the sport of tennis with his tie breaker, one that would go on to make tennis the multimillion dollar celebrity sport it is today. But how would he get it accepted? His persistence would help and also, he hoped, his sense of humor. All his life when something important happened that caught his interest—whether it be the abdication of the Prince of Wales or Ted Kennedy's disastrous accident at Chappaquiddick—he sat down and wrote a poem. His struggle for the acceptance of VASSS was no exception.

VASSS was accepted early for intercollegiate matches

> VASSS TENNIS plays the same as LAWN
> With all the bugs removed
> It eliminates "Advantage"
> So the schedule may be grooved.
> This holds the game to seven points
> The set to six games all,
> Add Nine points for the "Tiebreak"
> Ninety-three points overall.
>
> For ninety years and more alas,
> In fact since it was born,
> The rules of lawn and common sense
> Have been at daggers drawn,
> The need to lead by two to win
> So basically unsound
> The wonder is the embryonic game got
>   off the ground.
>
> VASSS brings pure drama —
> The thrill of Sudden Death.
> Which tests the player's courage,
> Makes the gallery hold its breath.
> VASSS simplifies the scoring terms,
> Its matches start on time.
> Where LAWN's rules are ridiculous
> VASSS NO-ADS are sublime.
>
>   —J. H. V. A.

Wakehurst

Chapter Two:
A Family of Privilege

If you went to the Casino—the "cradle of American tennis"—during the 1950s or '60s when Jimmy Van Alen was president, you might have caught a glimpse of him, a nattily dressed figure in almost constant motion. The driver of a yellow Rolls Royce with a "VA" on the hood in place of the standard RR, he was a mixture of *noblesse oblige* and all-American sportsman. His short stature—outfitted in bright colors, his bald head covered with a planter's hat, he was hard to miss. You might wonder about this iconoclast who loved games, but wanted to change their rules so that everyone would have more fun—this activist for sports and physical fitness, this unique guy with the terrific drive. What sparked him to pursue what he did? And why?

To trace Jimmy's steps onto the court, it helps to trace the Van Alen family's entry onto the Newport scene and even go further back to their settling in Colonial America. Long before Jimmy was born, successful members of previous Van Alen generations—the first born in each generation all named James—had already made significant contributions to American society. They had sailed from Holland in the seventeenth century to settle in the Hudson River Valley. Jimmy's great-great-grandfather, James I. Van Alen, was the half-brother of Martin Van Buren, eighth president of the United States. Others also were involved in politics, their prominence in their communities being assured by their own initiatives and the family fortune. Eventually, as they accumulated wealth, the

Van Alens were able to spend more time in leisure activities, a situation which became evident in the construction of Wakehurst, the family seat in Newport—the site where Jimmy's playfully competitive nature was born and cultivated.

The Van Alens had been landowners in Newport since the late 1840s, long before other big moneyed families like the Vanderbilts, Astors, and Goelets, who arrived in the 1870s and '80s to build their summer "cottages"—vast structures along Bellevue Avenue or overlooking the sea, modeled after European palaces and designed by America's foremost architects. James John Van Alen built his "cottage" on land the General, his father, had bought near Ochre Point. He named it Wakehurst because he had admired Wakehurst Place, an Elizabethan country house in Sussex built in 1590, and he commissioned his architect to copy it.

Wakehurst was the setting for many impressive Van Alen rituals – like the birthday party given for Jimmy by his grandfather, James John Van Alen, when Jimmy was eight. No expense was spared to make it an extravaganza. The Tudor mansion had been built by James John Van Alen in the 1880s after the death of his wife, Emily Astor, who died while giving birth to their third child.

The eighth birthday party held from 3:30 to 6:30 p.m. on August 27, 1910 spread out over Wakehurst's vast lawn, which was studded with tents and umbrellas for the occasion. The guests arrived by fashionable pony cart and novel automobile. A large throng

Jimmy as young boy with his mother, Margaret

gathered: almost one hundred children, their nurses and maids, parents and their friends, including the best of Newport society, like the Condé Nasts, the John Nicholas Browns, the Payne Whitneys, the William Astors (Mrs. William Backhouse Astor was the birthday boy's great-grandmother), plus waiters, entertainers—and reporters. Some mothers may have been thinking of a match to try someday for their daughters.

The entertainments may have overwhelmed the children and even the grown-ups. There were games for prizes, a vaudeville show from the Freebody Park Theater, Sam Watson's Barnyard Circus with its performing animals, and Herrman the magician. The Seventh Artillery Band from Fort Adams played throughout the afternoon, a local newspaper reported.

The birthday boy, "Jimmy" to all his friends, would live a long life, never content to limit his activities to what was considered acceptable for someone enjoying family wealth with no need to work, and always looking to have fun. His grandfather James John, the host of the party, played a big role in his grandson's lively life. Celebration to him was not something saved for special occasions like birthdays, rather, it was a way of life—a view that would be a running theme through Jimmy's earlier years and onward. He loved sports, he loved organizing, and he was born into the right set to do this.

The Van Alens were rich, cosmopolitan, and sports-loving. They had good times doing things together at the large estates where they gathered. They collected art, they traveled widely, and they hunted for deer, pheasant, and grouse. A big part of the family fun was, not surprisingly, tennis. After Jimmy began to play tennis when he was five, it

soon became a constant in his life. He played tennis with his uncle Will at Tuxedo Park, a resort north of New York City where athletic events were the rage, and as a child and teenager, he played often in Newport. As a teenager he played often in the south of France where his grandfather took a house. By the time he reached Cambridge University he was good enough to make the tennis team and respected enough to be chosen its captain.

Not only did he play himself, but a characteristic that came out early in his life was to persuade everyone else to play with him. As his brother, Sammy, described it, from an early age Jimmy was not only full of fun but he was keen for others to have fun under his direction: "Jimmy taught me to catch a baseball and hit a tennis ball; and he taught me to dance; he taught me to play the mandolin; and his love of teaching never was satisfied." This urge to organize and teach could become annoying. Once Jimmy threatened to hit Sammy over the head if he didn't start playing better.

The source of the family fortune, well established by the time Jimmy came along, was the pharmaceutical and dry goods business of his great-great-grandfather, James Isaac Van Alen (1776–1870). He came down to New York City from Kinderhook, near Albany, in 1815. The company was called Chesebrough & Van Alen. It later made a successful product, Vaseline, which was marketed beginning in the 1870s and was the foundation for the Van Alen fortune.

Two Van Alen ancestors were especially important to the family. Jimmy's great-grandfather and namesake, James Henry Van Alen (1819–1886), a friend of Abraham Lincoln's, was a hero to Jimmy throughout his life. His son James John Van Alen (1846–

1923), Jimmy's grandfather, was also a big influence. Jimmy was exceptionally proud of his great-grandfather because James Henry Van Alen had used his wealth and determination to recruit and equip the 3rd New York Volunteer Cavalry and take command as its colonel during the Civil War. He was soon promoted to brigadier general and then appointed military governor of Yorktown, Virginia, after its capture. In 1862, like a few other Union commanders, he attracted attention when he anticipated the Emancipation Proclamation by issuing an order, promptly countermanded by his superiors, that all Negroes "contraband and otherwise" be allowed full liberty and receive rations. Later, he served on the staff of "Fighting Joe" Hooker, the commander of the Union army defeated in the battle of Chancellorsville. James Henry retired soon after the victory at Gettysburg. Inspired by his ancestor's heroic exploits, Jimmy wrote a poem about him called, "Pickett's Charge," which told the exciting story of the Battle of Gettysburg. It was the official poem for the nation's 1963 centennial celebration.

President Lincoln recognized James Henry's service in the army, as "valuable to the country and honorable…". Van Alen became a friend of the president and on April 3, 1865 wrote a remarkable letter warning him to "guard his life" and to avoid exposing himself "to assassination as he had by going to Richmond" on April 4, after Union troops had taken the city. On April 14, Lincoln began his reply: "My Dear Sir: I intend to adopt the advice of my friends and use due precaution…". Later that night Lincoln was assassinated.

James Henry, "the General," was the first Van Alen to come to Newport in the 1840s, long before it became "the queen of resorts."

By this time the Van Alen family wealth had been invested in New York real estate—its price steadily climbing. With their fortune thus enhanced, the Van Alens were able to establish their place in the pleasant Newport milieu. They joined wealthy Southern families who came to the New England watering place to escape the heat.

Initially, Newport had been enjoyed by "old money" families from New York City, such as the August Belmonts—Mrs. Belmont was the daughter of Commodore Matthew Perry of the U.S. Navy—the Delancy Kanes, and the occasional intellectual like Henry James, or Edith Wharton, who grew up there as a child and lived there until 1900. It was after the Civil War that families of new wealth came. By the time Jimmy's grandfather, James John Van Alen, the General's son was coming of age in the 1870s, Newport was entering its famous Gilded Age period as those with enormous new fortunes arrived.

James John created the world in which Jimmy grew up. He had become part of Newport's social whirl by marrying well and was known for his playful personality and activities, qualities which Jimmy would observe and imitate. James John died in 1923, when Jimmy was 21, and therefore Jimmy knew the eccentric *bon vivant* during Jimmy's formative years. James John had created a lifestyle of expatriate living, of sports and leisure time activities that Jimmy took part in.

Wealthy, spirited, and full of *joie de vivre*, James John considered the world his playground. As a young man, he attended Harvard for a short time. He attracted adventure everywhere he went. Like the General, he spent much of his time abroad and adopted a rather English demeanor. He had married into the Astor family in 1876, after an alterca-

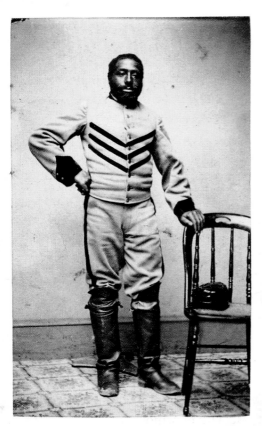

Brady.   Washington.

General Van Alen's valet by Matthew Brady

Washin

General Van Alen, Jimmy's great-grandfather,
namesake and hero, by Matthew Brady

tion between William Backhouse Astor, Jr. and James John's father, the General, during which a duel almost took place. For some reason, the Astors did not approve of James John at the time of the engagement and Mr. Astor used his influence to slander his future son-in-law. But General Van Alen, a man to be reckoned with, challenged him to a duel. Mr. Astor, who knew nothing of firearms, eventually backed down.

The marriage and the resulting children put the Van Alens at the very heart of Newport's social world. James John's mother-in-law, Caroline (Mrs.William Backhouse) Astor was the queen of Newport and New York society—her cottage, Beechwood, was the scene of gala summer parties. Marrying into the Astor family was marrying into one of the greatest, if not *the* greatest, fortune in America. Emily's great-grandfather John Jacob Astor was the richest man in America when he died in 1848. When Emily's brother, John Jacob Astor IV, went down in the Titanic in 1912 he was worth 160 million, or two billion in our dollars today.

Although the Van Alens had come to America in the seventeenth century and John Jacob Astor not until 1780, the Astors had quickly outpaced other successful moneymakers, both financially and socially. John Jacob As-

James J. Van Alen's Wakehurst

The den at Wakehurst

The hall at Wakehurst

tor was not yet an American "rabbit skinner"—that is, a fur trader—at the time James John's grandfather's half-brother, Martin Van Buren (1782–1862), was in the White House (1837–41). Still, when James John Van Alen married Emily Astor in the 1870s, the Astors were on the top of the social hierarchy and Van Alen could be said to be "marrying up."

For James John's mother-in-law, Mrs. Caroline Astor, New York City's premier hostess, society was "a religion." Her parties were always the subject of great anxiety, excitement, fervor, and plenty of headlines. As the self-proclaimed queen, she dressed accordingly. One party she wore a "massive tiara that seemed a burden upon her head, and she was further weighed down by an enormous dog collar of pearls with diamond pendant attachments. She also wore a celebrated Marie Antoinette stomacher of diamonds and a large diamond corsage ornament…She was a dozen Tiffany cases personified." Her court chamberlain dared to call her a "walking chandelier." The Astors were in the center of an exclusive society that money alone did not guarantee entreé into. The Vanderbilts, who had made their money in railroads just a mere generation after the Astors, were initially barred entry and were looked down upon by the Astors.

But Jimmy's grandfather wouldn't be in the Astor circle for long, for his wife Emily Astor, died in 1881 at the birth of their third child. James John was left a widower with three children. His father, the General, gave him a house in Newport: gave him land and a substantial sum of money, and said, "Do whatever you want with it." So in 1882 James John tore down the house and built Wakehurst, near Ochre Point, which took six years to complete.

Wakehurst, the first of the Gilded Age mansions, showed James John's flair for extravagance as well as his taste for architecture and antiques. It was modeled on Wakehurst Place, "an E-plan Elizabethan stone manor house or 'prodigy house' in Ardingly, Sussex, near Brighton, completed in 1590," which he had visited in England. The Newport mansion was furnished "with rooms he got from various houses that were being torn down in Europe." According to the family story, the den was the dining room of Lady Fitz-Herbert, George IV's morganatic wife. "The yellow room" was the first Adam room to come to this country. The dining room was Belgian, from a house that was being torn down in Bruges.

The official housewarming party for Wakehurst in 1888 was described by the local newspaper as "one of the grandest fetes ever given in Newport..." an accolade of some weight, given the scale and lavishness of the entertainments in that resort. "On the night of the party, Wakehurst shimmered in romantic candlelight—223 candles in the ballroom alone—as Van Alen preferred using the old English-style illumination to gaslights. Seen from the ocean, the diamond-paned bay windows glowed like beacons in the night."

Town Topics, known for its delight in lampooning society, had little good to say about the mansion, describing it as filled with "a cargo of sumptuous furnishings" brought back from Van Alen's European trips, purchased "with a lavish disregard for cost, and, as some of his acquaintances assert, of even good taste." But Archie Chanler, a cousin of James' wife, Emily Astor, who was welcomed there during a visit to his Astor cousins in Newport in the summer of 1888 said, it was "the handsomest house I ever was in."

Contemporary admirers noted that it was an ideal summer home, amid magnificent surroundings. The grounds were enclosed by a high massive granite wall, which hid the house itself. Beds of choice shrubs and flowers flanked the beautiful iron gate. It had its own park and garden, and wonderful trees. The layout was made to resemble an English park—with grouping of trees and the high wall giving the grounds a secluded effect. The landscaper was Ernest W. Bowditch—he included a sunken garden south of the house in addition to the plantings of trees and shrubs.

Other grand Newport "cottages" would soon follow the building of Wakehurst. It was, however, the first British extravaganza. The shingle-style mansion Ochre Point nearby, designed by McKim, Mead & White for Robert Goelet, after the success of the Casino, had been built earlier than Wakehurst, between 1882 to 1883. Ogden Goelet, his brother, completed his house Ochre Court, a Richard Morris Hunt French Gothic design, in 1892. The Vanderbilts were also building—Cornelius Vanderbilt II and his family moved into the Breakers, modeled after Renaissance palaces in Turin and Genoa, in 1895, and Marble House, a white marble mansion in the French style, had been ready for his brother William and his wife, Alvah, three years before, in 1892.

After his wife's death, James John attracted notice wherever he went with his boisterous style and great wealth. Eventually he was chosen for the appointment of ambassador to Rome. But one prominent newspaper campaigned against him when he refused an interview, calling him fat, ignorant, a slob, and so on. As a result, Van Alen refused the embassy appointment, even though the Pres-

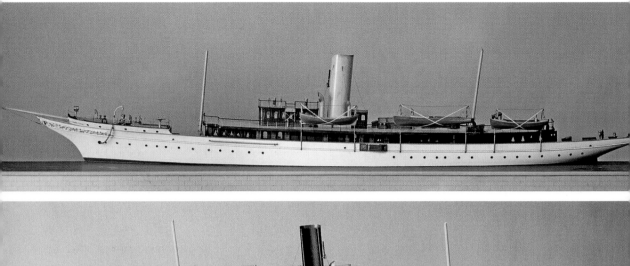

Model of the yacht Vanadis in which James John Van Alen,
Jimmy's grandfather, cruised with Edith Wharton in 1888

ident personally asked him to reconsider. A rumor circulated that if he took the post, "he undoubtedly would have bought the Coliseum and turned it into an athletic club for his friends." In a letter to his mother, Edith Whartons's friend architect Ogden Codman mentions that Teddy Wharton was rumored to be Van Alen's choice of a secretary if he took the Rome post.

Acting on his appetite for experiencing life, Van Alen embarked on a cruise of the Mediterranean with his good friend Edith Wharton and her husband, Teddy, in 1888. During these times most in proper society wouldn't dare to travel the Mediterranean seas, as they were notorious for brigands who looted boats and murdered travelers. But Wharton, also attracted to

the excitement of a new adventure, could not say no.

Van Alen, as adventurous as always, planned an extravagant itinerary for the three of them. Wharton was captivated. For the sake of propriety, the Whartons insisted on paying half the expense, a share that turned out to be equal to their estimated income for the year, from Edith's trust and Teddy's allowance. Edith's much older brothers and her mother and Teddy's father delivered their condemnation in chorus: Mediterranean cruises were a "fad for the wealthy" like James Van Alen. But Edith remembers a wonderful moment: "But my husband said, 'Do you really want to go?' And when I nodded, he rejoined, 'All right. Come along then.' And we went."

The cruise began in Algiers and ended in Ancona, Italy, and covered a lot of the Eastern Mediterranean. The travelers stopped at Malta, in Sicily at Syracuse, Messina, Taormina, Palermo, and Agrigento, then went on to the Cyclades, Rhodes, Smyrna on the Asia Minor coast, Mount Athos, Athens, and the Ionian Islands, and the Dalmatian coast, Spalato (Split), Ragusa (Dubrovnik), and Cattaro.

They traveled in the grand Van Alen style. Wharton described their luxurious yacht: The *Vanadis* was an impressive steam-yacht over 167 feet long and weighing 333 tons. On deck there was a pleasant deck house, with seats along the sides, and a table. Below there was a large saloon, and one of the two tables was used to dine at, the other for writing, reading, and looking at maps. Aft of the saloon were the Wharton's two state rooms, occupying the full width of the yacht, and comfortably "fitted with shelves, drawers, hanging closets and large bath tubs." Forward were the rooms for James Van Alen plus "two rooms for the maid and valet, and a fourth in which they took their meals." The boat had 16 in crew—"the captain and mate, two engineers, two firemen, the boatswain, five able seamen, two stewards and two cooks" and Wharton also brought along her lady's maid and Teddy and James John, their valets.

Jimmy had a sense of the lavish lifestyle of the past while visiting Newport and staying at Wakehurst, with its beautiful stained glass windows through which the light streamed, its dark paneled walls, its many artifacts, and its Old World atmosphere. It was the magical place of Jimmy's boyhood, a house as impressive as the European counterparts his grandfather owned or rented—such as Rushton Hall, his house in the English countryside, and his hunting lodge in Scotland. It became one of the important backgrounds of Jimmy's childhood. It remained in the family until 1968, and later was the setting for many gatherings of impressed tennis players who were invited to experience its Gilded Age ambience.

The creation of the house attests to James John's imagination and great energy. He probably spent more time on building and collecting for the house and on his travels to acquire its furnishings than he did seeing his three motherless children, James Laurens, Jimmy's father, and James Laurens' two sisters, Mary, known as May (1876–1959), and Sarah, known as Sally (1881–1963). The children lived in England and traveled around Europe like poor little rich orphans taken care of by governesses and tutors. As James John grew older, however, he liked being surrounded by his children and grandchildren and became more of a family man.

For Jimmy, occasions with his grandfather were full of festivities and expatriate adventure. With the passage of the Eighteenth Amendment in early 1919 and the onset of Prohibition, James John announced his plans to leave the United States for good. He decided to resettle in England saying, "If the Empire can be run by 100,000 whiskey-drinking Englishmen, then England is good enough for me." In December of 1919, a month before Prohibition took effect in the United States, he sold his four-story house at 15 East 61st Street in New York, claiming that he was only one of many "who will leave the United States and make their home in countries where the laws are not so strict." Although he continued to summer in Newport, Europe became his home. Because of Jimmy's grandfather's love of Europe, Jimmy and his brother, William,

["Whitehall Gazette" Copyright
(Painted from Life)]

"ANTI-PROHIBITION."

*James John Van Alen, Jimmy's grandfather left
the country with the passage of the Eighteenth
Amendment in early 1919*

OPPOSITE: *Margaret Post Van Alen*

always called Sammy, and his sister, Louise or Lulu, were very much a part of their grandfather's travels during his long life—he died in 1923.

Besides his houses in Newport and New York, James John owned a large country estate, Rushton, in England where the family gathered. Rushton was often featured in society columns. In a story run by The *New York Times* in 1909 entitled, "J.J. Van Alen Has Big Shooting Party," he is described as entertaining his guests "on a princely scale" and organizing shooting that was "most successful." The guests identified were the Duke of Manchester, the Marquess of Douro, and other titled princes, princesses, and countesses. The article notes how Van Alen was spending "great sums of money" to decorate his seat of entertainment, including 900 pounds to a dealer for a particular Adams fireplace that would suit the style of a room. It goes on to say: "the gardens are very fine, and the conservatories are among the best in England, and the house is full of beautiful things," for which "their present owner is said to have paid fancy prices." Jimmy and his family were entertained there as well.

While Jimmy witnessed his grandfather's exuberant life, he and Sammy remembered their father, James Laurens Van Alen, as more reserved. He had attended school at Eton, was very quiet, and in poor health. When Sammy was in his eighties he collected his memories in a memoir called *Sammy's Book*. As he remembered, his father "had bad eyes and he had to give up reading for two years, so he did not go to college." Fluent in French, he translated from French to English for Colonel Edward M. House, an American diplomat and foreign policy advisor to Woodrow Wilson, during the First World War. He preferred Europe, and never felt at home in the States. Sammy described his father as an unhappy person whose mere upbringing perhaps spoiled him for every day life. "He didn't understand that people went to work every day. People didn't go to work where he'd come from in Europe. He wanted to buy a chateau in France, Azay-le-Rideau, and live there, but he was talked out of it by the family. Perhaps if he had been able to live in the environment in which he was brought up, he would have been happy."

In 1900, at age twenty-one, James Laurens married Jimmy's mother, Margaret Post, nicknamed "Daisy," a young beauty from New York City and Rhode Island. She, too, had lived in Newport as a girl and was a good friend of Consuelo Vanderbilt, later Duchess of Marlborough. The newlyweds promptly moved into their house on 40 East 50th Street. Each year, after returning from Europe, James, Daisy, and later, their three children, Sammy, Jimmy, and Lulu, would leave their city house and take a private train embarking from Grand Cen-

Jimmy sailing to Europe with his mother

Jimmy on board the Aquitainia with mother, father, Sammy, & Louise

tral Station, heading for Newport, where they would summer either at Rosetta, the Bellevue Avenue cottage of their mother's family, or at Wakehurst, their grandfather's mansion. The upper-crust milieu of Newport during this time was captured in a poem Jimmy wrote on the occasion of his mother's ninetieth birthday. Beginning "Dear friends," it goes on to describe Daisy's deep roots in Newport's high society, the same high society in which Jimmy was raised:

> She's not keen on
> viewing her lady
> guests' knees,
> So at "Wakehurst" they'd
> better be careful,
> Or they'll find that she's
> not above speaking
> her mind
> If she thinks that their
> limbs are too bareful.
>
> She alone can remember
> the eighties and nineties
> With concerts and balls at
> the brand new Casino,
> Where 'debs' all long-
> skirted coquetted
> and flirted
> And no one had heard of
> Las Vegas or Reno.
>
> And ladies wore stockings when going
> in bathing
> And coaches and fours toured the drive
> by the ocean
> And the triflingest phrase from the
> queen of those days,
> Mrs. Astor, would bring on a social
> commotion.

> Her link with the past is the Newport
> Casino
> At noon where she strolled to the
> orchestra's strains
> And then in the cool of the soft summer
> evening
> She polka'd and waltzed to the latest refrains.

James Laurens Van Alen, Jimmy's father

The Van Alens were typical of the rich Americans who travelled in Europe often in the early years of the century. Until the age of twenty-six, Jimmy lived half of his life in Great Britain and France. He, too, was fluent in French and all his life he felt he had a cosmopolitan point of view that was valuable. He also considered himself to "have an understanding of English and French psychology." Later he would travel twice around the world, twice around South America, make two expeditions to Spain for the Museum of Natural History, visit many different countries to promote his tennis scoring system, including Greece, Australia, and South Africa, and maintain homes in Spain, and St. Croix in the Caribbean, as well as New York City, Newport, and Long Island.

Jimmy's first trip to Europe was in March 1903, when he was six months old. The family stayed at Claridge's in London and spent June at Folkestone. By September they were in Paris and again in April the next year, by June in England and back in Newport at Ro-

Van Alen Family at the hunting lodge in Scotland

setta, his mother's family house, for the summer. In October 1904 they were at Uncle Fred Vanderbilt's house at Hyde Park.

The pattern was somewhat predictable if peripatetic, including winter stays at the Van Alen house at 40 East 50th Street in New York City. The house, near Saint Patrick's Cathedral at Fifth and Madison Avenues, had been given to his mother as a wedding present by her "Uncle Fred" Vanderbilt, the husband of Daisy's Aunt Louise. Jimmy, therefore, grew up in the lavish transcontinental atmosphere of the rich during America's Gilded Age: Europe in the early spring—Paris and the south of France or Normandy—and in November and winter months back at the 50th Street house, the summer either at Wakehurst or Rosetta. These early memories included his parents' "yearly pilgrimage to Paris where the ladies bought dresses at Worth while the gentlemen went to the races at Longchamps with a get-together for pre-dinner libation at the Travelers Club on the left side of the Champs-Élysées."

Another early expatriate episode featured him and his father in transit: When he was three years old one Atlantic crossing ended with him and his nurse Lizzie Cooper spending "eight long enough hours" in a ship's tender off the coast of England. "I was all attired in frills and laces with an ostrich plume in my hat." Jimmy was fortunate enough not to get seasick. His father, on the other hand, was not as fortunate. He had long grown accustomed to drinking champagne to fend off *mal de mer*, but "ship's tenders in those days were definitely long on beer and short on the rarer refreshments."

In Europe the boys' grandfather, James John, created wonderful opportunities for his grandchildren's outdoor fun. Each fam-

Hunting in Scotland

ily place was maintained by a large staff of servants, butlers, maids, and manservants who also played a part in the children's lives. At the enormous hunting lodge Kindrogan House in Enochdhu, Scotland, the servants not only served the family but joined the children in their sports. As Sammy remembers: "We had a soccer team at the house in Scotland. Some of the servants were pretty good soccer players. John the valet was a good soccer player. A footman, Charles, was a good soccer player. Gowing was goalkeeper and he was not very good. We played against the village and then, we took them back and fed them whiskey and stuff." Following the post-game celebration, the village players "were spread all about the countryside. The policeman fell off his bicycle into the ditch and was there all night."

Jimmy's outgoing and dominating personality, his always wanting to lead others in sports and wanting to win and have fun doing it, comes out in stories of his boyhood at the different family estates. They also show his great love of the outdoors. He expresses a fondness towards the stalkers—the men who aided in the deer hunts in Scotland—saying that he enjoyed going out on hunts with them, and later cited them as an influence on his musical development.

Sammy described one brotherly adventure from their youth: "One day at my grandfather's rented shooting estate in Scotland, Kindrogan, the gamekeeper told us if we got up before daybreak we could go rabbit shooting while all the rabbits were out. So out we went. The rabbits had beaten us to it. We got one rabbit. That's all. And then, when the gamekeeper wasn't looking, we

(Front row) Daisy Post and friends from left to right: Daisy Post, May Goelet, Edith Gray, Marion Fish, Consuelo Vanderbilt, Josephine Brooks, Lily Oelrichs; (back row) Harry Havemeyer, Willie Vanderbilt, Bertie Goelet, Cyril Hatch, Charlie Oelrichs, Harold Vanderbilt

Three Generations of Van Alens

shot two pheasants that flew across in front of us, although they were completely out of season. And we upset the man terribly."

"The pheasant was reserved for grandfather. In the off-season you didn't say it was a pheasant. So this dish was offered to grandfather and he took some on his plate and tasted it and he said to the butler, 'Gowing, What is it?' Gowing said, 'It's bird, sir.'"

" 'What do you mean bird?' "

" 'It's bird, sir.' "

" 'What is it?' "

" 'It's bird, sir.' "

"That's all he could get out of the man. He didn't want to admit that we shot pheasants in the middle of August."

Sporting events were always a chance for Jimmy to develop new friendships. He had

Jimmy, his parents, Lulu, and Sammy

nice relationships with the family help, with teammates on the tennis team at Cambridge and with others with whom he organized events like tournaments and hunts.

As Jimmy's father wasn't a big tennis player, Jimmy was coached by others. In 1907, when he was almost five, his younger brother, Sammy, was born, and Jimmy was dispatched to Tuxedo Park to stay with his uncle Will Post, his mother's brother, who was an ardent bat and ball player. A barrier was put up in one of the passages of the club in Tuxedo and he hit his first tennis ball. As Sammy said later, "He never looked back. Tennis was, from then on, his game."

Uncle Will, his mother's brother, was an important influence when Jimmy was growing up. Will Post was an example to

Jimmy in many ways. He was a good tennis player, he enjoyed music, singing, acting in plays, and giving toasts. Many of his toasts—like those Jimmy would give later, were so lengthy that the eyes of guests began to glaze over. Jimmy had taught himself to play the piano like Uncle Will, playing only chords at first. Then, as he told his nephew Bill Van Alen years later, "After I took typing lessons I learned how to play notes!" The songs and poems that Jimmy sang or recited were of his own composing. He loved to be the center of attention and he did so by regaling the assembled company with his amusing compositions.

Tuxedo Park, where Jimmy visited his uncle, was a more natural setting than Newport. With everything from tennis

Jimmy Van Alen as a teenager

When Jimmy was learning to play in the first decade of the century, Teddy Roosevelt, then president and larger-than-life sportsman, was a big tennis enthusiast. He saw the sport as a gentleman's game. He was against professional sports and said "when money comes in at the gate, the game goes out the window." He built the first tennis court on the presidential grounds, and played there with his close friends, who came to be known as his "tennis cabinet." Roosevelt felt that indulging in demanding sports was a way of "cultivating a vigor of mind and character."

Jimmy's tennis debut was during the era of Bill Larned, who won the championships seven times and was number one in the country eight times. In 1907 the racquets used would be almost unrecognizable now; the attire would be equally out of date: long white flannels for male players were de rigeur, and women wore lengthy dresses.

Tennis had started in America as a "gentleman's game" and it continued as an elite sport. In the years between the wars, however, it soon became a sport for everyone as youngsters in cities and towns all over America began hitting on the courts in parks and public places.

Early on, Jimmy developed an aggressive style. According to his brother, Sammy, "He was asked to play with the older people when he was about twelve and he did." But in what became a hallmark of his game, "he dropped the ball a little bit short on a lady and when the lady rushed up and scooped the ball back, he tried to hit her with it." His game later in his life was called "cerebral." His serve was not extra powerful, but bounced high. He thought about his strategy and was good at placing and slicing the ball.

courts and golf courses to a toboggan run and bridle trails, Tuxedo was the preeminent spot for the well-off who preferred to be closer to New York City. Pierre Lorillard, formerly of Newport, created the woodland retreat in eight months between 1885 and 1886. Moneyed New York families built large comfortable houses and enjoyed a less formal atmosphere. (Here the short evening jacket was first worn when gentlemen dined amongst themselves or with ladies in the country. This dinner jacket, which replaced white tie and tails, was called, therefore, the "Tuxedo.") Many families, like the Posts, the Kanes, and others, frequented both Newport and Tuxedo.

Will Post or Uncle Billy who taught Jimmy how to play tennis and the mandolin

Jimmy playing tennis as a young man

Also typical of Jimmy from the start was organizing games that overwhelmed his partners or opponents. Their sister, Lulu, had memories of Jimmy's single-mindedness. Later on he entered her as his partner in the handicap mixed doubles tournament on the Riviera. She didn't want to play, but, felt she had no choice. In the first round their opponents turned out to be a formidable pair: a Spanish lady champion, Lili de Alvarez (seeded No. 2 at Wimbledon in 1927–28), with the King of Sweden as her partner. Lulu remembered "Jimmy said to me, 'this is an easy game. Alvarez is the champion. But you lob over the king's head, she'll chase it back and I'll put it away.' So we began and I was horrified that I would hit the poor old thing's teeth. He was standing quite straight at the net. Of course I hit everything out. It went from bad to worse. I kept hitting into the net. I was terrified that I'd hurt his teeth. It ended at four double faults, mine."

Jimmy could be a great tease in addition to being a good athlete. Sammy later recalled his older brother's enthusiasm for pranks and games, which included locking Sammy in the tower of one of their enormous houses: "He never knew when to stop," said Sammy. And this was true of his personality—he was known for his constant lobbying for his tennis causes, his long-winded toasts at parties, and his over-the-top enthusiasm for everything from establishing the English robin in the United States to pulling out his ukulele and breaking into songs of his own composing. Later on, at Newport dinner parties, a host might hide Jimmy's ukelele in the closet to forestall any performance.

The family were early participants in tennis play at the Casino, although his grandfather had a tennis court at Wakehurst. Sammy remembered that at Newport's Casino in those days, there were "twenty-two grass courts as well as six clay courts... and in the afternoon the children were allowed to go down there when they were old enough to play tennis." The Casino, designed by McKim, Mead & White and built in 1880, was located on Bellevue Avenue, the handsome tree-lined thoroughfare that stretched from the town's historical center toward the sea. It would become the most successful play place of Newport for generations to come. By the time Sammy and Jimmy traded groundstrokes on the immaculate green grass, the Casino was famous as the site of the first lawn tennis national championships. In 1915, after 35 years, the championship tournaments were moved to Forest Hills, Queens.

The year before, the Van Alen family stopped their energetic European traveling and returned to America. The children had been attending school in England—Jimmy

Mother & Father before the Bristol Hotel, Paris

at Ascham St. Vincent's at Meads in Eastbourne — and spending vacations in France. Although they felt at home on both sides of the Atlantic, Sammy recalled that before the family returned each spring he would practice his "American accent" so that he would not be teased. In the summer of 1914 they were at the Grand Hotel Vichy in France and they sailed July 28th. The war started that August, just before Jimmy's twelfth birthday, transforming Europe and sending most well-off American travelers home.

His father, James Laurens Van Alen, loved cars. In Paris he had become one of the earliest automobiliers. During the war he donated an ambulance to the French army and a patrol boat to the U.S. Navy. He expected to command it, but due to his poor eyesight, he was unable to pass the physical.

Now back in the States, Jimmy went to a number of American schools. He was at St. George's in Newport in the fall of 1915 and then at the Lake Placid School in upstate New York from 1916–19. Sammy recalled that the Lake Placid School asked Jimmy to leave in 1919, when he tried to take over the school. "Jimmy had organized a group to counter the authority of the school." As Sammy remembered, "Jimmy was not a very good influence on the school. He hated it and did everything in his power to upset the headmaster. He whistled when he wasn't supposed to. Finally, he got kicked out." It was typical of what would be his later style. When the authorities were running things in a way he disliked, he was there to tell them how to make reforms and do things his way. This strategy of Jimmy's reforms—his wish to be the authority himself and to do things his way—was not always popular, but it would be a key element in his exuberant personality.

A carte postale of Jimmy and his father enjoying a mock plane trip

Jimmy and friends in the south of France in the Rose Parade

H.C.A. Gaunt *Kings*   E. Reed *Trinity*   H.K. Lester *Jesus*

R.G. MacInnes *Trinity*   J.M. Hack *Peterhouse*   J.W. Van Alen *Christs*   J.J. Dezard *Trin Hall*   D.K. Putnam *Trin Hall*

Cambridge University Tennis Team, 1924

Chapter Three:
Cambridge

In August of 1925 a New York paper reported an unexpected upset: "A native son of Newport furnished the main thrill of the second day's play in the Newport invitational tennis tournament." A surprise feature at the tournament was James H. Van Alen, "English Oxford-Cambridge tennis star," who maneuvered "the most startling upset of the tourney to date" by eliminating George M. Lott Jr., number nine in the national rankings. Lott was "outsteadied by his English rival. Van Alen got everything that Lott pushed over the net and frequently slipped over a neat placement." Lott was the best tennis player Jimmy ever beat in a tournament.

At the same time, the family drew notice in other ways: The *New York World* reported that "the dance given this evening by Mrs. J. Laurens Van Alen, [Jimmy's mother], at Wakehurst, attended by many of the tennis players in the annual invitation tournament at the Casino and a number of the younger set, was the principal entertainment in the colony." The Tudor mansion was set aglow as its large ballroom was lit up by candles.

Jimmy had perfected his tennis game at Cambridge University. After the War, he had gone to Harvard for a year and then to Cambridge, where he became a resident of Christ's College, which, when Jimmy was a student, was one of its twenty-two colleges. He may have hated Lake Placid School but his feelings about Cambridge would be entirely different. It was there he made a place for himself and was successful in what he cared about. As he liked to say later, at Cambridge he "took a first in tennis...I was a full blue," a special achievement comparable but even more prestigious than a varsity letter in the States. It meant he had played at the highest level of competition, like on a varsity team here, and had competed against Oxford. (For this achievement, players were awarded a light blue jacket, hence the designation "full blue.") At Cambridge he won the singles and doubles championships and was the first American ever to captain a major sport there. His tennis game had become outstanding—he was a member of the lawn tennis club and the Marguerites. The Marguerites Club was one of the oldest surviving societies in Christ's College, founded in the late nineteenth century and made up of distinguished student athletes. It claimed to represent something more than just athletic distinction.

His marks were mediocre: he read history for two years, receiving Third-class honours (or "a Third") each year, the lowest honors degree classification for an undergraduate at Cambridge. During his third year he switched to law, receiving another Third. He learned, however, in other ways. He admired the values at Cambridge and Oxford and became aware of his talents. Later, he was to write that before he was captain of the university tennis team where he ran all the varsity tennis tournaments, he was "just one more sheep following along the same old path, my eye on the tail of the sheep in front of me who had its eye on the tail of the sheep in front." In 1924 there were 127 entries

It's the taxi from the station
Chugging past Saint Mary's Church
With your trunk tied insecurely,
Swaying wildly on the top–
Bulging, full to overflowing
And you fear at every lurch,
The frazzled rope has had it
And is surely going to pop.

Cambridge by James Van Alen, drawings by W.R. Dalzell

on eight grass courts and "the rain tumbling down." There was always the "threat of a match turning into an uncontrollable marathon…" At Cambridge he got the idea of shortening matches. It was not only that he conceived this idea that would lead to his tie breaker, but also that he began to see himself as someone who could break from the line of sheep. Jimmy stayed at Cambridge for four years instead of leaving after three so he could be captain of the team one more year.

He wrote later that Cambridge and Oxford had a code of honor and behavior which defined the actions of the students both on the playing fields and off. He objected to a piece in the Tattler on undergraduate life at Cambridge that made the university seem "an overgrown Café de la Paix with a wine shop attached." "It makes one thankful for the fresh air of the playing fields of public schools and colleges and healthful athletic competition between Cambridge and Oxford in which victory depends on strong legs, lungs and hearts, rather than an elastic belly and a hollow leg."

He was attending one of the great universities of England, just after the First World War, when England's empire still extended over the world. Christ's had been founded in the 1430s and was originally named God's House. It moved to its present site in 1448 and was renamed Christ's in 1505 when Margaret Beaufort, Duchess of Richmond and mother of Henry the Seventh, endowed and expanded the college. Christ's had many illustrious graduates, including Charles Darwin and John Milton. It was housed in Tudor buildings, which might have reminded Jimmy of his grandfather's mansion, Wakehurst, where the light streamed through its stained glass windows in a similar way. He

became a member of the Hawks Club, a club composed of jocks and a particularly special honor reserved for those excelling on the top teams. And this was at a university where sports meant success—whether it be in rowing or rugby or cricket. And at Cambridge, lawn tennis was an important sport.

In a poem twenty pages long entitled "Cambridge," written thirty years later and published privately at his own expense, Jimmy vividly recalled the details of his Cambridge experience. The first verse begins with his arrival at Christ's—taking a taxi from the station, chugging past St. Mary's Church, with his trunk, his mandolin and ukulele tied insecurely, "swinging wildly on the top." He was certain that his overflowing, bulging trunk was going to pop the ropes that tied it.

After being greeted by the porter at the great gate of Christ's, Jimmy met his tutor and had his first encounter with his "gyp," slang for "domestic servant." He immediately noticed how far away the baths were from his rooms and the fortitude in winter months needed to make the trip. Once inside the gate at Christ's he'd find himself in the First Court, with its buildings of students' rooms surrounding the yard. Beyond stretched the lovely gardens with the famous tree where the Marguerites historically held one of their important rituals. Each year during May week the President of the Marguerites would climb the very old tree in the court and make a speech.

For Jimmy there was a lot to recall at Cambridge: his success at sports, the parties, May Week, the games, the boat races on the River Cam. But there were "hollow feelings," too, and "pangs." He felt the "hollow feeling" when hungry—"craving for ham and eggs

It's the welcome from the porter
In his lodge beside the gate,

It's the Sunday morning kipper
With its rich familiar smell,

It's the College crests and colours
Of the blazers caps and ties

It's Fenners' emerald solitaire,
Rose cut, in cinder setting

It's the pang you felt on hearing
That a pal upon your stair,

It's the River Cam meandering
Past the wall of Queens' to King's,

The Prentice Cup — Harvard-Yale v. Oxford-Cambridge, NEXT PAGE: *J.H. Van Alen Cambridge Captain,* FOLLOWING PAGE: *Jimmy playing doubles at Cambridge International Club*

for tea," for "your inner youth needs stoking like a furnace constantly, and rowing, squash or rugger makes the need felt worst of all." There was the "creepy hunted feeling when you slink back late at night," without your cap and gown and hoping the proctor will not see you. There were the hangovers when your breakfast guest arrives for Sunday morning kipper "looking anything but well, from a birthday celebration sparked by something more than beer." There were the friends with tripos troubles who must "go down" earlier than they wanted. And he himself, never an outstanding student, would look at the first questions on an exam

of Caesar, French or algebra and know that he could "only hope to squeak through by the most astounding fluke."

And then there were Rugger Night and Boat Race Night and Spring on the River Cam, with all its delights. And lawn tennis, which he organized, being the captain of the team, on "Fenners' emerald solitaire" [the lawn tennis courts] where you heard "the ping of ball on racquet on the Vars'ty courts" and the matches were so engrossing "that you find yourself forgetting exams and buttry bills."

A stanza from Jimmy's Cambridge poem identifies the likely source of his lifelong urge to put initials, particularly his own, on

The Universal Game.

Lawn-Tennis Notes and Sketches by
H. F. Crowther-Smith.

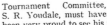

I SUPPOSE one can follow Bill Shakespeare's lead and say that all the lawn-tennis world's a stage, and all the men and women merely players. Certainly they have their exits and their entrances, though not quite in that order, for it is necessary to enter for a tournament before you can get knocked out. At least that is how I understand it. The entry comes first and the exit afterwards. And if leaving out the infant age, and still keeping in view the idea that all the lawn-tennis world's a stage—we inquire why the schoolboy is whining, we shall probably be told that the poor lad is smarting under the fact that the headmasters of our public schools are not in favour of the game. Perhaps that is why at the end of the holidays he creeps like snail unwillingly to school.

However, thanks to the enterprise of the Queen's Club officials, there are no whining schoolboys during the summer holidays. For the sixth time in succession the lawn-tennis tournament specially arranged for them has proved a boon and a blessing to hundreds of boys. At the time of writing there seems little doubt that H. W. Austin (Repton), the holder of the open singles, will again carry off the cup.

H.W. AUSTIN, (Repton).
Winner of SCHOOLBOYS' competition

He is, of course, the brother of Joan Austin, famous for her success in doubles in partnership with Evelyn Colyer. Young Austin is certainly a player of great promise. In this schoolboys' competition he stands out as the winner of it as certainly as "Little Bill" Johnston did (head and shoulders) above the rest of the competitors in the Wimbledon Championships last year. I understand that, on leaving school, Austin will be favourably situated, from a business point of view, to be able to keep up his lawn-tennis.

Turning from the actual schoolboy, let us pause for a while to consider the doings of the more advanced type of youth *in statu pupillari*—the undergraduate. Here we have genuine cause for rejoicing and congratulations. For we find that the combined talent of Oxford and Cambridge—that strange mingling of the Dark *Half* Blues and the Light *Full* Blues—has triumphed

K. Plaffman, Capt. HARVARD

over the united strength of Yale and Harvard Universities.

This was the fourth of these inter-university contests, and the first time that we have succeeded in beating the Americans. A. S. Watt, the Oxford captain, distinguished himself at Wimbledon by taking a love set from Washburn in the fourth round. He was expected to beat W. Ingraham, but, after leading him 4—1 in the final set, he lost the next five games. A fine performance on the part of the Harvard man, and one in which an exceedingly fast service played no small part. Van Alen, the Cambridge captain, beat K. Plaffman, of Harvard, 6—3, 6—2. He was at the top of his form. C. H. Kingsley, Oxford, was rather disappointing in his match against Arnold Jones. After winning the first set, 7—5 (in which he was led 5—3), the next two sets went to America's undergraduate, 6—2, 6—4. Kingsley recently won the Scottish lawn-tennis championship at Edinburgh — an honour held in the two previous years by the South African, P. D. B. Spence. The final result of the contest was a win for our universities by fifteen matches to six. Van Alen and "Lizzie" Lezard (this sounds like a mixed double, but, of course, it wasn't) really put the seal on our success when they defeated Arnold Jones and Ingraham in the doubles.

The European section of the Davis Cup competition was, as everyone expected, won by France. The brilliant array of French talent will now be shipped across the Atlantic to America. There they will meet Australia, and the winners of this round challenge America, the holders. Mexico were able to put up no sort of adequate opposition to the Australians. They lost both singles; and the Patterson and O'Hara Wood partnership in the doubles was far too powerful for Borbolla and Gerdes, who were beaten in three straight sets, 6—4, 6—4, 6—0.

Bournemouth brought a very successful meeting to a close in real summer weather. That energetic member of the

D. S. MILFORD, (Rugby).
Runner-up in the SCHOOLBOYS' COMPETITION.

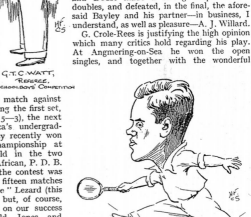

G.T.C. WATT, REFEREE, SCHOOLBOYS' COMPETITION

J. H. van ALEN, the CAMBRIDGE Captain.

Tournament Committee, S. R. Youdale, must have been very proud to see his fellow-countryman, J. M. Bayley, winning the open singles, which carries with it the Hampshire championship. It was Bayley who caused such a sensation at Wimbledon by defeating Randolph Lycett in the second round of the championship.

Here, at Bournemouth, his opponent was that experienced New Zealander—a master of courtcraft—F. M. B. Fisher. Fisher has often been in the final of this event. He won it in 1919, 1921, and 1922. Last year Brane Hillyard deprived him of the title; and now Bayley—by reason of his youth and quickness on his feet — proved too much for Fisher. The latter's brain was moving fast enough; but the physical side of him could not carry out the cleverly conceived tactics. Bayley won 6—4, 6—3. Eames and Doust made a strong couple in the doubles, and defeated, in the final, the aforesaid Bayley and his partner—in business, I understand, as well as pleasure—A. J. Willard.

G. Crole-Rees is justifying the high opinion which many critics hold regarding his play. At Angmering-on-Sea he won the open singles, and together with the wonderful veteran, M. J. G. Ritchie, also carried off the men's doubles.

Another player who has achieved considerable success lately is A. C. Belgrave. He was "runner-up" in the recent Hurlingham Club grass court tournament, making "Flaneur" go all the way in a five-set match. Since then he has won the open singles at Sandown, where Sir G. A. Thomas was defeated in the final, after playing all five sets—the last of which ran into eighteen games. Miss Ryan had a great time at this meeting, winning all three events.

What a tremendous number of tournaments there are at this time of year! Nearly a dozen every week. The great seaside Wimbledon will very soon be coming along—that is, of course, Eastbourne.

After that the hard court comes into general use again. When will the grass surface be abolished as being utterly impracticable? The last few weeks have surely hastened its end. Certainly there is an increasing expression of the hope that—in the words of Gordon Lowe— "grass courts in a few years' time will have departed into the limbo of the past."

All the Sports of Interest to You are fully illustrated and described in the "Illustrated Sporting and Dramatic News" each week. So are all the amusing Theatrical Events.

everything—on his Rolls Royce, shirts, ties, and everything VASSS-related:

It's the college crests and colours
Of the blazer caps and ties
Of the Clubs, the centers of the world
Of games and sports and talk
Which as the term wears on,
   unconsciously
You start to recognize
Crusaders, Lions, Leander
And the emblematic Hawk.

The Hawks were the athletes. Jimmy would always take pride in being a member, recognized for his lawn tennis skill. The end of his poem suggests the unquenchable optimism Jimmy, at age 22, still feels about his own future and at the same time his fondness for what he experienced as an undergraduate there:

It's your picture on the Senate steps
In gown, white tie and tails,
An undergrad no longer
Your degree held in your hand.
You had no way then of telling
Which way fate would tip the scales,
The future still unshadowed,
All the world a promised land....

To Cambridge days then Cantabs rise
And lift your glasses high,
Whenever and wherever
By design or chance you meet,
Though you live to be a hundred
Years or more, until you die,
None will ever be more precious
None will ever be more sweet.

Cambridge would be a pivotal experience in Jimmy's life. After his second marriage he chose to return there with his wife, Candy Alig, for their honeymoon—called their "wedding trip"—and each year after they came back to visit.

In the summer of 1921 Jimmy Van Alen had joined the combined Oxford and Cambridge lawn tennis team that was first invited to America to compete with a combined team from Harvard and Yale. They played matches at Princeton and the Westside Club in Forest Hills. The visit was sponsored by the U.S. Lawn Tennis Association. The English players were given "private" hospitality from USLTA members, and President of the USLTA, Julian Myrick, gave a dinner in New York. These matches were the beginning of many intercollegiate British–American matches Jimmy would take part in.

A different kind of tournament between Oxford-Cambridge and Harvard-Yale began later that year, and Jimmy was one of the first Cambridge players to compete. The international tennis tournament pitting the two combined teams against each other is known today as the Prentice Cup, the first international intercollegiate tennis event ever held, and at present, one of the very last bastions of truly amateur tennis played on an international scale. The inspiration for the Prentice Cup came from a similar competition—a track meet—between the combined teams of Oxford-Cambridge and Harvard-Yale in 1899. In both competitions, the idea was to hold a sporting event pitting the two oldest universities in England against two of the oldest universities in the United States. The site of the competition alternated between England and the United States. In England, matches were held at the All England Lawn Tennis and Croquet Club, which also plays host to the Wimbledon tournament. When it was America's turn to hold the tournament, the teams competed at the Newport Casino.

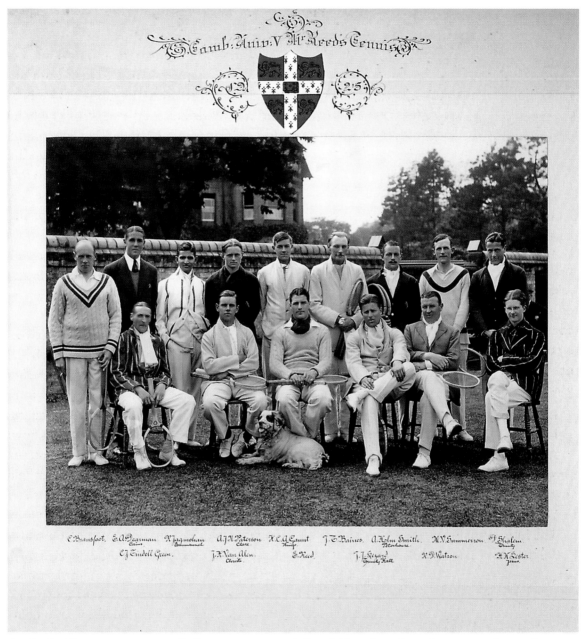

Cambridge University vs. Mr. Reed's Tennis, 1925. Jimmy's friend Edward Reed put the team together to play against the Cambridge University team, which was captained by Jimmy.

The Casino continued to host the Prentice Cup until 1952, when J. Upshur Moorhead, chairman of the Prentice Cup Committee and a former player, had the competition transferred to the Seabright Lawn Tennis and Cricket Club in Rumson, New Jersey.

Jimmy sharply disagreed with the move, and a heated argument broke out between them.

Jimmy had already played for Oxford-Cambridge once—in 1922 at Eastbourne—when Prentice donated the trophy, making Jimmy one of the earliest competitors in the

Prentice Cup on either side of the Atlantic. He played doubles with R. B. Barbour from Oxford, and as a sports writer recorded: "Van Alen and Barbour can never have shaped better individually than in this match," and "Van Alen was always stimulating to watch, and in doubles he did many fine things." But as Jimmy said of the matches that year, "I made the team in 1922 by the skin of my teeth, but the less said about the outcome the better for my compatriots against whom we were battling gave us a sound beating."

He played again in 1924 at Eastbourne and then at Newport in 1925, "an historic year in the annals of Harvard-Yale and Oxford-Cambridge tennis, as it was the first time the Prentice Cup was placed in competition." It was an historic year for Jimmy as well, as it was the first year that players from all four universities wore the special blazer, sweater, and tie designed by Jimmy for the tournament. As captain of the Cambridge team, Jimmy was "largely responsible for the organization [of the matches] and in the course of my duties I thought how nice it would be to have a blazer and a tie to commemorate playing in the match," a typical Jimmy idea. They blended the logos of a number of his favorite sports venues. "So that's how the Maroon blazer, the pocket of which I'm happy to say I designed, came to be." The tie used a maroon background which also stands for Harvard and a light blue strip for Cambridge and thinner dark ones for Oxford and Yale. The width of the stripes followed the lines of the Hawks Club, Cambridge's great athletic club. Jimmy also generously offered instructions for those who wished to "avail themselves the privilege" of purchasing their own blazer. "It was my one contribution to the Prentice Cup and it always makes me feel happy when I see someone wear the colors."

Jimmy faired well in the last Prentice Cup matches of his tennis career. In 1925, he and Lezard, his doubles partner, were both undefeated in their respective singles matches. An intense and heated competition lasting for three days was finally decided on July 18, when Harvard-Yale reclaimed the title of champion from Oxford-Cambridge by an overall score of 11 to 10.

Should the Prentice Cup tournament and trophy have been transferred to Seabright from Newport's Casino? Seabright, after all, prides itself on being one of the first tennis clubs in America, having opened in 1877. The first tennis matches at Seabright were held in the spring of 1877, when the new equipment from England arrived. Then came the attractive shingle-style clubhouse, a great spread of grass courts, and beginning in 1879, the annual club championship tournament. An invitational tournament began five years later, in 1884, and continues to this day. Whenever the club put on a tennis tournament, the wealthy community pitched in with evening entertainment, houses opened for the players, and young members of the club manning the lines and acting as ball boys.

The club also boasted a roster of famous players who had competed in the famous invitational tournament, including members of the Davis Cup teams of Spain, France, England, Australia, Canada, Mexico, South Africa, Japan, and—before it became a U.S. state—Hawaii. Some of these players included Olympic gold medalist Lawrence Doherty of England, Australian Championships winner Gordon Lowe, and Manuel Alonso of Spain, the World No. 2 ranked player in 1929.

Seabright clearly had the reputation to host the Prentice Cup. But there was a better reason, Moorhead argued, that Seabright should play host for America. The Prentice Cup received its name from Bernon S. Prentice, a former Harvard tennis captain (class of 1905) and then-chairman of the U.S. Lawn Tennis Association's International Intercollegiate Committee, who donated the tournament trophy that became known as the Prentice Cup in 1924. Prentice had been the president of the Seabright Lawn Tennis and Cricket Club from 1922 to 1938. For Moorhead, it was only right that the tournament should be played at the Club that Prentice himself had belonged to. Although Moorhead was successful in transferring the tournament location, Prentice, who died in 1948, did not live to see the matches played there.

Jimmy said later that being the first American to captain a major sport at Cambridge "went down well with some, not so good with others." In *Granta*, the Cambridge publication, a profile sees Jimmy as the "diminutive person," who could be seen "bustling up Jesus Lane in voluminous gray flannels with a small white hound trailing behind." Jimmy, it added, was "a considerable personage who shines in any society," and that at college he "learned to perfection the various lessons his tutors had to teach him, of which not the least important was the perfect manipulation of all stringed instruments from ukuleles down to real tennis racquets," and concluding that "...if America has any more James Henrys, let's have 'em—they go down over here!"

While at Cambridge, Jimmy met Edward Reed, a fellow student and member of the Cambridge lawn tennis team. Their friendship would blossom at the university, and the two would share an almost sacred love of the sporting lifestyle and all it embodied. This love of sport later developed into a lifelong camaraderie.

Reed was a popular student and loved parties almost as much as Jimmy did. Reed's son, Gavin, comments that his father "was always looking for fun" and was "always keen on having a good time. That's why I'm sure, with Jimmy's help, they had a wonderful time." Like Jimmy, Reed was a "good leader" and "always a very good organizer" at Cambridge, and they both played on many of the sports teams. They even traveled to the south of France together to play tennis, and were beautifully entertained there.

As their friendship strengthened even outside of school and the team, the two men would often go hunting and deer stalking together in Scotland, and Reed kept very detailed diaries of these experiences up in the Scottish highlands. Deer stalking, which differs from deer hunting in that no hounds are used to track the deer, refers to the stealth tracking and shooting of wild deer on foot. Stalking usually occurs around a large country estate where the hunters and their guests stay for a few days or weeks. As the word "stalking" suggests, this type of hunting requires extreme caution and wariness on the part of the stalker so as to not scare the deer away. Usually a guide—called a "gillie" or "ghillie"—who is more familiar with the terrain is hired to locate the deer's dwelling, where shooting is easier. In England and Scotland, deer stalking is often an initiation into masculinity, with the entrance into manhood corresponding to the shooting of one's first stag. Gavin Reed, Edward Reed's son, recalls how his father was pleased when he shot his first stag.

An excerpt from Edward Reed's hunting diaries, dated October 1, 1937, gives an idea

Jimmy at Cambridge graduation

of how careful the deer stalker must be during the hunt. As Reed writes, "Immediately below us were four stags and a few hinds—only one of the stags was any use, he a fair 10-pointer with cups but no great length or strength of horn. A few other beasts were waiting here and there so we decided to lunch on the ridge and try to locate them…" After having lunch, Reed and Jimmy "had nothing better than the 10-pointer down below so we commenced a long and careful crawl from rock to rock generally in full view. Eventually we managed to get down and walked along till 150 yards from the stag, which was out of sight. Presently, however, he came round a rock and offered an awkward shot as he was half-concealed by a large stone, which I feared to hit. The shot was just behind the heart and he stood for

some time with his back turned before rolling over apparently dead. I took my camera and went forward and was just about to take a picture when he rolled over and staggered to his feet. The poor beast could barely move and gave two steps before he fell again for the last time."

Jimmy's verses about Scotland and the hunting expeditions are notable for their emotional investment and appreciation of the landscape. Jimmy took hunting seriously, and he loved the location as well as the details of the wildlife. In the poem "Scotland, My Scotland," he captures the scene:

> The Highlands, the wildlands, where
> ptarmigan nestle
> Close to the rocks on the edge of the
> snow,
> Where the eagle is monarch and soars
> in the heavens
> Receivin' his subjects the stag and the
> doe.
> …
> Dear Scotland, the land of the miniature
> mountain,
> The purplin' valley, the burblin' stream
> Of the pipes, kilt and tartan, clans, reels
> and sweet ballads,
> Wherever I be 'tis of these that I dream.

As World War II approaches Edward Reed's diaries take on a more foreboding tone, as both Reed and Jimmy, who are hunting together years after leaving Cambridge, sense that their world will never be the same. One of the passages reads: "Over the weekend the international situation, which all along had lowered over us, assumed even more threatening an aspect. So on Monday we set out for our day's stalking feeling that well it may prove our last and that 'ere many

Stalking at Culachy—a highland pony being loaded up with a stag, 1929

a days had passed we might be the hunted listening to the crack of bullets." The next diary entry reads, starkly: "Sept. '39—War broke out."

While at Cambridge in the 1920s Jimmy's annual allowance was 400 English pounds or about $2000 at that time—nearly $25,000 in 2010 USD—and this was meant to support him, his valet, and his dog Tim. Unlike most students he brought a servant with him. The allowance was raised to 2000 pounds (over $150,000 in 2010 USD), when he reached twenty-one. Jimmy's formidable allowance placed him high in the ranks of moneyed university students at Cambridge, particularly in the post-war years.

Jimmy himself recalled that at Cambridge, "I really couldn't live a life of luxury with the money I had, but, if I could get over to Cannes during the holiday, where my parents and grandparents had places, then I was living." "It was wonderful there," he said, "with some really great people playing tennis...the King of Sweden, people like that. And a lot of pretty girls. Oh, I was quite the thing—if I could get there, that is. It was, I think, the last pleasant era of playing tennis." His tennis was good and he was getting notice in the French press when he played in the south of France and back in the States, when he played at Newport.

Early in Jimmy's Cambridge years, in the winter of 1920-21, the Van Alen family lived in Cannes, renting a beautifully remodeled house next door to the Church of England. Facing Nice, it was perched up on a hill near the city's edge and sported such modern accoutrements as a tennis court, put in at the request of Jimmy's father.

The south of France was a particularly good place for a tennis player to visit during the early 1920s. Tennis champions from around the world came to tournaments in Marseille, Cannes, and Nice to showcase their skills. One of them was Bill Tilden, who won both the U.S. Championships and Wimbledon by the spring of 1921. France's Suzanne Lenglen, who won 31 Grand Slam titles between 1914 and 1926, was also playing during that time in matches all over the Riviera, and practicing constantly at the Nice Tennis Club. Her flamboyant prima donna personality had made her an overnight sensation—particularly after 1919, when she vanquished seven-time champion Dorothea Douglass Chambers in the final match at Wimbledon. While other women were wearing dresses that covered everything save face and hands, Lenglen was turning scandalized heads by playing in short-sleeve dresses cut above the calf. The French press, which nicknamed her *La Divine* ("The Goddess" in the Anglophone press), helped to make her the first female celebrity athlete.

Tilden and Lenglen had an intense and often bitter rivalry. Both were celebrity athletes at home and abroad: while Lengen's "audiences invariably included kings, rajahs, and international tycoons, Tilden always attracted the queens of Broadway and Hollywood." Neither could stand feeling ousted from the limelight by the other—a frequent occurrence, as both were in their prime during the 1920s. Interestingly enough, the rivalry began in France right around the time Jimmy began taking summer vacations there. On May 27, 1921 Tilden and Lenglen were honored guests at the same lunch in Saint-Cloud (on the outskirts of Paris) where, after "all the speeches and the hilarity, [Lenglen] allowed herself to be drawn into a one-set challenge in singles with Tilden." Tilden, not to be upstaged by anyone, especially a woman, easily beat Lenglen 6–0 the following day. When asked about the results in her dressing room, however, Lenglen simply shrugged and coyly replied, "Someone won 6–0, but I don't recall who it was."

Suzanne Lenglen was more upset than she led the press to believe. Not one to take such a defeat lying down, Lenglen challenged Tilden and his partner, Arnold Jones, to a doubles match the following day. She and her partner, Max Decugis, an eight-time French champion, realized how embarrassed Tilden would be if he and his partner lost to a mixed-doubles team. And embarrassed they were—Lenglen and Decugis beat Tilden and Jones with a single-set, 6–4 victory. The fierce rivalry between Tilden and Lenglen that would last for years had begun.

Jimmy's tennis playing in France in the early '20s was featured in an article from *Le Miroir Des Sports* of 1922. Jimmy is in the third and final photo in a triptych featuring Swiss champion Aeschliman on the left, and none other than Suzanne Lenglen in—where else—the center. Underneath Jimmy's photo, the caption reads: *"Le jeune Americain Van Alen s'est révélé comme un champion de l'avenir"* (literally, "The young American Van Alen revealed himself as a future champion").

Suzanne Lenglen playing in the South of France, 1921

This phase of Jimmy's life ended in the 1920s. He graduated from Cambridge in 1924, a year after his grandfather's death. Uncle Fred and Aunt Lulu Vanderbilt, Daisy's aunt and uncle, came to stay with the family in Cannes, where, upon their arrival, they took up the task of dividing up James John's possessions. His many cars were driven back to Paris in an entourage comprised of maids, chauffeurs, valets, family, and "four Rolls Royces, a large Renault and an open car." Sammy recalls talks of the trip from his father's valet, "...John, who could be fairly risqué, telling us about all the prostitution areas of various towns which they passed such as Avignon."

Not everyone was notified of James John's death in 1923. When he was in London he stayed at the Cavendish Hotel, which was, as Sammy recalled, "where mostly single men were apt to stay in London, my grandfather among them. As most people know, Rosa Lewis was a very famous mistress of a prominent person who gave her the Cavendish. She had started as a kitchen maid in a royal household somewhere and was a very amusing woman."

She had remodeled her hotel in 1901—the first year of the reign of Edward VII—in the style of the country houses in which she was accustomed to cooking. Fashionable and attractive, it offered suites that had a club feeling with their own dining rooms—even

1922

LE TOURNOI INTERNATIONAL DE TENNIS DE CANNES

UN REVERS DU SUISSE AESCHLIMAN — UN DRIVE ATHLÉTIQUE DE SUZANNE LENGLEN — L'AMÉRICAIN VAN ALEN EN ACTION

Le tournoi international de tennis de Cannes a réuni quelques-unes des meilleures raquettes d'Europe et d'Amérique. Le Suisse Aeschliman, en compagnie de l'Anglais Fisher, a gagné sur Morgan-Watson la finale du double messieurs par 4-6, 10-8, 6-4 et 6-4. Mlle Lenglen, avec Fisher pour partenaire, a enlevé la finale du double mixte sur Mrs Sattherwaite-Hillyard, par 6-1 et 6-0. C'est assez dire que notre championne a retrouvé sa forme. Il est dommage que Mlle Lenglen ait cru devoir s'abstenir, pour raison de santé, de l'épreuve de simple dames, qui a opposé, en finale, l'Irlandaise Mrs Sattherwaite à l'Américaine Miss Ryan. Le jeune Américain Van Alen s'est révélé comme un champion de l'avenir.

"L'Americain Van Alen en action"

---

one (probably seldom used) for the king. As one historian put it, "Rosa's circle had always been decadent and now her hotel had become the flagship for the fashionable but racey." It was definitely a place where the well-off could enjoy their sexual adventures.

"After Grandfather died, the funeral service was almost directly across the street from the Cavendish at St. James. Mother kept the whole thing out of the papers somehow because there was no notice anywhere. Mother didn't want Rosa Lewis and all her girls at the funeral. And, of course, they would have come."

A few years later when Sammy was at Cambridge, he went to the Cavendish and met Rosa Lewis. She said, 'Van Alen, Van Alen, huh. Any relation to Jimmy Van Alen, my friend Jimmy Van Alen?' And I said, 'Yes, he was my grandfather.' She said, 'You know, the damndest thing, he died, and we never even knew it. We didn't find out for a week. So, we called him 'Dead-a-week Van Alen.'"

Four years later, in 1927, James Laurens died at the Ritz in Paris. Although Jimmy was more in tune with his grandfather's interests than his father's, he was a very affectionate son. In one of his poems, a child is in awe of his father:

Why can't I be like father, Lord
Shoulders broad, strong of limb
With the look in his eye of eagles, Lord,
Why can't I be the spit of him.

After his father's death Jimmy wrote of "family ties and family bonds," and expressed the significance of losing his father when he was a young man as the loss of a guide or mentor:

My dear father knew and understood
   these things
As few others ever have,
And it is our loss, for all time,
That he was taken away
While still a young man,
And we, unready to take on
The full weight of the cloak of maturity.

One wonders if Jimmy was thinking of his own father's welfare later when he wrote the sequel to Clement Moore's "A Visit from Saint Nicholas," which makes sure the father in the poem is tucked in safe and sound in bed on Christmas Eve.

With James Laurens' death the next generation came into great amounts of money. The wealth was partly Van Alen money from the family business and wise investing over the years, and partly money inherited through family connections to the Astors and later, the Vanderbilts. Since Jimmy's grandfather, James John, had married Emily Astor, daughter of William Backhouse Astor, Jr. and Caroline, as a result, James John's three children—Jimmy's father, James Laurens, and his two sisters, Mary and Sarah—were beneficiaries under the will of their maternal grandfather, Astor, who died in 1892. A codicil to Astor's will left New York City real property worth exactly $466,667—over $10 million in 2010 USD—to each of the grandchildren. Now, at James Laurens' death in 1927, Jimmy, Sammy, and Lulu inherited their father's share of both the Astor money and James John's fortune, which, according

to Jimmy, was worth somewhere around $23 million dollars—over $270 million in 2010 USD (the papers said between 15 and 20 million). As Sammy said: "Father died at the Ritz Hotel in Paris. After he died, I was rich. I had my own horse at Cambridge and a beautiful new automobile, a LaSalle. Eventually Jimmy and I had polo ponies."

A share of the Vanderbilt fortune would later be provided to the Van Alens by Frederick William Vanderbilt, who had been married to Daisy's Aunt Louise. He would die in 1938. Frederick Vanderbilt (born in 1856) was the son of William Henry Vanderbilt, grandson of the Commodore and brother to George Washington Vanderbilt, Cornelius II, and William Kissam who, like Frederick, built enormous mansions.

After two charities, the Sheffield Scientific School at Yale and Vanderbilt University, Frederick's will made Margaret "a niece of my wife," and her sons the principal beneficiaries. Margaret was left immensely valuable real property: his house at 1025 Fifth Avenue, eight lots in mid-Manhattan, and "my estate at Hyde Park." Hyde Park was Vanderbilt's enormous white-columned house overlooking the Hudson River, designed by McKim, Mead & White. After the death of her husband, James Laurens, Jimmy's mother, Daisy, had made herself Frederick's companion and caretaker. She often went to Hyde Park, where she had her own bedroom. He wanted to marry her but she declined and remained Mrs. Van Alen until she married Louis Bruguiere in 1948. Jimmy and Sammy were each left 2.5% of his residuary estate, plus 25% to them on Margaret's death, after a lifetime trust for her benefit. His estate was valued at $78 million in 1938—over $1 billion in 2010 USD. Frederick's wife, Louise, had died in 1926 and her will left half of her estate to Margaret's sons [Jimmy and Sammy] after Margaret's death. Sister Lulu, however, was left out. It was speculated in gossip columns that Frederick did not approve of Lulu's two marriages to brothers, each a self-proclaimed Russian prince.

The rumor came from Paris—and would eventually prove true. Lulu Van Alen, younger sister of Jimmy Van Alen, had sparks of romance in the late 1920s when "handsome" Prince Alexis Mdivani of Georgia was a guest at the Van Alen home in Newport. The papers all carried varying stories of their rumored engagement, with headlines such as, "Will the Prince Take Louise Away? Van Alen, Society Bud, to Wed Indian Prince," and "Astor Kin to Wed Mdivani Prince." Lulu is described as "fashionable," a "leader in the younger social set," as well as "immensely wealthy," while the Mdivani Prince, Alexis, whose father lost his entire fortune in the Russian Revolution, has been forced to "make his own way." Was it a marriage for money? The Mdivani brothers, Alexis and Serge, were rumored to be climbers, but in truth, they had first befriended Jimmy and Sammy Van Alen years before while they were all at Cambridge.

Lulu and Alexis were married on May 15, 1931, in the drawing room of Wakehurst. In applying for the marriage license, Alexis Mdivani listed his occupation as "gentleman." The ceremony was held in front of the mantle piece, where white roses and lilies were simply arranged. Lulu did not wear a wedding gown, however, but instead a "brown traveling costume." They later headed to New York,

boarding the Ile de France to Europe for their honeymoon. They were to settle in Paris.

But the marriage between Lulu and Alexis did not last. As Sammy Van Alen writes in his book, *Sammy's Book: Family Memories*, Alexis "went off with Barbara Hutton," but Sammy notes that Alexis' second marriage was also doomed to failure: "I don't think that marriage went very well because he was killed in an automobile accident in France motoring with somebody else entirely, another lady." Lulu later fell in love Alexis' brother, Serge Mdivani (who had already been married to Pola Negri, an Austrian silent film actress, and been divorced), and married him. Unfortunately, it seemed Lulu was destined for trouble in marriage; just six weeks after their marriage, Serge was killed in a polo accident. John Winslow, a family friend, remembers when he was a student at St. George's school seeing Lulu Van Alen, heartbroken, arriving at the cemetery in a Rolls Royce and placing orchids on Serge's grave.

After World War II had ended, a friend of Lulu's, Lydia Strauss-Foote, introduced her to her cousin, Alexander Saunderson. As a British officer in the war, Alexander had been imprisoned for four years by the Nazis, and was, as Sammy writes, "in rather dreadful shape." Brought to Newport by Lydia for rehabilitation, Alexander met Lulu, and they fell in love and got married. They later moved to California and had a wonderful life together.

With the death of their father and their new state of independent wealth, the Van Alen brothers would move into their adult lives. From their trans-Atlantic and affluent childhood the two brothers—Jimmy and Sammy—started their lives in privileged circumstances. They didn't have to work for a living and they had witnessed the leisure time activities of the very rich, were good at sports, and loved to travel. They now pursued different careers. Tennis would eventually become Jimmy's *raison d'être* and his passion later in his adult life as a player, a manager, and an innovator. Sammy, on the other hand, became an architect. After marrying Betty Kent, daughter of Atwater Kent, who held patents for an auto ignition system and was the first mass manufacturers of radios, they moved to Philadelphia where he practiced architecture and became involved in charitable work. The two brothers stayed close, however, through playing tennis and court tennis and many family celebrations. Sammy was the more relaxed of the two while Jimmy was always determined to act to change things and became obsessed and even single-minded about his causes. They contrasted but complemented each other.

Though much of Jimmy's sense of identity was built upon the figure of his grandfather who saw life as a chance to have fun, Jimmy's character was a writerly one as well. Every time something significant happened he sat down and wrote a verse or a song. His long poem of his impressions of Cambridge, though written later in life, was a commemorative poem cel-

PRINCE WEDS ASTOR DESCENDANT

Prince and Princess Mdivani.

Special to The World-Telegram.

NEWPORT, R. I., May 15.—After a simple marriage ceremony in the living room of the Van Alen estate here at 8 o'clock this morning, Prince and Princess Alexis Mdivani, the former Miss Louise Astor Van Alen, left for New York, where they will sail at 4:30 o'clock this afternoon on the Ile de France for Europe.

The bride, a direct descendant of John Jacob Astor, founder of that family, is a great-granddaughter of the late Mr. and Mrs. William Astor and of the late General James H. Van Alen, of Civil War fame.

She is a granddaughter of the late James A. Van Alen, American Ambassador to Italy during the Cleveland administration, and of Mr. and Mrs. William Post, of New York. She is the daughter of Mrs. James

Laurens Van Alen. Van Alen.

Prince Mdivani of the late General, aide de camp an court of Czar N His brother, Prir was married las McCormic, Chic after a previous Negri, the movie divorce. Another David Mdivani, Murray, the mov

The wedding the simplest in Astor family. O atives were pr were dispensed v was attired in a

The Rev. Stan tor of Trinity which the brid Lilies and white tate decorated t

Louise A. Van Alen Weds Prince Mdivani of Georgia At Wakehurst in Newport

Simple Ceremony Without Attendants; Couple to Live in Europe

Newport, R. I., May 15.—(AP)— Miss Louise Astor Van Alen of Newport and Prince Alexis Z. Mdivani of Georgia were married at Wakehurst, the bride's Newport home, today.

The ceremony was performed by the Rev. Stanley Carnaghan Hughes, rector of Old Trinity Church. It was one of the simplest and least ostentatious society weddings held in Newport in many months.

Neither the bride nor the groom was attended. Less than a dozen persons, all members of the bride's immediate family, witnessed the ceremony and the family of the prince was not represented.

The bride wore a brown traveling costume instead of the customary gown. Simple floral decorations of white lilies were set in front of the big mantelpiece at one side of the large drawing room, where the ceremony was held.

Immediately after the ceremony the bride and groom left by automobile for New York, where they were to board the steamship Ile de France later in the day. They planned to motor in England and then go to Paris, where they will make their home.

The bride, a direct descendant of John Jacob Astor, is the daughter of Mrs. James Van Alen and granddaughter of the late James J. Van Alen, once United States Ambassador to Italy. She was educated abroad and she and her mother travelled extensively in France and England prior to her father's death in 1927. She made her debut here last year when she was 22 years old. Her engagement was announced last June.

Prince Mdivani, who is 23, is the son of Zakaart Mdivani, who was an adle-de-camp and general at the court of the late Czar Nicholas of Russia. The prince's family are from Georgia in the former kingdom of Transcaucasia, absorbed a century ago by the Russian empire. The prince is the brother-in-law of Mae Murray, screen actress, whose husband is David Mdivani. A second brother, Prince Serge Mdivani, is the divorced husband of Pola Negri and was engaged to marry Mary McCormic, the Chicago opera star.

In applying for a marriage license, Prince Alexis listed his occupation as "gentleman."

LOUISE ASTOR VAN ALEN

Louise Van Alen weds Prince Mdivani of Georgia

Margaret and Louis Bruguiere

JHVA with his mother and Sammy

ebrating his years at the university. Van Alen had even commented in a letter that of the other poets who had attended Christ's—both Rupert Brooke and even Milton—"neither ever really did a thorough job on Cambridge," and it was "on account of this slip up," as he called it, that he set out to write his long poem. So it seems clear that Jimmy felt, like many writers, the ambitious need and creative responsibility to document his memories and experiences, although his verses are in a lighter vein than those of the serious poets he mentions.

The brothers seemed to gravitate toward the passions of creation and control, both building creative "spaces" in their own way—Sammy with buildings and Jimmy with everything from his amusing verses, to opinion pieces, to songs, to orchestrating the social scene of Newport tennis. Writing, like architecture, is involved with building—an intellectual and creative building of symbolic space on the page and in the reader's mind. How appropriate, then, that Jimmy evolved from writing poetry like "Cambridge" and editorials on politics and World War II for several Long Island newspapers to aid in the creation of tennis culture itself.

Jimmy and Sammy, the team of brothers

Jimmy with his pooch

Chapter Four:
The War

After graduating from Cambridge in 1924, Jimmy had decided, "I wasn't going to be the world's best tennis player. Anyway I had fallen in love with a beautiful girl whose family was active in polo and fox hunting. I immediately set out to become the greatest horseback rider in the world." Jimmy was no stranger to this life, as he had grown up riding and playing polo in Newport and Palm Beach.

His fiancée, Eleanor Langley, came from a socially prominent New York family. At what was said to be one of the most important and notable weddings of the season, Jimmy married Eleanor in October of 1929 in the small Church of the Advent in Old Westbury, Long Island, the outside of which was decorated with white chrysanthemums and autumn foliage. The gossip columns and society writers made much of the fact that he was "one of numerous descendants of John Jacob Astor." Pictures of the newly-weds appeared often in the newspapers. The *New York Herald-Tribune*'s description of the bride noted that "She wore a princess gown of deep ivory-colored satin, severely plain, without embellishment of lace, the skirt quite long, according to the prevailing fashion." Eleanor's passion as a horsewoman—a passion which Jimmy now embraced—could be seen in the golden carriage pulled by four steeds that carried the couple away from the ceremony. The couple would spend their honeymoon traveling to California, proceed onward to Honolulu, and then continue on a six-month cruise around the world.

At first the match seemed a good one—Jimmy shared in Eleanor's love of horses and sporting, and after they had children the young boys, too, became avid riders. At the birth of their first child, on April 30, 1931, the *Daily News* headline read, "Van Alen Stork Brings Prestige Plus," announcing the birth of the couple's first child, James Langley Van Alen—they would call him Jay. Sam, their second child, was born in 1934.

Both busybodies and doers in every sense of the word, Eleanor and Jimmy Van Alen led very active lives. Eleanor was raising their two young boys, managing the household, and was a coordinator for the war-relief effort in Nassau County, a trustee of the town hall, and also head reviewer of the publication *Current History*.

Slowly, however, cracks in the seemingly perfect marriage began to appear. Soon after their engagement, a newspaper writer called attention to the public scrutiny that Eleanor, as Jimmy's wife, would be subject to. He noted that Eleanor would be basking in the social sunshine of Newport. And although he thought she met "the inspection of the colonists with the aplomb of an experienced individual," to Jimmy and his mother's dismay Eleanor did not take to the Newport scene. She simply didn't like it—and their visits to the island became fewer and fewer. Jimmy, on the other hand, was often the star of the party and the social scene; a man who felt at home as host and often entertained his Newport circle of friends with his music and poems.

"I had fallen in love with a beautiful girl whose family was active in polo and fox hunting. I immediately set out to become the greatest horseback rider in the world."

And while Jimmy continued to be passionate about his hobbies and other interests, the fact that he had no established career soon became an issue for Eleanor. Though he was always busy, Eleanor preferred that he have steady work in addition to his numerous causes. She was happy when Jimmy eventually took a position at the Farrar Straus publishing house. But their marriage was slowly dissolving—and it seemed Jimmy was not destined to meet his true soul mate until several decades later. His revived interest in horseback riding, to please his wife and her family, did not check his enthusiasm for tennis in any form. He became the protégé of the legendary Pierre Etchebaster, who for twenty-six years would be the world's title holder of court tennis. Etchebaster soon turned Jimmy's lawn tennis prowess into the right stuff for playing what the English call "real tennis," derived from the medieval sport of kings played inside a castle courtyard. *New York Times* sports columnist Allison Danzig, showing off his understanding of the complex game, reported in 1933 that Jimmy had beaten the reigning United States champion, William C. Wright, to win the national amateur court tennis crown. Danzig would become a great friend of Jimmy's and cover his Newport tournaments and later his VASSS efforts. He praised Jimmy for "murdering" his opponent's railroad serve, laying down chases, "timing every shot with meticulous precision, getting down to the ball with his shoulder well into the stroke and cutting into it with a bite that brought the ball down sharply to the floor." Jimmy repeated his success as U.S. amateur champion in 1938 and 1940.

By taking up court tennis, Jimmy was narrowing the field in which he could excel. There were fewer than ten courts in the country and they were very expensive to build. It was played, therefore, by those who belonged to the clubs that housed the courts—the Racquet Clubs in New York and Philadelphia, Green Tree on Long Island, Tuxedo Park north of New York City, and at the Casino in Newport. Court tennis differs radically from lawn tennis. It is played in a large room with walls that are key to the play of each shot. It was a good game for Jimmy,

Wedding Nears

(By Pacific & Atlantic)
ENGAGED to be married are James Van Alen and Eleanor Langley, who move in upper realms of society. Don't they look it? Their marriage is expected to be the most important nuptial of the autumn, unless prince of Wales does it.

James Van Alen and Eleanor Langley are engaged

as he was quick, good at angling the ball, and excelled at cutting, slicing, and placing the ball into corners for shots that were hard to return. As Danzig wrote, "Jimmy had beautiful classic strokes. I wouldn't say he was the best amateur in this country, but he was a very smart player who got the most out of his abilities."

At the same time he had changed his focus in athletics to horseback riding, hunting, and court tennis, Jimmy began working in New York, spending a year in training at Chemical Bank and Trust in New York City. At the end of his training, however, he decided to leave the bank and take up a position as the Managing Editor of the prestigious *North American Review*, one of the nation's first literary magazines, founded in Boston in 1815. He was also urging Long Island readers to adopt his opinions on the worsening world situation in columns he wrote for Long Island newspapers.

His desire to write came from his constant need to express himself and make changes and reforms to the status quo, as he had done as a child and at Cambridge, and as he would later do in the world of tennis. And Eleanor, an established book reviewer who was interested in writing, was also active on the *North American Review*.

By the end of the decade his combativeness, his willingness to fight for what

MRS. JAMES H.
Van ALEN,
Formerly Miss Eleanor
Langley, Daughter of
Mr. and Mrs. William
Clark Langley, Who Was
Married Recently at
Westbury.
(New York Times
Studios.)

MISS LANGLEY WEDS JAMES H. VAN ALEN

Ceremony in Church of the Advent, Westbury, L. I., and Reception at Langley Home.

REV. DR. POPE OFFICIATES

Father Gives Bride in Marriage—
Couple to Make Trip Around
the World.

Special to The New York Times.

WESTBURY, L. I., Oct. 11.—In the Church of the Advent here this afternoon Miss Eleanor Langley, only daughter of Mr. and Mrs. William Clark Langley of 136 East Seventy-first Street, New York, and Westbury, was married to James Henry Van Alen, a direct descendant of the original John Jacob Astor in this country, who came to America in the middle of the eighteenth century and was the founder of that family in the United States. Mr. Van Alen is the elder son of Mrs. J. Laurens Van Alen and the late Mr. Van Alen, and a great-grandson of the late Mr. and Mrs. William Astor, who held a prominent place in New York society

While comparatively small, the wedding was one of the most important of the Autmun. Only near relatives and a few close friends were asked to the ceremony, which was performed by the Rev. Dr. Richard Pope, rector of the church. Autumn foliage and white chrysanthemums decorated the picturesque little edifice.

There was a program of organ music while the guests were assembling. The bride was escorted by her father to the chancel steps, where she was joined by the bridegroom and his brother, William L. Van Alen, who was best man. The bride was given in marriage by her father. She wore a princess gown of deep ivory colored satin, severely plain, without embellishment of lace, the skirt quite long, according to the prevailing fashion. Her veil of tulle fell in billowy folds over the long train, which was a part of the skirt. Instead of a bouquet the bride carried an ivory prayer book which had been used by her aunt at her marriage.

Miss Laura Robinson, daughter of Mr. and Mrs. Thomas L. Robinson, a cousin of the bride, was maid of honor and her only attendant. She wore a frock of cream-colored georgette with a velvet jacket of the same shade. She wore a close-fitting, cream-colored velvet toque trimmed with a band of russet-colored velvet ribbon. Her bouquet was of Pernet roses.

At the conclusion of the ceremony Mr. Van Alen and his bride left the church for the Langley home, where the reception was held, driving there in the Arrow, the coach of F. Ambrose Clark.

Mr. Van Alen and his bride will go to California for the first part of their wedding trip, and from there will sail for a trip around the world. On their return they will live in Roslyn, L. I., the estate of Mr. and Mrs. Sidney Webster Fish, which Mr. Van Alen recently purchased.

Eleanor Langley Van Alen

Right—MRS. JAMES H. VAN ALEN, the former Miss Eleanor Langley, who was married on October 11.   *Ira L. Hill*

he believed, and his obsessions filled the pages of his short weekly opinion pieces called "Between the Lines" for local Long Island newspapers. Many of his pieces were devoted to domestic political and social concerns. He now had a forum from which to expound upon "the unsound, half-baked philosophies with which the New Deal has experimented." Always the entertainer, his astute journalism was often countered by quirky remarks such as, "My inner man wanted to get up and shout, but the little bird that whispers in my inner man's ear said, 'Keep your shirt on, big boy, or you're liable to lose your pants.' So I stayed pretty still until the anti-third term resolution was proposed. At this point I did all I could to make a public exhibition of myself."

Accordingly, Jimmy was a big Wendell Willkie fan, supporting his nomination as the Republican presidential candidate in 1940: "everyone else has said every good thing about Wendell Willkie's nomination. Even if they hadn't my heart is too full for articulate expression. Divine Providence has looked down on this soft and subsidy ridden nation, and given it another chance…".

By September 1939, World War II had begun in Europe, but the extent of Germany's military ambitions was not yet clear to the world. On July 20, 1939 Jimmy began his piece in "Between the Lines" with the haunting question, "Will 1914 Be Repeated?" "Europe is balancing on the brink of war," he wrote. "1914 is here again. A day, a week, a month may see the start of it if something isn't done and done quickly…". Jimmy's columns often covered the war in Europe and he steadfastly warned that the Allies must take the offensive and that the U.S. must join in.

Soon the onset of World War II would alter the course of his life. After Germany attacked Poland in 1939, Jimmy enlisted in the navy and was commissioned a Lieutenant in the U.S. Naval Reserve. The navy's response was to sign him up for Naval Intelligence: when mobilized, he agreed to be stationed in Paris. Until mobilization he was ordered to keep a secret: "Keep this matter of your assignment to yourself. It's confidential. No one is to be told about it." When called to active duty in July 1941, however, it was first to the Office of Public Relations, assigned to the book and magazine section in New York City.

Everyone's life changed radically with the war. And those involved in leisure-time activities like tennis found their lives changing, too. Careers were interrupted, with normal play put on hold, and the very good players found their expertise was put to use in the war effort.

President Franklin D. Roosevelt encouraged the playing of tennis in the services to boost morale, and so while serving in the navy, Gardnar Mulloy, one of the best players in the late 1930s, was assigned to be tennis instructor to the trainee flyers. Mulloy considered this appointment as not beneficial for either party. "They resented me because they were so tired each evening after their flight training, and I resented having to give tennis instruction to a bunch of kids who did not know how to play and did not want to anyway." In spite of setbacks, his game was still thriving during this period. After he left the flight trainees he saw considerable action, commanding LSTs in Sicily, Italy and southern France. His best years were after the war in the '40s and '50s. Mulloy won a national title while playing doubles with Billy Talbert and gained a No. 3 ranking. He also

Virginia - bred Eleanor Van Alen can take the jumps with the best of them, and does.

Brookville Show to Aid Children

Ever since there's been a Brookville Charity Horse Show the name of Mrs. James H. Van Alen has been high on the committee list. It's there this year with the designation of chairman beside it for the one-day show set for Sept. 28.

Host to the forthcoming display is Victor Emanuel, who is turning over some of his Brookville acres. There will be both a show ring and outside course and complete emphasis on riding rather than side divisions.

Since everyone connected with the show contributes his services without charge, it's possible to turn over the entire proceeds to Nassau County's Society for the Prevention of Cruelty to Children, for which the show is held. Last year that amounted to the tidy sum of $1990.

Members of the executive committee with Mrs. Van Alen are Mrs. Rigan McKinney and Mrs. Norman K. Toerge. Sponsors will include Mrs. Bradley Delehanty, Mrs. James M. Austin, Mrs. Harvey D. Gibson, Mrs. Samuel Register and Mrs. Charles S. Payson.

The Brookville show is not only a benefit for children; it's also a show for them. All morning classes, plus those in the early afternoon, are devoted to the youngsters. Their parents take over after that.

Support of the show by members of Long Island's riding set is enthusiastic because the cause is so good. The society maintains a shelter for under-privileged and maltreated children.

Rain at a show is no treat, as witness this Piping Rock picture of Mrs. Van Alen.

Family class events often find young Sammy Van Alen and father Jimmy successful competitors

Jimmy, Eleanor, Jay and Sam Van Alen

Mr. and Mrs. James H. Van Alen and their sons, Sammy and Jay

The RIDING Van Alens

felt that the war disrupted his improvement as a player. "I would have been better had I not gone to the War," he says.

Just at the time Bobby Riggs wanted to turn pro, in April of 1942, he got a letter saying he was drafted into the navy. He had won the U.S. Championships at Forest Hills in 1939, but lost his title to Donald McNeill in 1940. He won again in 1941, beating Frank Kovacs. Instead of becoming pro, he went to boot camp and spent the war years giving tennis exhibitions and clinics. He was asked to play tennis with a number of high-ranking officers who fancied their game and he generally put on exhibitions at hospitals, recreations centers, camps, and clubs. He was playing on rough asphalt courts on the base instead of the carefully manicured lawns of Forest Hills. Racquets and balls were scarce because most materials, especially rubber, were diverted to wartime use. Players used withered old balls that were overplayed, without any bounce and with covers worn thin, or recycled balls that were lively but lost their covers on the tenth hit. As Riggs' biographer concludes, "the game proved incredibly popular on base, with long waits for courts and most play limited to just a single set. A base tournament in 1945 drew 158 singles players and 67 doubles teams." Good crowds always turned out for Bobby's exhibitions.

By 1945, the service decided to put on a series of matches between army and navy players and Bobby found himself playing against Don Budge. The matches were played on islands in the Pacific where American forces were stationed. The conditions were difficult; they played under hot sun on courts made of coral, surfaced with a mixture of broken rock and sand. The traditional tennis outfit of white shirt and white trousers was discarded for cooler clothes to help players withstand the scorching heat. Budge won the first match. The second was on the island Peleliu and Budge won again, but by not so much. Bobby won in straight sets on the island of Ulithi (6–1, 6–1) and on Saipan he won 6–3, 4–6, and 6–1. The next was played in early August on Tinian and Bobby won 8–6. At the same time, the atomic bomb was being assembled at the other side of the same island and on August 6th, it was loaded onto the Enola Gay. The war was over days later.

In civilian life, tournaments were cancelled or limited to women during the war. Newport's Casino suspended its tournaments. The Forest Hills matches limited their sets to the best of three until the finals, and at Seabright, only eight men and four women competed in 1945. The International Tennis Federation, organizer of the Davis Cup, expelled nine countries from participating—including Germany, Italy, and Japan.

In Great Britain, the All England Tennis Lawn and Croquet Club—the site of the Championships at Wimbledon—suspended the tournament but technically remained open, despite severe staff shortages. Even so, most of the Club's premises were occupied by British military and civil defense operations, including fire and ambulance services, a decontamination unit, and troop drill exercises. To make matters worse, a German bomber dropped 500 pounds of explosives directly over the Club in October of 1940, striking the famous Centre Court and destroying 1,200 seats. The damage took months to repair. Aside from a few matches played between Allied servicemen on the old No. 1 Court, Wimbledon saw little competition until 1946, when the Championships finally resumed "despite a shortage of racquets,

Gardnar Mulloy, 1955, champion doubles player of the 40s and 50s

years was among the smallest and least diverse in the tournament's history. But after the December 7, 1941 bombing of Pearl Harbor, not even the United States cared much about competitive tennis. And the meticulous skills required for a lot of workers to maintain grass courts for tournament play were otherwise useful in the war effort.

Even players who did not serve felt the effects of war. Only eleven years old in 1941, Tony Trabert—an American player who would go on to win five Grand Slam titles just over a decade later—remembered that in his hometown of Cincinnati, "Racquets were hard to get, tennis balls were very difficult to get. I remember my dad bought a wire wheel that you put a tennis ball in and turn the wheel and it roughed up the ball so the balls would last longer, and so you used them until they were actually rubber balls."

Tony's career, however, thrived in the postwar years. He ended up winning the Paris Championships, the French Championships, and the Italian Championships, as well as a tournament played at The Butler Club in Monte Carlo, thanks in part to his mentor, Bill Talbert. Talbert, who won nine Grand Slam doubles titles during his career, was one of a very few diabetics in sports at a highly competitive level. As he was exempt from the draft, Talbert's improvement was not disrupted, which perhaps accounts in some way for his success and more positive take on the war. "The war's increased competition only freshened my appetite," he says. "I had something to prove again, to myself and to the tennis public. Some of the best men had been out of the lists at the time I was winning my laurels, and I couldn't really be satisfied until I had defeated them in tougher post-war competition." This complicated time period can

balls, and court equipment and with a large section of the center court cordoned off."

Other Grand Slam tournaments were interrupted as well. The French Championships (now the French Open) disappeared in 1940 with the fall of the Third Republic, and the Australian Championships (now the Australian Open) followed suit a year later. Neither tournament resumed until the end of the war. The only Grand Slam tournament that survived the war was the U.S. National Championships (now the U.S. Open), but the pool of competitors during the war

be best described in his words: "In the special view of tennis players, World War II was the period between the 1939 Challenge Round and the 1945 National Championships. Even as the Forest Hills tournament got under way, MacArthur's troops were landing in Japan to carry out the surrender terms. Tennis, like every other kind of activity, began to emerge from wartime restraints. There was an atmosphere of release."

In the early '40s, Jimmy channeled his energies into war work—first during his navy years, when he became one of the officers in the book and magazine section of the Navy's Office of Public Relations, and later when he managed an overseas assignment.

Beginning in 1941, he became the boss of a young man who would be an important publisher in the American book world—Roger Straus, fourteen years Jimmy's junior. His work with Straus in the navy's publicity efforts pleased Eleanor, and the happy coincidence of the arrangement also worked for Jimmy. Caught as he was in a less-than-happy marriage, he directed his passionate nature and creativity into the navy work, and

Tony Trabert, during Davis Cup Match, 1955

Mulloy, on nearside, playing Pancho Gonzalez at the Casino, August 1949

later into his role as a promoter of Straus's burgeoning publishing endeavor.

Roger and Jimmy's friendship was legendary, and constitutes a most fascinating period in Jimmy's life. They saw each other both at play and at work. Jimmy and Eleanor, then living in Roslyn, New York, invited the Strauses over frequently. Dorothea Straus looked forward to the evenings with the Van Alens. Jimmy had a way with people. "Jimmy had all the charm...and he was fun." And he had the ability to smooth over tense situations. One luncheon party Dorothea distinctly remembered could have been a disaster. It was before Pearl Harbor and the Van Alens had invited Charlie Chaplin, along with Josée Marie, daughter of Pierre Laval, and her husband, René de Chambrun, a Nazi sympathizer. (Laval, Vice-Premier of France under the Vichy government, was later convicted of high treason and executed for his part in the collaboration with the Nazi regime.) "Really and truly, we were sitting with the enemy. I mean really, Chambrun!...He was really a Nazi...I don't know why [the Van Alens] thought it was a good idea to have this lunch with this French Nazi, and us, and Chaplin, all being Jewish. But, it was a lovely luncheon and Jimmy handled it beautifully. He [Chambrun] didn't counter anyone. Jimmy was charming and made it all go smoothly."

After lunch, Charlie Chaplin and his right-hand man, and Roger and Jimmy went off to do what Jimmy loved to do—play tennis. Roger and Jimmy were the better players and were beating them hands down. As Dorothea recalls, "Charlie Chaplin was not a good sport, and as soon as he saw they were losing, he started putting on the act, twirling around, walking this way and that. And Jimmy, with his good nature and charm, he carried it off, and it all became a very amusing spectacle."

Dorothea also remembered, "Later, Roger was overseas in the Pacific, not in action because he had had a spinal surgery when he was twenty that was done poorly, and consequently did not heal properly. It prevented him from being active in the forces. When Roger was overseas, Jimmy would call me occasionally and we would go dancing. And it was fun, because he had so much strength, he wasn't at all flirtatious, he was just fun. And Eleanor was just a killjoy."

Working together at the Public Relations Office, Roger and Jimmy set about the task of interviewing writers who wanted to go overseas as journalists. After evaluating their credentials and their personality they would either accept or reject them. According to Dorothea Straus, "Jimmy was the most wonderful boss. He and Roger got to be friends. And as you know, Jimmy was not a demon-worker! My husband was appointed to be Jimmy's aide. Well, Jimmy, who was shrewd, took one look at Roger. Here was a way of doing good and passing the heavy work on to this young man, because, as you see, my husband was just the opposite. He was a dynamo of work."

One successful project Jimmy initiated and managed was 1942 publication of *They Were Expendable*, William L. White's account of the P.T. boats at war in the Philippines. Jimmy Van Alen went to *Reader's Digest* on behalf of the navy around May of 1942 with the request that the magazine do an article about a group of P.T. boat officers who had just returned from the Philippines. *Reader's Digest* publisher DeWitt Wallace accepted the navy's invitation to interview the officers and assigned White to the story. In September 1942 *Reader's Digest* published the condensed version of *They Were Expendable* shortly before the book was published. It went on to become one of the most popular books written on the war.

It was working under Jimmy at the navy's Book and Magazine Section that got Roger Straus excited about publishing. Dorothea recalls, "Roger was fascinated. Before that Roger wanted to be a newspaperman. But this completely changed him. He realized that he liked working in an office." A few years later Roger decided to start his own publishing house. As a close friend and fellow-admirer of literature, Jimmy offered to help Roger with this endeavor and determined that he would invest a considerable amount of his family's money into the business. A meeting was set up with Jimmy's mother, Margaret Bruguiere, at the Ritz Hotel. Dorothea remembered how "he put in some money and told us that his mother would be happy to put in all the money needed. So she came to the old Ritz and had lunch with Jimmy and Roger. But after they'd been talking about the plans for the new company for some time, she turned to Jimmy, with Roger sitting there, and said, 'What makes you think that I am going to put up money in a Jewish firm?' Roger said that Jimmy was really shocked. He turned white when he heard his mother's response." Unlike his mother, Jimmy did not hold the

JHVA meeting with fellow officers at naval base in England

Time out for reading

anti-Semitic attitudes of others among members of his social class. Instead, Jimmy invested in the firm and according to Dorothea Straus, "For a very short time the firm was called Van Alen and Straus."

Roger Straus's publishing company went on to publish such renowned authors as Alberto Moravia, Edmund Wilson, Nadine Gordimer, Philip Roth, T.S. Eliot, and many Pulitzer Prize-winners and thirteen Nobel Laureates. Roger himself became a mainstay of Manhattan's literary community, holding salons regularly at his Upper East Side home. As for Jimmy's connection to the company, he continued to suggest book subjects and he maintained his connection through the stock he owned. Later, his second wife, Candy, was on the Board. But after his marriage to Candy and his move back to Newport, Jimmy saw less of Roger and Dorothea.

Like many desk-bound reserve officers, however, Jimmy pushed hard for more active duties. After his brief tour in Paris, he eventually succeeded in getting himself assigned to a course of study at the Naval War College in Newport, thanks to a plaintive memo to the Bureau of Naval Personnel, which concludes: "I have been at present shore duty for more than a year and a half and am anxious for the opportunity of fitting myself to take a more acute part in the war."

Jimmy's son Jay remembered that "at the War College they were showing a series of graphs that they were trying to maneuver to go into battle with. The graphs looked clumsy to him. So, he refigured the navy's presentation of a battle between two ships. And this was accepted, but just like anything else, at first the navy was opposed to it. And then they realized Jimmy's solution was better."

Jimmy left his impression on the navy in other ways as well. Even during his enrollment at the Naval War College in Newport, he maintained an enthusiasm for sports and competition. In his War College thesis, exhaustively titled "Policies and Conditions Leading up to the Present Conflict between Japan and the United States, including Notation of the Parallels between the Opening of the Present Hostilities and the Opening of the Russo-Japanese War (1904)," he managed to integrate sports and organized play into an otherwise somber piece of academic writing. The thesis is peppered with sports metaphors. It was Jimmy's goal to demonstrate how both the Second World War and the Russo-Japanese War of 1904 offered two examples of the same imperial impulse in Japan's military policy, and to outline the conditions in Japan that enabled these expansionist efforts. At the same time, Jimmy could not help but see the war as a kind of playoff in the grand game of international politics. As he puts it in his thesis, "For a nation to reach the starting line in a race for world domination—for a nation's 'time' to have come—certain specific conditions are sure to be present in varying degrees."

One of these conditions, which Jimmy identified in wartime Germany as well as Japan, was the presence of what he called "a docile yet brutal lower class willing to serve as a patriotically fanatical football for the military to kick in any direction considered best." Elsewhere, in a more complex and extended metaphor, he compares Japan's imperial prospects during the nineteenth and twentieth centuries with those of a hunter who arrives too late in the day to make a kill. As Jimmy puts it, "Japan was bound to go a-huntin'. However, unfortunately for the peace of the world, by the time Japan was

Jimmy exercising his men

ready to hunt most of the birds had been shot and all the best shooting land was posted. Africa, India, North and South America (South America posted with Monroe Doctrine sign boards) Australia, New Zealand, Indo China, the Dutch East Indies, Burma, Borneo were all plucked and in the larder, as far as Japan's dreams of expansion were concerned." And in his historical analysis of the events leading up to the bombing of Pearl Harbor, he interprets the Japanese military's seizure of then-Indochina as a badminton game against the United States, in which "Indo China was the controversial shuttlecock, which was batted backwards and foreward [sic] between the State department and the Japanese Embassy."

Unfortunately "such a game," Jimmy noted, "can only last as long as the players don't get tired." Japan presumably grew weary

of playing badminton around December 7, 1941—the day the Japanese military bombed Pearl Harbor and pulled the United States into the Second World War. From these events, Jimmy concluded his thesis with the strikingly sober observation that "one must pay for one's fun—in other words, the price of democratic freedom is unpreparedness for war." The admiral who graded his paper judged it "a very good thesis showing originality of thought and expression."

Having submitted his thesis in late May of 1943, Jimmy officially completed the "staff preparatory course" in June. At the graduation ceremony, the Secretary of the Navy spoke to his class and distributed their diplomas. There is no record of Jimmy lobbying him, but they did shake hands, and overseas he went—to England—with a lieutenant commander's half-stripe added.

In England he would be assigned to the U.S. Naval Advanced Amphibious Base in Dartmouth, where everyone was intensely committed to D-Day landing preparations. Jimmy would be involved, assisting to load landing craft with army equipment and personnel. He then was the Commanding Officer at the Sandridge Naval Base from 1944 to 1945. Next he headed up public relations for all U.S. naval installations on the English coastline, and finally he was the Commanding Officer at the Vickerage Naval Base at Plymouth for six months, until May 1945.

In England during the war he would become a legendary figure. As usual he also made sure there was fun. He cornered the market on lobsters in the south of England for his men's pleasure and also helped pay for a sailors' club in London. When a fellow officer was billed $150,000 for its construction "Van Alen used his old boy friendships with the British to see to it that the bill was charged off against lend-lease."

After Normandy he ran a rest and rehabilitation center—just the thing for him to do, as he was so sports and health conscious. His men all followed him for a daily six A.M. run. As Jimmy described running what he called his "Rest and Rehabilitation Base" in Devon: "When I say 'ran' I mean it literally; I ran the troops a mile a day myself as part of the program. This experience gave me a very good opportunity of countering 'gold bricking' in many of its forms and also impressed me with the generally low grade of physical fitness of much of the combat naval personnel."

Jimmy—who could never resist trying to improve or reform—was not only critical of his physically unfit subordinates in the navy, but of his superiors as well. In a poem entitled "The Annapolis IF"—a twist on Rudyard Kipling's "If"—Jimmy offers a cheeky assessment of what makes a "five star Admiral":

If you can kiss your Admiral's hand
    And smack your lips with glee
If you can lick your Captain's boots
With loyal humilitee
If your Admiral's jokes convulse you
Tho' they're not remotely funny
And you court his cross-eyed daughter
And acclaim that she's a lovey
If you can dodge decision
Like the acne or the plague
And foil a searching question
With an answer dim and vague

…

If you can take these qualities
And roll 'em into one
You'll have the makings
Of a five star Admiral my son!

Sam and Jay Van Alen with Eleanor (above) and Jimmy (below).

Of course the impulse behind this poem, like the impulse behind his rest and rehabilitation center, was anything but malicious. Jimmy liked the navy and was well-liked by his men and his superiors, and was promoted several times during the war.

Jimmy's fellow officer, Jack Ormsbee, the supply officer of a U.S. naval base at Dartmouth when Jimmy was in charge of the R&R camp attached to the base, described how "Jimmy's exploits and eccentricities were legendary even there and then. When there was a shortage of beer in the U.K., Jimmy bought a brewery in Wales just so the guys in his rest camp could have their brew. (He picked up a Welsh Corgi at the same time to snap at their heels.) He used the camp's stewards' mates to beat the bushes in the woods while he hunted birds in a Sherlock Holmes hat." His dress was unusual for wartime—"constantly out of order, but intriguing. He wore the blue naval officers' jacket with his two gold stripes as if it were a blazer, combining it with grey or white slacks when he felt like it, and occasionally throwing in white shoes and a striped shirt to boot." He was popular with the admirals, who competed to have him entertain at their parties.

Having spent his war years on the coast of southern England—partly in the east near the mouth of the Thames and partly at Torquay and Plymouth further west in Devon—he returned to the United States in September of 1945 after the war was over.

His patriotism, however, continued in his presidency of the Soldiers, Sailors, and Airman's Club in New York City.

Back in New York, Jimmy worked as a part-time columnist of the Griscom Publications newspaper in Glen Cove, Long

Island—a business he also co-owned—and was an officer of Farrar, Straus until 1954. As the publishing company was starting up, Jimmy and even his wife, Eleanor, took part. A fellow worker, Arthur Ormont, who shared one of the three new offices at Farrar, Straus with Jimmy, then Vice President, remembered how impressed he was by Jimmy's style and his status as a court tennis champion. Ormont figured Jimmy was perhaps the fourteenth richest man in America—he wore Peale shoes and chalk-stripe suits, which Ormont was sure had been tailored for him on Savile Row. Jimmy spent only an hour or so each day at the office, talking on the phone to people like Douglas Fairbanks, Jr., the Duke of Bedford, and Pierre Etchebaster, the court tennis master. "Once Jimmy took me to see him play a court tennis match at the Racquet and Tennis Club on Park Avenue. Watching Van Alen stroking for the dedans gave me fantasies of ending up—hadn't other enterprising aliens like Irving Berlin and Benny Goodman done it?—with a glamorous socialite wife." The lovely Eleanor Van Alen came in the office to read manuscripts for the firm, "and that summer, when she and Jimmy invited me to their country place on Long Island for a Sunday afternoon, and we had lunch at the Piping Rock Club, the blonde beauty of the young girls left me stunned with desire."

Jimmy and the beautiful Eleanor were unhappy together, however, and before long Jimmy would have an encounter that would change his life. It began on an evening in 1948 at a New York cocktail party. Jimmy asked the host to introduce him to a young lady sitting by herself. The introduction was auspicious; the two talked late into the night, unaware that everyone else had left. At the time Candy Vanderlip was living in New York City and working as an editorial writer and assistant to the editor and publisher of the *Herald Tribune*, Whitelaw Reid. Her newspaper career had started as a war correspondent in Europe during the Second World War. She had been married before to Kelvin Vanderlip and divorced and vowed never to marry again but to concentrate her efforts on her career: "Never was I going to get married again. I had finished that." But that evening she had met a fellow who would prove to be irresistibly charming. He walked her home, and the next morning Jimmy arrived at her doorstep hoping to escort her to the office. That week he wooed Candy with caviar and champagne and remarkably, by Friday, even though he was married to Eleanor, he asked Candy to marry him and she accepted. Candy felt, "Jimmy was so bright. You have no idea. After all these people that I was seeing every day, he just stood out. Clever and amusing. Very, very informed."

Candace A. Alig was born in Louisville, Kentucky, and lived a varied and cosmopolitan life—spending weekends at the Hearst Castle in San Simeon, California, taking tea with Eleanor Roosevelt, and studying and traveling abroad. Bright and ambitious, she attended good schools, Rosemary Hall and Vassar College, and Radcliffe, the Sorbonne, and Columbia University for postgraduate studies. Her first job was in public relations but she soon found her true calling as a journalist.

World War II offered many women like Candy the opportunity to enter the workforce. In 1945 she became a correspondent for the International News Service and was stationed in Paris. She once met Nobel Prize-winner George Bernard Shaw, and interviewed him for an article. She asked him what he thought of the atomic bomb, and he said, "The bomb's old-fashioned. Nobody's going to use that anymore. Who wants to use that? When you go to war, you take over a country that you could use. You don't want to take over a country where the land has been ruined and nothing can grow on it, the people are ill from the effects of the bomb." Though newspapers would censor much of her article, she continued, quoting him saying that "one day the U.S. would be taken over since it had so much to offer."

Later she would work not only for the *New York Herald* but as a contributing editor of *Vogue*, and a columnist for the *New York Daily News* and the *Chicago Tribune*. Candy was suited to Jimmy's creative and intellectual endeavors, as they shared a love of writing, good times, and adventure.

And Candy, unlike Jimmy's first wife Eleanor, not only loved Newport but she got along with Jimmy's mother. She also accompanied Jimmy on a long honeymoon trip overseas. Jimmy was keen to show Candy his English life. Through the English Speaking Union they found a family in Cambridge to receive them as guests. The Bevan family was prominent in Cambridge—Dr. Edward Bevan was Prince Charles's doctor when the Prince was a child. He and his wife Joan had also been hosts to Ludwig Wittgenstein. Later on their son Anthony would become a regular at Jimmy's sporting events in England and in Newport.

The wedding trip included a visit to Jimmy's old friend and tennis teammate Edward Reed. His son Gavin, then a teenager, remembers them showing up in an enormous Hudson car and it made a big impression on him. Stalking with the Reeds in Scotland was included and Gavin's sister, Jimmy's goddaughter, was on the hunt with the grownups. At one point she spied Jimmy and Candy departing from the others and skinny dipping in a stream.

Since Jimmy was still married when he met Candy in 1948, they were forced to be apart while Jimmy was in Reno, Nevada, attaining a speedy divorce. He wrote constantly to Candy, giving her updates on the situation and describing the scenery for her. They refer to a routine of "daily letter writing" in their correspondence, and it seems that the bond between them, though they had not known each other for very long, was immediately strong. In one letter written in the summer of 1946: "It still doesn't seem true that we had that week of paradise—I have to pinch myself." After a phone conversation with Candy he writes her again: "I can't explain what hearing your voice did to me—really hearing it, I mean. The nice little whispers that have come over the phone have done me the opposite of good—just made me ache—this was different. But one thing it certainly brought home to me," he writes, talking about the distance between them, "separation at the present time is just plain murder." In yet another he writes, "I've just spoken to you on the phone so will progress from there. What is on my mind? Would you really like to know—just your happiness, my darling. All my love, J."

With the divorce finally granted, Jimmy was inspired by his former unhappiness in his first marriage to write a poem:

A man doesn't want his faults explained
He knows them only too well
When he's been unwise
He instinctively shies

From someone whose going to dwell
On the wherefore's and whys
Of his mistakes
He's longing for someone to tell
Him that he just didn't get the breaks
The rest can go to hell
He's looking for peace and comfort
Not scoldings and ranting and tears
And if his wife denies his needs
He'll find some other ears
That will force him into lies
For a man loves approbation
He loves to be petted and praised
He hates to admit to the one he loves
That some situation has fazed him
Even if just for a moment
In her eyes he wants to seem wise
He wants her to think he's as smart as hell
Right up to the day he dies.

Jimmy and Candy were well matched, and the marriage lasted 43 years. George Herrick, in a tribute piece to Candy in *Newport This Week*, said that "it was the variety and quality of their experience that made the Van Alens such a memorable couple." Both well-traveled, both intellectual and creative, both social animals—one could say Jimmy and Candy were made for each other. Candy encouraged Jimmy's pursuits, especially his ideas about tennis and his VASSS reforms. While observers sometimes found Jimmy's endeavors silly or unnecessary or annoyingly obsessive, she was always for them. One could say she was his biggest supporter. Friend Ralph E. Carpenter describes Candy's care toward Jimmy: "When Jimmy was not well, she was absolutely with him all the time, took the best tender care you could give anybody. She would take him to events and stay right with him."

Jimmy and Candy

Later in Candy's life, when people would ask her where she lived, she would reply, "In a suitcase." She lived in the moment, much as Jimmy did: "As we all know, nothing makes time fly like happiness. The high point of my life is the now-present. Always, it has been so. When I look back at the past high peaks that were the present, I wonder how I thought everything was so great when it is indefinitely more so now."

In addition to their writing pursuits, Candy, with her endless support and dedication, would lead Jimmy back into tennis life as a founder of the Tennis Hall of Fame.

AMERICAN LAWN TENNIS

S. W. MERRIHEW
PROPRIETOR AND EDITOR

Official Organ of United States
National Lawn Tennis Association

Vol. XIV
Established in 1907

AUGUST 15, 1920

No. 7
Whole No. 200

THE CHAMPIONSHIP COURT AT NEWPORT ON AUGUST 14

Sensational Final Round Match Ends with Defeat of Champion W. M. Johnston (in foreground)
by C. J. Griffin, 6-3, 4-6, 2-6, 6-4, 6-3

PRICE 30 CENTS

The Championship Court at Newport on August 11th, 1929

Chapter Five:
The Casino—Cradle of American Tennis

In Candy, Jimmy had found a partner who championed his many projects. She joined him in writing his columns for the Long Island newspapers; she acted as hostess for his parties. She was an enthusiastic traveler. Some of their excursions ended up as articles in *Vogue*, like the one called "We Chartered a Baby Submarine, We Painted It Yellow So Whales Wouldn't Swallow It." She got along with his strong and dominating mother, and—perhaps most important for Jimmy's future which now would be molded out of his past—she liked Newport.

Jimmy often said, "Newport can be hard on women." Candy, however, would share Jimmy's love for everything Newport—for his Astor lineage, his passion for tennis, for the family's history, and for Wakehurst, the enormous house built by Jimmy's grandfather on the Ochre Point lot. She appreciated the fact that Jimmy's mother, Daisy Post Van Alen Bruguiere, then Wakehurst's chatelaine, now in her seventies, was Jimmy's greatest champion.

Jimmy's mother, one of Newport's *grandes dames*, was a formidable presence. She lived very formally and liked to maintain an anachronistic grandeur. After the death of James Laurens, Jimmy's father, she had returned to the town where she had deep roots. She was born in Newport in the summer of 1877. Her father's family, the Posts, were from New York and her mother's father, Charles Lee Anthony, was from Bristol, Rhode Island. According to her son Sammy, Newport "was always where she wanted to go back to."

Proud of her Newport background, she was not above reminding others of it. The Misses Wetmore who owned Château-sur-Mer were, in her son Sammy's words, "very stylish indeed," and "considered themselves to be very old Newporters." One day one of the Wetmore sisters said to Mrs. Van Alen, "You don't go back really far in Newport history, the way we do." Margaret was able to show them the deed by which General Van Alen, her husband's grandfather, sold them the land on Bellevue Avenue where they had built their house after his house had burned down in 1852. The house had burned in a fire before James Henry Van Alen could live in it, but the Van Alen out buildings—including the stables and the gate house—are still there today.

Newport, when Jimmy and Candy returned, was the place of handsome houses and pleasant diversions—tennis, sailing, and golf—although it was not the super-affluent watering place it once had been.

In the early 1950s they bought a house. The estate, known as "Avalon," was designed and built during 1906 and 1907 by architect Grosvenor Atterbury. The sprawling, 25,000-square-foot mansion was constructed in the style of a Mediterranean villa, with stucco walls, arched sash windows, a terracotta-tiled roof, and a large pergola over the porch. A circular driveway lined by meticulously trimmed hedges and sculpted shrubs greeted the guests to Avalon, who would enter the mansion through a set of stately French doors and find themselves in a grand round foyer lined with

James and Candace Van Alen, 1950s

fluted square columns and decorative corbels. Behind the house, an ivy-covered wall enclosed an impressive garden populated with wildflowers, trees, and classical statues.

Avalon was originally the summer home of lawyer and financier Edward Stephen Rawson, who commissioned Atterbury to design the house in 1906 and oversaw major renovations to the property from 1916–1917. In 1920 Rawson sold the villa and the surrounding 34 acres to Vera Scott Cushman of New York—one of the early American leaders of the Young Women's Christian Association (YWCA)—and her husband, who owned the nearby property of Moorland Farm. In 1952, the Van Alens purchased Avalon from the Cushman estate.

The elevation of Avalon—which sat atop some of the highest ground in Newport—afforded the Van Alens a stunning view of both land and sea. To the south, Avalon overlooked the gently breaking waves of Price's Cove and, further out, the Rhode Island Sound. On an especially clear day, one could see Block Island on the southwestern horizon welcoming a steady stream of fishing boats. Ocean Avenue, a grand beachfront road dotted with Gilded Age mansions, stretched out along the rocky coastline below the estate. To the west, Jimmy and Candy could survey the meticulously manicured greens of the Newport Country Club. Perhaps it was after he took up residence in Avalon, with thousands of grieving golfers as his neighbors, that Jimmy first thought to reform the rules and regulations of that game—an effort he would take up more seriously during the 1970s and 1980s.

Twelve years after they bought Avalon, Jimmy and Candy also purchased extra acres next door, the old Wrentham Estate, a stone and shingle house designed by Richard Morris Hunt and Frederick Law Olmstead, for $85,000. Jimmy converted the dozen or so acres of land around Wrentham House into a gaming preserve for his hunting guests.

The Van Alens bought Avalon in the early 1950s

After settling back into Newport life in 1951, he was elected president of the Casino. He had taken on a job with lots of problems. Like many resort clubs that enjoyed prosperity before the War, the Casino had suffered. The magnificent complex, once the epitome of Newport's Gilded Age grandeur, was way past its prime and showing its age. During the war the large complex was used as an officer's club, and there had not been much upkeep. American lifestyles had changed drastically after the war, and the appearance of the Casino had changed too. Hence, when Jimmy became president of the Casino in 1952, the job came with a considerable amount of repair work to undertake, and a dismal financial situation to go with it.

And to make matters worse, in 1953 a fire destroyed the whole north wing. On April 18, 1953, a *Newport News* headline described how a "General Alarm Fire Destroys North Wing

of Newport Casino Block." A dog barking at the smell of the smoke had alerted the night watchman just before 5 A.M.—and a firefighting apparatus was rushed to the scene. After an hour's battle the blaze was brought under control, but not before the north roof and upper walls of the historic building had collapsed. The first story ceiling had fallen into a litter of tangled debris. It looked like the entire north wing running back from the Bellevue Avenue stores might need to be razed. The damage was estimated at $75,000, a large sum in those days. The fire was the last thing the aging tennis complex needed.

Just before Jimmy took over, Henry Phelps had been president from 1945–1951. Under Phelps, tournaments restarted one year after the end of the war, in 1946, when Gardnar Mulloy beat Ted Schroeder 6–1, 2–6, 14–12, 6–3 and Jack Kramer and Schroeder won the doubles against Bill Talbert and Robert Falkenberg 4–6, 6–3, 7–5, 6–3.

Jimmy was a good choice for the new head of the Casino. He knew its history, he

The Newport Invitational Tennis Tournament in the 1930s

loved to run tennis matches, and he was full of ideas. He met regularly with the board of governors and the executive committee to oversee the large property and devise ways to ameliorate the financial situation and improve the attendance at the tournament, which was one stop on the amateur circuit each July. One big idea, which Candy had thought of, was creating a Tennis Hall of Fame. Other ideas were to have round robins instead of the usual tennis tournament format, to have more women's events, to have fashion shows, and even a prize fight. The last suggestion was turned down.

Creating a Tennis Hall of Fame would help save the Casino. Jimmy's son Jay Van Alen remembered how Jimmy "had seen the Baseball Hall of Fame in Cooperstown, at some point. And he had seen the Football Hall of Fame," and it seemed a logical step to create a

Tennis Hall of Fame at the Casino. The Hall of Fame could be set up in the Casino's complex. One of the first challenges was to get the USLTA to recognize the Casino as "the true cradle of tennis in America." Such a step might make possible a way of making money and making the Casino a tax-exempt entity.

The Casino was well worth saving. Its origin is one of the great Gilded Age stories. It was also an architectural monument of note as soon as it was completed. As Robert Stern writes: "An accident of social history gave the resort a social center that provided a focus for the lively sports-oriented community and, coincidentally, was one of the consummate architectural creations of the Shingle Style." As the story goes, in 1879, James Gordon Bennett, Jr., the immensely rich publisher of the *New York Herald*, had been entertaining a visiting British army officer, Captain Henry

Augustus Candy. Captain Candy was challenged to ride a horse through Newport's most prestigious club of the day, the Reading Room. The officer obliged, and maneuvered his horse up the front steps and into the main hall of the revered place. As a result, Bennett was barred from the club. Piqued, Bennett set out to build the Casino as "a livelier center for summertime frolics."

Bennett, publisher of the *New York Herald*, which had been founded by his father, was a powerful media tycoon along the lines of Joseph Pulitzer and today's Rupert Murdoch. Thanks to Bennett father and son, journalism had changed from only reporting politics and the personalities of the editors and publishers to covering society, sports, shopping, and business news, and stories from all over the world, which were telegraphed or cabled to the paper. There was something for every reader. Court cases were newly featured. Bennett Jr. made the *Herald* the most read paper in the post-Civil-War years, and with this success came a large fortune. While his father was credited for starting the newspaper, the son was well known for his "escapades"—skippering and winning the first trans-Atlantic yacht race, keeping a disagreeable Parisian mistress, building the Casino, introducing polo to America—while at the same time, he ran three metropolitan newspapers. He was also the person who commissioned Henry Stanley to find David Livingston in Africa.

After the Candy escapade, Bennett bought the Sidney Brooks estate called "Stone Villa," which was opposite an empty lot on Bellevue Avenue, and on this lot the Casino was built in a quick six months. He commissioned McKim, Mead & White to design it, giving the firm its first commission. The Casino opened

JAMES GORDON BENNETT,

James Gordon Bennett, Jr., circa 1895, whose idea to better the Newport Reading Room became the Casino

in 1880, in time for the summer season. "To Bennett's satisfaction, it quickly became *the club* in Newport."

The *Newport Mercury* described how in the spring of 1880, the town was alive with anticipation of the coming lively season, "and the most watched operations are the Casino lot. The tennis court is a novelty for Newport and its construction is a curiosity." By July, "the block with its handsome stores filled with rich and rare goods, the picturesque building painted in dark colors with trimmings of brownish red, recall the pictures of scenes a hundred years ago." The first court was embellished with flower-beds, and there was also "a fountain." Beyond the first piazzas, with their quaint lattice work, "stretches the magnificent lawn." The Casino would be formally opened when Bennett returned from Europe.

The first National Lawn Tennis tournament, held at the Staten Island Club, Camp Washington, New Brighton, Sept. 1st, 1880

Casino in the 1880s

Once completed, the Casino, with its green-shingled horseshoe-shaped piazza, created an appealing and pleasant site for tennis, social gatherings, theatrical programs, balls, and concerts. It "combined classical and Roman planning with motifs and materials from both vernacular American and French architecture" to provide a wonderful gathering place. The visitor entered from Bellevue Avenue where fashionable shops lined the

street. He found himself facing a big expanse of green turf with a horseshoe-shaped piazza in front of him where spectators could watch the play on the grass courts. To start with, the Casino had only three lawn tennis courts, but by 1888, seven had been added, and even more when Jimmy and Sammy started to play.

A tower adjoined the entrance inside. Its purpose was to break up the linear geometry of the shop-lined street and orient the visitor to the rounded shape of the large inside space. On the tower was a huge clock with a yellow face, which looked down on the turf and the goings-on below. Beyond the piazza where spectators gathered to watch the tennis, was another expanse of turf for more courts. The numerous green grass courts marked daily with fresh chalk during busy periods beckoned tennis players to take part in the new sport. They would be the site of decades of games between white-clad opponents enjoying the quickly growing popular pastime.

It was at the Casino that the first United States championships were held in 1881 and the fledgling game began its competitive history. The tournament drew twenty-five players for the singles and thirteen pairs for the doubles. Since there were no grandstands, the spectators sat on "camp stools or light chairs set out in rows of two or three with latecomers standing to watch the action." Richard Sears, America's first national champion, described the matches: The nets were not the same height across but were four feet at the posts and three feet at the center. This meant "avoid[ing] lifting the drives over the highest part of the net along the sidelines." Sears said that all he had to do "was to tap the balls as they came over, first to one side and then to the other, running my opponent all over the court." Sears won the championship in 1881 and in the following six years.

Sears also described the look of the players who "wore knickerbockers, with blazers, belts, cravats, and woolen stockings in the club colors. Their shoes were rubber-soled and generally of white canvas or buckskin. They all wore caps or round hats with a rolling brim that could be turned down in front to ward off the glare of the sun."

Play evolved quickly. Sears also explained how in the second year of the championship "all the players [were] serving overhand with more or less speed, mostly less, with everyone coming in to volley as soon as any good opening presented itself." Sears and his partner, James Dwight, out lobbed their opponents because their shots were too short, making it easy for Dwight and Sears to hit them back with a great deal of speed.

Although the Casino and Newport claim to be the site of the first championship event, other places also vie for that distinction. There are two versions of how lawn tennis got started in America—the Boston story and the New York story. The early players were possessors of an Englishman's innovation: Major Walter Clopton Wingfield's "box" and its contents, the kits he had introduced in England in 1874. Each contained bats, balls, and "a portable court" to be erected on any flat surface. The most popular surfaces were the green lawns used for croquet. Players needed only to set up two posts and a net and mark the ground with lines within which they could then play the new game of lawn tennis, which Wingfield called Sphairistike.

The Boston story credits two Bostonians, James Dwight and Frederick Sears, who, in 1874, found one of Wingfield's boxes at a

James Dwight (left) and Richard Sears

BELOW: *Richard Sears, the first National Champion at the Casino*

Major Walter Clopton Wingfield, creator of the Wingfield "box"

country house in Nahant owned by their friend William Appleton. They opened the kit—which was a gift that Appleton's son-in-law, Arthur Beebe, had brought from London—and they proceeded to play two sets. Even though a rainstorm started, it did not discourage them. They banged the ball around at the Sears estate in Brookline called Longwood, which, by 1890, was the site of the Longwood Cricket Club, a popular venue for tennis which took off immediately. Sears was the elder brother of Richard Sears, the first national champion, and James Dwight became known as "the father of American tennis."

The New York story credits Mary Outerbridge of Staten Island as having imported one of Major Wingfeld's boxes in 1874 from Bermuda. The first tournament in Staten Is-

land was played on September 1, 1880. It was a beautiful site with "the sunset over the bay, the elegant ladies in their colorful dresses," and the attraction of a "handsome silver cup worth a hundred dollars showing, on one side, the engraving 'The Champion Lawn-Tennis Player of America.'" The winner was an Englishman, O.E. Woodhouse, a finalist that year at the All England Championships. But the event was not without its controversy: the scoring, the height of the net, and the size of the ball were all complained about. The next spring the first meeting of the United States National Lawn Tennis Association (USNLTA) took place at the Fifth Avenue Hotel in New York. On May 21, 1881, "The thirty-six delegates, representing nineteen clubs and having a proxy to vote for another sixteen, agreed to adopt the rules of the All England Club for a year. The assembly also resolved on holding an official championship." What they needed was a venue and as early as June the executive committee, on the question of the venue, decided in favour of the newly built Newport Casino, Rhode Island; the date, 31 August 1881." Thus did Newport's Casino become the "cradle of American tennis."

Once the championships were held at Newport in 1881 they continued to be played on the Casino's carefully cultured turf courts for thirty-four years. As Allison Danzig later described it: "Strains of the string orchestra on the horseshoe Piazza" wafted out to the spectators who were "elegantly gowned women in full length skirts and ruffles under parasols" chattering away in chairs encircling the championship court. The world's most famous players, British, American, and Australian—such as Sears, the Dohertys, Larned, McLoughlin, Johnston, Whitman,

Campbell and Huntington, U.S. National Doubles Champions, 1891–1892

U.S. National Lawn Tennis Tournament, Hovey vs. Smith, Aug. 22, 1891

U.S.N.L.T. TOURNAMENT. HOVEY -VS- SMITH AUG.22,1891

Campbell, Brookes, Wilding, Gore, Clothier, Wrenn, Ward, Slocum, Davis, Wright, and Hovey—took part in some of the country's best tennis matches.

Maud Howe Elliot, chronicler of Newport history, claims that the Newport milieu detracted from the seriousness of the sport. She wrote that Newport's attitude toward tennis was social rather than sporting: "The beautiful women and their gay parasols served as a moving background that was trying for the players." In 1915 the championships were moved to Forest Hills. Although Elliot attributed the loss to Newport's social atmosphere, it was more than likely the move was made because tennis was becoming even more popular, more democratic, and less patrician in its appeal, and the size of the layout at Forest Hills was better and easier to get to. Championship tennis had outgrown Newport.

When the national championships went to Forest Hills the Casino entered a new period. It became host to an invitational grass court tournament that was an important stop on the tournament circuit. There were other amateur tournaments on the East Coast—at the Longwood Cricket Club near Boston, at the Seabright Lawn Tennis and Cricket Club in Rumson New Jersey, and the Meadow Club in Southampton. The circuit play culminated in late August at the national grass court championships at Forest Hills. All the tournaments were big, serious, and impressive—big for the spectators and a big job for the organizers or managers. When Jimmy became president of the Casino—in the early '50s, part of his job was to make sure their tournament could continue.

After the Casino lost the national championships, Newport was still an important venue, and the tournament there drew some of the best amateurs in the world. Tournament organizers went to Wimbledon—to sign up the players for their invitational, which preceded Southampton, Longwood, and Forest Hills on the grass court tournament circuit. There was no play in the war years of 1917 and 1918, but the tournaments resumed in 1919. Bill Tilden won against "Little Bill" Johnston to begin the play of the 1920s—a great decade for the sport. In 1915 Craig Biddle, head of the tournament committee at Newport, invited fifty-five players.

Months of planning by the Casino governors made all of this possible. James Stewart Cushman took over the Tennis Committee after Craig Biddle. "He took a keen interest in the happiness of the players, and in their careers, although Wilmer Allison, the 1934 Newport winner, writes of a 'good, kind Mr. Cushman who could never understand why we did not want to go to some socialite luncheon after playing five hard sets in the morning with five more facing us in the afternoon.'" A steadfast churchman, Cushman could not be convinced to schedule finals on Sundays.

Spectators and residents of Newport enjoyed the festivities as well. Eleanor Elkins Widener (later Mrs. Hamilton Rice – her Widener husband had gone down on the Titanic) started her famous Tennis Week Ball at Miramar, a gala event that went on through 1937. The servants were dressed in livery like those at Versailles with knee breeches and powdered wigs, and there were two orchestras – one in the ballroom and a Hungarian orchestra on the lawn. It was the highlight of the Newport season. The former Rhode Island governor R.L. Beekman who had been the runner up in 1886 gave an entertainment and there was a celebration at the Clambake

A group of prominent Newport Cottagers watching the Annual National Tennis Tournament at the Casino, 1880s

Club, an exclusive club looking out over Narragansett Bay.

In the years leading up to the Second World War, tennis week at Newport was a great occasion. Spectators would repair daily to the Casino courts knowing that that was the place to see everyone and the place to be seen. What could be more fun than to sit out in the sun or under awnings on a glorious day and watch the best tennis in the country? The prominent families had their own boxes: the Curtis Jameses, Mrs. Watts Sherman, the John Nicholas Browns, the Cushmans and Gillespies. The silver trophies gleamed in the sun on a table and the suspense was who would carry them off at the end of the week. The sport was visually beautiful with the green grass that was mowed and chalked daily and the white-clothed players competing in the pleasant summer weather.

The participants liked the tournaments at Newport because it was a beautiful place to play, the best players competed, and there was a kind of gravitas or dignity to the proceedings. According to an early sports writer "Ichiya Kumage, the Japanese player was the surprise of the 1916 Invitational. He defeated Bill Johnston 6–1, 9–7, 5–7, 2–6, 9–7 in a match of suspense and sportsmanship long remembered." Mr. Kumage told Japanese papers of his good time and raved about the superb hospitality at Newport and the genial Newporters who "invite tennis players as honorable guests." He described "the quavering heat waves of the August day," and made light "of his uncertainties on the grass surface." Against his opponent Bill Johnston's "beautiful refined technique" Kumage's "awkward country style" held-up. After a victor's jazz-band party at Bailey's Beach,

LEFT: *Linesman watching the match, 1894*

ABOVE: *Early court roller*

BELOW: *Casino, 1915*

NEXT PAGE: *Newport Stars in 1892*

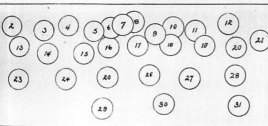

KEY TO THE PICTURE.

NEWPORT STARS IN 1892

(From an old print, by courtesy of C. C. Gunther.)

1. Mrs. J. Borden Harriman
2. Thomas Cushing, deceased.
3. Mrs. Fernando Yznaga, now Countess Bela Zichy
4. Señor Padelia, of the Spanish Legation
5. Miss Anna Sands
6. Mrs. Stuyvesant Fish, who died last Summer
7. Whitney Warren
8. Fernando Yznaga, deceased
9. Miss Maud Livingston, now Mrs. Henry Worthington Bull
10. Lloyd Warren
11. Miss Sallie Hargous, now Mrs. Douglas Gill, of England
12. Hamilton W. Cary
13. M. LeGhait, the Belgian Minister
14. Mrs. Ogden Mills
15. Miss Tooker, afterwards Mrs. Wadsworth Ritchie, deceased

16. Mrs. Victor Sorchan, then Miss Charlotte Hunnewell
17. Mrs. Sidney Dillon Ripley, now Mrs. Charles R. Scott
18. Mrs. W. Butler Duncan
19. Count Boni de Castellane
20. Mrs. W. R. Travers, now Mrs. Frederick C. Havemeyer
21. Frederick O. Beach
22. Count Sierstorpf
23. Mrs. George Barclay
24. J. F. D. Lanier
25. Miss Edith Cushing, now Mrs. Blair Fairchild
26. Mrs. L. M. Rutherfurd, now Mrs. W. K. Vanderbilt
27. Mrs. John Astor
28. Mrs. Whitney Warren
29. Victor Sorchan
30. Duncan Elliot
31. Winthrop Rutherfurd

Ladies dressed in Gay Nineties attire for Tennis Week, 1956

Courtside seats, Casino, late s

Kumage and two dozen other players boarded *Whileaway*, Harry Payne Whitney's yacht, to sail across Long Island sound to the next battlefield, Southampton.

The players would not only join the customary Newport merriment, but also enjoy the Casino's atmosphere. Francis Hunter, four-time Wimbledon champion, preferred playing at Newport to playing before the crowned heads of Europe. "One was competing before a knowledgeable gallery," and the courts were perfect, and "courtesies and niceties," always existed there. José Alonso, whose brother Manuel was runner up to Tilden at Newport in 1927, remembered, "The doors were always open for us in all the clubs, and Bailey's Beach was a meeting place."

The tournaments resumed after World War II, but the Casino buildings were deteriorating and Jimmy was faced with the problem of bringing it back to its former glory or having it replaced by a mall. The Van Alen family had been involved with the institution for generations. His grandfather James John Van Alen was a member of the board of the Casino Corporation back in the 1880s and his mother was an avid supporter of its theatre. Jimmy had played on the courts as a boy and as a young star beginning in the early 1900s. Realizing the value and prestige of the place, he was determined to save it and, in the process, to make the most of the organization's interesting history, and to bring tennis into the present.

Tennis match at Casino, 1955. BELOW: *JVHA gracefully taking an overhead*

In 1956 he organized an historical happening for the Casino's Diamond Jubilee—one of many benefit events to raise desperately needed funds. *The Providence Daily Journal* reported on the "spectacle of lovely ladies, colorful costumes and horse drawn carriages" which were assembled there to celebrate the 75-year-old tradition of staging "the finest amateur tennis players in the world" on its grass courts every summer. Jimmy turned out in a swallow-tailed coat and a bright red "Life with Father" mustache. He regaled the galleries "with some of the old-time court etiquette," and then a group of players from that year's tournament re-enacted the championship matches of 1881 using antique racquets and wearing the long white pants and shirts of the former era to bat the ball back and forth. There were also female spectators in period dress: voluminous-skirted gowns and broad-brimmed hats. They sat along "the sidelines and managed, between chuckles, to cheer the 'old boys' on." Such events were appealing to backers of the Casino, but didn't raise large amounts of money. Amateur tournaments played on grass courts at the northeastern clubs were disappearing; therefore, a continuing challenge was to preserve the Casino's annual invitational tournament, which had been played at Newport since 1915 when the national championships had gone to Forest Hills. Another challenge was to revitalize the old place, which now was only frequented by the summer residents during tennis week. At one time, for summer colonists, and especially teenagers, the Casino was enormously popular and had monopolized tennis in Newport. But since the 1938 hurricane, when Bailey's Beach installed its own tennis courts, Newporters chose to play tennis there and the Casino suffered from this competition. The Casino was forced to respond, and offered reduced rate tennis packages to corporations, business clubs, and professional guests. Jimmy had many ideas for breathing new life into the old place and the best one would be the Hall of Fame.

Forest Hills, 1951, where the U.S. National Championships were played before being moved to Flushing Meadows in 1978

Tennis at the Hall of Fame

Chapter Six:

The Tennis Hall of Fame

In the late 1940s and early 1950s, it was not only the Casino that was being threatened by erratic economic conditions, zealous real estate developers, and a capricious Mother Nature; Newport's other historic buildings were vulnerable to change as well. Over a decade of economic depression had bled Newport of its moneyed residents, the town's most important asset. The presence of the U.S. Navy—especially at the Naval War College on Coasters Harbor Island and the Torpedo Station on Goat Island—acted as a temporary tourniquet during both World Wars, when the federal government poured millions of dollars into Newport's naval operations and thousands of sailors and their families took up residence in the town. But as combat ended both in Europe and in the Pacific, Newport once again faced an identity crisis. With no industrial base for the town's economy, developers sought to tear down much of Newport's historic real estate to build malls, retail stores, and parking lots. Colonial monuments such as the Rhode Island Union Bank were in danger of demolition or condemnation, and the palatial "cottages" of the Gilded Age were selling for a fraction of their original value. When liquor magnate Edson Bradley had his Newport summer home of Seaview Terrace built in 1925, the mansion cost around $1 million (over $10 million in

Casino Clocktower entrance

2010 USD); in 1949, his daughter sold it to a developer for a mere $8,000 (just under $70,000 in 2010 USD).

At the same time, a desire to preserve the tangible evidence of that strange, vanished period—the Gilded Age—emerged as a response to these rapid redevelopment and renewal efforts. In 1945 the Preservation Society of Newport County was founded by about a dozen residents—including Katherine Warren and her husband, George Henry Warren—with the aim of preserving some of the grand mansions. The Preservation Society's first project was to purchase the Hunter House on Washington Street. One of Newport's grand colonial treasures, Hunter House was built and expanded from 1748 to 1754. Throughout its long history, it had been the home of wealthy merchants, powerful statesmen, and for a brief period (1780–1781), a number of French troops en route to the battle of Yorktown.

By 1945, however, Hunter House belonged to St. Joseph's Catholic Church of Newport, which used the building to house some of its nuns. When the parish planned to sell the paneled interiors of Hunter House to the Metropolitan Museum of Art in New York, the newly formed Preservation Society stepped in and bought the house with the aim of restoring it. In 1946 the Society purchased the house for $16,000 and began

*Board of Governors of Tennis
Hall of Fame, 1957*

*Meeting at the Hall of Fame, 1961;
back: Henry Heffernan, Archbold
van Beuren, William Sherman,
George Morrison; front: James
Van Alen, Mrs. George H. Warren,
Mrs. Kenneth Clinton, Mrs. James
Van Alen, Mr. John O'Donnell,
Mr. Monroe*

*Jimmy presiding at the Board of
Governors meeting, 1973*

NEXT PAGE: *Board of Governors
standing on the steps of the Hall
of Fame Museum, 1973*

extensive renovations to the interior and exterior. In 1953, the House was opened to the public, and its beautiful colonial furniture was showcased. Inside, it was discovered that there were outstanding examples of early Newport cabinetmakers' furniture, many by the Goddards and Townsends. Their shops had been located near Hunter House.

The success of Hunter House spurred on the work of the Preservation Society. Seven years earlier, in 1946, the Countess Gladys Szechenyl, youngest daughter of Cornelius Vanderbilt II, who had inherited the family's enormous pile, The Breakers, had agreed to lease the mansion to the Preservation Society for $1 per year and open it to paying tourists and visitors. The Breakers quickly became a popular tourist attraction, drawing thousands of patrons each year. The success of The Breakers encouraged the Preserva-

tion Society to purchase and restore more of Newport's grand, historic real estate for the public to see. Other preservation efforts followed. In 1968, Doris Duke founded the Newport Restoration Foundation to preserve the town's many colonial and pre-Revolution monuments, allowing the Preservation Society to focus most of its efforts on the grand nineteenth century mansions lining Bellevue Avenue and Ocean Drive.

Jimmy was on the same wavelength. He feared the loss of his beloved but ageing Casino. The success of projects like Hunter House and The Breakers suggested that he could save the Casino if he could transform it into a tourist attraction. He attempted to do just that by converting the old complex—the site of some of the earliest tennis matches in the United States—into a national Tennis Hall of Fame, an idea of Candy's. With a Tennis Hall

Ceremony at the Tennis Hall of Fame; left to right: Julian S. Myrick, George Morrison, S. Peabody Gardner, William L. Van Alen, Allison Danzig, David S. Niles, Archbold van Beuren, William J. Clothier, William A. Sherman, James H. Van Alen

Jimmy with the Marquis de Rochambeau who has just cut the ribbon

of Fame, Jimmy would be able to save an important bit of Newport history and also to maintain the Casino's tournament and beautiful grass courts. He had a few major hurdles to jump over, though. The first was to get the permission of the USLTA and sell the idea to the Casino's Board of Directors.

In August of 1952 meetings were held to see if the Hall of Fame idea would fly, and the Newport Casino executive committee brought the Casino's board of governors into the planning. On March 11, 1953, Jimmy wrote to James H. Bishop, president of the USLTA, and stressed the Casino's history as the site of the National Championships from 1881 to 1914, the site of the Newport Invitational Tournament, one of the regular stops on the amateur circuit, and the Casino's unique architecture, all as reasons to create a Tennis Hall of Fame in Newport.

Emphasizing the history of tennis from way back, Jimmy wrote to Bishop: "I can assure you that every effort would be made to make the hall a fitting shrine and the museum an interesting and correlated history of the game since a racquet, a ball, a net and a court were first dovetailed into the game of tennis as played by Henry VIII at Hampton Court in the Sixteenth Century."

A year went by in which Bishop was trying out the idea on the USLTA leaders. On May 1, 1953, Jimmy wrote again sending a more detailed proposal to Bishop. He described the site— two rooms on the first floor of the south wing of the Casino (where the

JHVA with Mamie Eisenhower and William Clothier presenting a trophy

Interior of the Tennis Hall of Fame museum

Tennis Hall of Famers: Three former stars yesterday inducted into the Tennis Hall of Fame at Newport Casino chat with James H. Van Alen, president of the Casino. Left to right are Johnny Doeg, Van Alen, Helen Hull Jacobs and Ellsworth Vines.

—Journal-Bulletin Photo by TOM VARLEY

Net Greats Honored at Newport

Helen Hull Jacobs, Ellsworth Vines and John Doeg, all former national champions, were enshrined in the Tennis Hall of Fame yesterday at the Newport Casino in ceremonies conducted in conjunction with the Newport Invitation Tennis Tournament.

Prior to the induction on the grandstand court with some 700 spectators present, the three net greats of a generation ago had been guests at a luncheon at the Casino.

At the ceremonies, presided over by James H. Van Alen, Casino president, who traced the careers of each recipient, induction certificates were presented.

Hall of Fame directors present at the event were Henry H. Heffernan, William J. Clothier 3rd, William L. Van Alen, J. Burk Wilkinson, Archbold van Buren.

Miss Jacobs is now a resident of New York City. Vines is a golf professional at the Inwood Country Club on Long Island summers and at the Thunderbird Country Club, Palm Springs, Calif., winters. Doeg lives in Colma, Calif.

Vines won the Newport singles title in 1931 with a five-set triumph over Fred Perry of England. Doeg and George Lott were Newport doubles champions in 1928 when they defeated Wilmer Allison and John Van Ryn.

*Net Greats Honored at Newport. National
Champions seated left to right: Johnny Doeg,
Helen Hull Jacobs and Ellsworth Vines.
Jimmy Van Alen is seated behind them.*

---

gift shop is now), and he outlined the process of picking inductees. They would be chosen by tennis writers. The Hall of Fame would ask players for memorabilia and donations. The climax of each year's tennis at Newport would be the inductee ceremony, to be held at the end of the Casino's Tennis Week. A research center would also be established.

What Jimmy and his committee got in September of 1953 was a five-year option, which later was stretched to ten years, during which time the Hall of Fame might be moved to New York or elsewhere, if Newport was felt by the USLTA to be too remote. Van Alen was delighted, and in September

1954 he called a meeting in New York City. William J. Clothier II, of Valley Forge, Pennsylvania, whose father had been U.S. champion in 1906, was elected the first president. Now they could start revamping the space and creating their tennis museum. A quest began for trophies, memorabilia, and other tennis souvenirs to remind visitors of tennis greatness gone by. The first inductees were decided on at a meeting of the board at the Harvard Club in New York in June of 1955 and the Hall was dedicated on July 9. In attendance were Rhode Island notables like Senator Green and Governor Roberts. Straight Clark of Philadelphia and Neale Fraser of Australia entertained with an exhibition match on the center grass court. Grace Kelly, then the close friend of Bill Clothier, was on hand to give out the trophies. A ball at The Breakers capped off the celebration of the new venture.

When the Hall of Fame first opened, its exhibits were modest. The Hall consisted of three rooms, one showing off such memorabilia as Beals Wrights' blazer patch as Davis Cup Captain in 1906, 1908, and 1911, and an autographed menu of a Delmonico dinner honoring the 1913 Cup team. There was also a letter signed by Tilden, Johnston, Hardy, and Washburn written when they were "in quest of the Davis Cup, November 1920." Upstairs there was a paneled room with court tennis exhibits—honoring Jay Gould, an early player and pupil of Tom Pettit's, the Casino's pro, and also honoring Jimmy. Teacher Pierre Etchebaster, World Court Tennis Champion from 1928 to 1954, was remembered in a statue, and the sporting trophies of Theodore Roosevelt Pell (cousin of Senator Claiborne Pell) were on display. In the doubles room there were photos of all the national cham-

Pancho Gonzalez receiving a trophy at the Casino

Ken Rosewall, Ham Richardson, and Jimmy Van Alen

pions. Jimmy was determined to also exhibit tennis dress, which in the mid-1950s was considerably more conservative than it is today. He managed to find a set of tennis dresses by the London designer Teddy Tinling, and an outfit worn by Mary K. Browne, champion between 1912 and 1914.

The Hall of Fame museum went through many stages as it developed. At some points the displays were skimpy and suffered from lack of funding. Other aspects of the place suffered too. Tony Trabert remembered being honored as an inductee in 1970 and being awarded an unimpressive piece of paper in a five-and-ten-cents store frame. The buildings themselves were always in need of repair. Today the exhibits of the Hall of Fame are impressive, and the Hall as an entity beautifully shows off the history of tennis in America.

Once the Hall of Fame was established, organizers decided that on Saturday of the yearly Newport tournament, enshrinement would take place. Sportsmanship and contribution to the sport would be equal to titles in qualifying for the honor. Richard Sears and six contemporaries were first, in 1955. In 1957, all four early luminaries were in Newport, on the center court: Mary K. Browne, champion from 1912–14, Hazel Hotchkiss Wightman, champion from 1909–11 and in 1919, Maurice McLoughlin, champion in 1912–13, and R. Norris Williams, 2nd, champion in 1914 and 1916. Henry Heffernan, treasurer of the Hall of Fame, was with Mr. McLoughlin when the tall, white-haired athlete caught his first sight of the courts through Stanford White's shadowy archway. 'That moment alone,' said Mr. Heffernan, 'justifies the entire Hall of Fame.'"

A new problem had emerged in the mid-1950s. In 1954 a Providence real estate developer appeared with an offer to buy the property for $150,000. Then another developer upped the bid to $160,000. These offers were very attractive to some of the stockholders. Even though the Hall of Fame had been launched by September 1954, the Casino and the Hall of Fame were still two separate entities and the finances of each were precarious. Nevertheless, the board met and voted to turn down the developers' offers. Other solutions for its bleak financial future were considered—a merger with either Bailey's Beach or the Newport Country Club. The 150 shareholders met to decide the Casino's future and one good thing that could be pointed to was one of Jimmy's accomplishments—his reorganizing of the spectators' seats. Since becoming president he had succeeded in having the two grandstand courts surrounded by the famous "umbrella seats," a reorganization of seating which created boxes with attractive umbrellas to shield spectators from the sun.

In his campaign to save the Casino Jimmy knew he had a winning argument—the need to continue its unique history, and many Newporters who cared about the town's traditions agreed with him. In a speech to stockholders in 1956 he emphasized the fact that "the sport for which the Casino has become world famous by its faithful and continuous support has been lawn tennis," and he reminded them of "the duties as laid down in the original charter" and the importance of the "perpetual continuation of the Casino and its nationally renowned Lawn tennis fixtures."

His big push to merge the Casino and Hall of Fame began in April 1959 when he wrote to the stockholders of the Casino "outlining the offer of the National Lawn Tennis Hall of Fame and Tennis Museum, Inc., to acquire control of this corporation by the acquisition of 51% of our stock by gift." If the Hall of Fame could obtain controlling interest in the Casino, the preservation of the Casino would make it "a center of lawn tennis activity." The Board of Governors suggested that the stockholders deposit their stock "under the escrow agreement with the Industrial National Bank of Providence which has been previously been mailed to them." The letter to the stockholders mentioned "the precarious financial state" of the Casino, and a "threat that the present management of the USLTA may withdraw its sanction for our Invitational tournament along with those of other grass court championships on the Eastern summer circuit."

Since the Hall of Fame was a non-profit organization it could solicit funds for the Casino's support "on a nation wide basis," and the continuance of the Casino under this arrangement was more certain than as a private club. The Casino had been appraised at $175,000,

Jimmy with Bill Clothier and Joe Leandra at Newport Casino

and there were 331 shares of stock outstanding, 12 of which were in the name of the Casino. The value of each share was about $540. Gifts of Casino stock would be tax-deductible and stockholders were urged to donate their shares and deposit them with the Industrial National Bank. It would turn out later that the Internal Revenue Service only allowed $100 per share as the deductible figure.

According to Jay Van Alen, Jimmy then used all his considerable influence to save the Casino by contacting and persuading Casino

1971 Enshrinement ceremony: Vic Seixas, Althea Gibson and Jimmy Van Alen

stockholders of the importance of saving the institution. "There were shares of stock that people had inherited from the people who had built the Casino, and there weren't very many of these. This guy wanted to develop the Casino into a kind of supermarket/plaza and Dad went out to each share of stock, and some people had two or three, and he went on bended knees and proposed making a tax-exempt organization out of the whole thing." He would call people first thing in the morning. "He would tell them 'you can donate your shares to the organization, and I'll get you a decent appraisal of the property.' And he was relentless, going around to all the people, and finally he got all the shares. I remember how jubilant he was when he could finally make the Hall of Fame a situation out

right. And then, of course, the trick was to get some funding in order to fix the place up."

Some stockholders fell right into line and some didn't. According to John Winslow, long-time president of Newport's Preservation Society, who gave over his stock right away, Jimmy and Candy would throw attractive dinner parties, seat the female stockholder next to Jimmy, who charmed her throughout the evening in the hope that he would receive a telephone call the next morning saying, "Of course, I will donate my stock."

The IRS had authorized tax exempt status to the Hall of Fame in 1955 and in 1960 the USL-TA was to recognize the new entity. Some stockholders were opposed to the merger and wanted to sell the Casino. They felt that the Casino Corporation was beyond saving and they were afraid of future assessments. Henry Havemeyer, a former Casino president, held 35 shares and was one of those against. His relatives owned 16 more. He was for the sale of the Casino to the developers; Newport's town leaders, however, were against the idea. The Mayor saw it as an asset to the City and the Newport Chamber of Commerce didn't like the idea of out-of-town ownership.

It looked like Havemeyer might win and the Casino might go the way of many Gilded Age monuments—razed for a site of modern buildings. At the last minute Jimmy and his plan were saved by a *deus ex machina* loophole—the language of the Casino Constitutional amendment adopted in 1881. "At all meetings of the Corporation each member owning one share shall be entitled to one vote: owning two shares or more, two votes and no more." As Alan Schumacher writes, " Thus, Havemeyer's 35 shares only entitled him to 2 votes. And his relatives, being non-members, could not vote their stock at all. At the meeting, however, shareholders left open the matter of a future sale."

And even though the Casino was seeking to be controlled by a tax-exempt organization, the Hall of Fame, that did not assure relief from future entrepreneurs who wanted to buy the property. There were later offers but luckily they were turned down. To obtain all the shares, however, was a process that took years. It would not be until 1976 that the final takeover of the Casino Corporation by the Hall of Fame would be complete.

In addition to observing his involvement in the Hall of Fame, Newporters got to watch Jimmy's usual iconoclastic mode and his efforts to apply his way of doing things in another preservation project. He now turned his focus to transforming

Clement Moore's home in Newport into a Christmas museum. Clement Moore, the nineteenth-century Classics scholar, is best known for his poem "A Visit from Saint Nicholas," beginning, "'Twas the Night Before Christmas...". Moore's poem is largely responsible for creating the cultural image of Santa Claus we are most familiar with today, transforming him from "a gaunt old man in bishop's robes who rode about on a white horse with gifts for good children and a birch rod for bad ones," into a fat, jolly, elfish old man pulled on a magical sleigh by a team of eight flying reindeer. Were it not for Clement Moore, the world would be lacking "the finest, jolliest Christmas present of all time: Santa Claus himself." The poem itself was probably written at Dr. Moore's summer home in Newport, a large white frame house at 25 Catherine Street, where he died on July 10, 1863.

Jimmy loved the Christmas poem, judging its message to be one "that fascinates children, brings vivid memories back to their parents, and has meaning for all." He felt that "the values we hope are instilled by this are ones we sadly need." At the same time, he thought Moore's poem as it stood was incomplete, and in 1958 he wrote an introduction and a 48-line addendum to the original 56 verses. As Jimmy recalled, "When I was a child, I always thought the poem ended too soon. It started so suddenly I used to get left behind. Besides, I used to worry about Father standing there by the open window as the poem closes." His solution, as with so many other things, was to write the poem his way—ending with Father sleeping soundly in his bed. "I was afraid he might catch cold, so now I've got him safely tucked into bed. I hope Dr. Moore doesn't mind."

Jimmy wrote his introduction to Moore's poem in rhyming couplets, intending to provide a prelude that would ease the reader or listener into the events that followed. Moore's begins *in medias res*, with the speaker—a father whose family has just gone to sleep on Christmas Eve night—recounting his meeting with Santa Claus. He awakes in the middle of the night to a "clatter" outside his home and, like any responsible father, rushes downstairs to investigate. There in a sleigh pulled by eight tiny, flying reindeer, is Santa Claus, who moments later slides down the chimney with his sack full of toys. The father witnesses Santa filling the stockings and the two exchange a conspiratorial moment before jolly old St. Nick ascends back up the chimney and soars away, wishing a "Happy Christmas to all, and to all a good night!" Jimmy felt the poem began too hastily, without evoking the proper setting for its readers—the Newport home of Dr. Moore, just before bedtime on Christmas Eve night. In his introduction, Jimmy paints this portrait where Moore does not:

Jimmy reading from "A Visit from Saint Nicholas"

The Doctor, children and his wife
Are gathered that the tale be read
Before the children go to bed.

In his afterword, a 48-line "sequel" to Moore's poem, Jimmy's goal was to bring "A Visit from Saint Nicholas" to a more peaceful resolution by latching the window and making sure the father would warmly sleep away the hours until Christmas morning like the rest of his family. Jimmy picks up right where Santa Claus shouts his famous "good-night" and takes to the sky. By the end of the afterword, there is little doubt that all loose ends have been tied up like ribbons on a Christmas present, and the father can comfortably reflect on the visit of his extraordinary guest:

Yes, Saint Nick had been here, it had not
been a dream,
He had come and he'd gone like a
phantom moonbeam,
But where moonbeams that vanish leave
never a trace,
Clear proof of his visit hung by the
fireplace.

As my eyes closed, I smiled at the
wonder there'd be
In the morn when I told what had
happened to me.
What questions and answers, what
jumping and dancing
The picture I conjured was truly
entrancing.

With my heart warm and happy my
nightcap on tight
I resettled myself for the rest of the night
And I whispered so only the Good Lord
would hear
"Bless my children, Saint Nick and his
tiny reindeer."

In 1953, Jimmy and Candy had begun an annual reading of "A Visit from Saint Nicholas" at Moore's home in Newport. Jimmy would dress up as Dr. Moore in a frayed frock coat and sit near the Christmas tree, reciting the poem from memory. But he wanted to share his love of the poem and of Christmas itself with as many people as possible. So after he finished his introduction and afterword to the poem, he solicited Radio City Music Hall in New York to host a reading by none other than himself. On September 12, 1960, he received a response thanking him for the offer, but politely declining it. He later wrote to the President, hoping to have his version read at the annual White House Christmas dinner and party, but received no reply. Although he gave up trying to read his version of Moore's poem to a larger audience, Jimmy continued to pursue his plans to convert Moore's aging white frame house into an authentic nineteenth-century Christmas museum for the children and families of Newport, even into the 1970s. He wanted it to be an authentic reproduction of Moore's house as it would have looked during the nineteenth century, and hoped to add a few flourishes from the poem itself, including a team of eight live reindeer. If the Casino could be saved so that more people could have the fun of playing tennis and reflecting on its history, maybe Christmas could be enhanced, too, by Jimmy's playful endeavors to create a fitting Yule museum. This never happened. However, he continued to dress up and read the poem to assembled children each Christmas in later years at the Newport Congregational Church and the Casino.

Spectators checking the draw on the VASSS Tournament boards

Chapter Seven:
Jimmy's VASSS Tournaments

Besides working at the Casino in the '50s and '60s and trying to establish the Clement Moore Christmas museum, Jimmy was traveling the world plugging the new scoring system. He felt his new system would improve the playing of tennis and make it possible for it to be easily televised. Owen Williams, South African tennis champion and later tournament manager of the United States Open, remembered being at his own tournament in Johannesburg when a helicopter approached the stadium. It circled lower and lower, terrifying the crowd. Who was it—the police? an attack? It turned out to be Jimmy with a big VASSS sign.

In 1965 his VASSS scoring system was being used in the intercollegiate matches to shorten the playing time, but in order to be taken up by the rest of the tennis world, it needed more publicity. As the President of the Newport Casino, Jimmy could easily influence the policies and procedures of tournaments there. But there was a problem—amateur tennis competitions were still subject to the rules and regulations of the International Lawn Tennis Federation (ILTF) and its American arm, the United States Lawn Tennis Association (USLTA), which mandated the traditional scoring system. To get around this, he decided to ignore the amateurs altogether and host an invitational tournament for professionals instead. This was iconoclastic— allowing professionals to play at Newport—the former site of the U.S. Amateur Championships, and one of the most famous venues for amateur competition in the coun-

try! It was unheard of. As professional player Butch Buchholz said later: "Pros at Newport! The green grass might turn brown!"

Without the USLTA breathing down his back, Jimmy would showcase VASSS for tournament play and would schedule matches according to his own method. The tournament format would start as a round robin. Ten matches of 31 points would be played each day, with service changing every five points and players changing sides on the fifth, fifteenth, and twenty-fifth points. Instead of the "love, 15, 30, 40, game" sequence of traditional scoring, Jimmy's tournament used ping-pong-style scoring of 0, 1, 2, and so on, up to 31—not 21—points. Along with a scoring system less confusing to spectators, the round robin gave fans a chance to see every player in action every day. After the round robin, the four players who had amassed the most cumulative points would compete in semifinal and final elimination rounds.

In addition, Jimmy moved the service line three feet behind the baseline, where service normally occurs, in an effort to blunt the impact of the power serve and encourage longer rallies of groundstrokes. The fans, Jimmy thought, were less interested in watching a quick succession of three-point rallies—power serve, weak return, put-away—than they were in watching players show off a variety of skills across the court.

The pros were glad to come back to Newport. In 1965 tennis was still a two-tiered sport, with separate tournaments for amateurs and professionals, and the division was bitter to

Van Alen pointing out special VASSS service line moved 3 ft. behind baseline, to a skeptical Adrian Quist at the Newport Casino

players on both sides. The best players who had turned professional were not allowed to play in the important grass tournaments such as Wimbledon, Forest Hills, and also Newport. Instead, pros played in exhibition matches or small-scale tournaments, usually on hard courts or clay, and sometimes even on a local basketball court. Although some made a decent living, the pros were looked down upon by the tennis establishment—by officials, fans, and even other players. And while amateurs were more esteemed, they had a difficult time financing their tennis careers and finding time to practice.

Just as Jimmy had hoped, the impressive $10,000 purse for the Newport Pro VASSS Championship attracted the best players. Rod Laver from Australia came. He was by 1965 the No. 1 ranked professional, having won fifteen titles and beaten his fellow Australian, Ken Rosewall, 13–5 in their matches during that year. Laver had turned pro in 1962, after winning all four Grand Slam singles titles of that year. Rosewall, who had turned pro in 1957, also came. He had won the French Pro, beating Laver.

Pancho Gonzalez of Los Angeles would make the most noise at the VASSS tournament. He was arguably the best player from 1954–1962, winning the United States Professional Championship eight times and the Wembley professional title in London four times. He whipped all of the best amateurs who turned pro, which included every Wimbledon champion for ten years in a row. Gonzalez' burning desire to win, coupled with his serve and aggressive net game, made him a lethal competitor.

The Ecuadorian-American Pancho Segura, whose forehand has been called "the greatest single shot ever produced in tennis," also showed up. By then he was an old timer, having been ranked World No. 1 player by the Professional Lawn Tennis Association in 1952. Segura had always been a fan favorite. "The fans would come out to see the new challenger face the old champion, but they would leave talking about the bandy-legged little sonuvabitch [Segura] who gave them such pleasure playing the first match and the doubles."

Other all-star pros at the tournament were Barry MacKay, ranked No. 1 in the U.S. in 1960, who stood out with his big serve and bold playing style; and Andres Gimeno from Spain. In 1972 he would become the oldest male to win the French Open. There was Mal Anderson, too, an Aussie player who became the first unseeded player to win the U.S. National singles championship and ranked No. 2 in the world in 1957–58. Luis Ayala from Chile played, an amateur ranked in the world's top 10 from 1958 to 1961. He reached the French final twice, the U.S. quarterfinals in 1957 and 1959, and the Wimbledon quarterfinals in 1959, 1960, and 1961, losing to Rod Laver. Butch Buchholz of St. Louis was one of the game's top players in the late 1950s and early 1960s. He was ranked the World

LAVER-BUCHHOLZ WIN DOUBLES — Earl Buchholz, at left, and teammate Rod Laver were given a surprisingly tough battle before winning a doubles match at the Casino's professional tournament yesterday. They defeated 44-year-old Poncho Segura and Barry MacKay, who was not up to par, suffering from a leg injury.   (Daily News Photo)

Pro Tennis

Aussies Net Points

A pair of Australians led their flights today as the $10,000 professional tennis tournament continued at Newport Casino.

Left-hander Rod Laver led in

In the second match Buchholz beat the sportsmanlike Spaniard. Andres Gimeno, by the same score, 31-27. This was also basically a serve and

31-27, this time in favor of Gonzales. Anderson played a fine game, keeping the score close, but he also had to deal with two interruptions due to

Rod Laver and Butch Buchholz playing doubles

No. 5 player in 1960, appeared four times in the U.S. Top 10 and played for the U.S. in the Davis Cup in 1959 and 1960. Buchholz turned pro in 1961 and toured until 1967, winning the United States Pro Championship in 1962 by beating Pancho Segura in the finals. Also, there was Mike Davies, a famous player from Wales who was to be an early advocate of the tie breaker.

The first match at Jimmy's Newport VASSS Championship was between Davies and Segura. After losing to Segura 19–31, Davies put on his best British scowl and lamented that VASSS "takes the tactics out of

Pancho Gonzalez and Jimmy at the 1965 VASSS Tournament

tennis." Under VASSS, every point was critical—players could not strategically throw a game or set if they were behind, in order to conserve their energy for a later one. But Segura, who had just beaten Davies, called it a "very good" system and "an equalizer." Segura was referring to the way in which VASSS blunted the impact of the power serve, making matches more contentious as players competed in long rallies of groundstrokes, rather than protracted, three-shot, "serve-rush-volley" games.

The second match was between Rod Laver and Luis Ayala. In a slightly closer outcome, Ayala beat Laver 31–25. Laver, who went on to the semifinal match based on his cumulative points, prematurely called VASSS "blooming hopeless," and was ready to give up on the tournament altogether. "You serve one bloody way all your life," Laver complained, "and Jimmy says you have to serve another way." Laver's notoriously powerful serve, which could win him a point in just three strokes, was suddenly powerless to save his game. Jimmy's plan to harness the power serve by insisting players serve three feet behind the baseline made Rod Laver very nervous: "With the server restricted to three feet behind the baseline, service was not the factor it is normally, nor was it followed to the net more than occasionally." For Laver, "his wicked-spinning southpaw service was of little help to him either in scoring or in getting him to the net." Ayala, smiling, told reporters, "In this game, now," raising an index finger to his head, "now you have to think a little." Ayala realized what Davies did not—namely, that the elimination of the power serve required players to develop new playing strategies that would win them long baseline rallies. Although a certain degree of

strategy was lost under VASSS, Jimmy's scoring system made up for it in other ways. As in most games, complaints about the scoring system generally came from the defeated, while the victors found a variety of reasons to praise Jimmy for his innovative thinking.

Jimmy also felt that if the power serve was harnessed, the result would be "that ground strokes would regain their rightful importance. Loss of service would become more frequent, and the net attack would again become a strategic maneuver as it was in the days of the Dohertys, Bill Larned, and Bill Tilden." This was proved at the VASSS tourneys. (Of course in the 1960s Jimmy didn't reckon on the way tennis is played today with the newer, stronger racquets and more fit players being able to return the serve strongly, making deep court rallies routine.)

But the most innovative component of Jimmy's VASSS—the tie breaker—had to wait to make its debut until a later match, when Davies faced off against Rosewall. Jimmy's objection to the traditional rules was that a game could only be won by a margin of two points. Instead of drawing out a match indefinitely until one player consolidated a two-point lead, Jimmy enforced a tie breaker at 30-all. Originally, Jimmy had envisioned the tie breaker, which he called a "hand," as an eight-point game, with the winner being the first player to reach five. If the score reached 4-all, the umpire ordered a replay. The tie breaker added suspense to close matches, but also made sure they ended in time for spectators to see other players.

In one tie breaker game between Rosewall and Anderson that reached 4-all, the two Australians—confused and unsure about how to proceed—asked Jimmy, "What do we do now?"

"Simple, gentlemen," Jimmy answered. "You play another tie breaker."

The inaugural tie breaker at the 1965 Newport Invitational proceeded according to these rules. After a particularly fierce back-and-forth battle between Davies and Rosewall, the score reached 30-all, and the first widely showcased tie breaker match in tennis history began. In an eight-point game that looked like it would inevitably end at 4-all, Davies finally managed to rally on the last two points to beat Rosewall 5–3.

Besides the thrill of watching good tennis, there was a lot more drama to be seen. As Bud Collins recalls, "Pancho Gonzalez demonstrated a remarkable lack of maturity in taking a 31–16 trouncing from Andres Gimeno on Saturday night in the fog. The big champion of the world yelped throughout the match, firing a linesman, moaning about the lighting and generally misbehaving like a tennis brat half his age. Pancho packed his bags after that walloping and stalked out of the dressing room, ready to desert his doubles partner, but he was physically restrained by his wife from leaving the Casino grounds."

As Collins remembers, "Well, Gonzalez was upset at a call. He hit the ball out of the court, onto Bellevue Avenue, or something like that. And Jimmy from his box came out down to the court to reprimand him. And there was all this suspense. And there was quite a disparity in height. Pancho looking down at [the little Jimmy] and saying, 'If you don't like it, I'll leave.' And Jimmy said, 'Then leave, if you can't behave like a gentleman!'"

Gonzalez had hit it out of the court because he was mad, and although he continued to play, he was fuming in the dressing room and about to explode. Gonzalez's wife, Madeline, was sitting in a box next to Candy

and she didn't know who she was and Candy Van Alen didn't know who she was. Pancho said, "Do you know what that Van Alen bitch said about me? She said that I must be horrible to live with." Pancho was saying this to one of the only guys who could get along with him, Pancho Segura. But Segura countered with, "She doesn't know the half of it, does she buddy?"

When it came time for the finals, the crowd assembled, eager to see who would win in this new, over-the-top event. The two players who had amassed the most points in the round robin to qualify for the semifinals and had won those matches were Rod Laver and—despite having lost the earlier tie breaker to Davies—Ken Rosewall. It was exciting. Laver started out with a 9–0 lead, sparking early predictions that he would crush Rosewall and easily clinch the match. But Rosewall rallied, nearly bringing the score to a tie. Laver then pushed ahead 15 to 10, but Rosewall quickly turned the game around and took the lead at 23 to 16. Laver persevered, scoring an impressive fifteen points to Rosewall's five, and came back to win the match 31 to 28. The crowd was ecstatic.

Besides the emotional reactions at Jimmy's tournament, there was plenty of good tennis to watch. Laver came away with a nice pot. Money, an unusual part of a Newport tournament, flowed nicely at Jimmy's Invitational. Van Alen had paid each singles player five dollars a point, with the doubles players splitting the five dollars for their points. Since Laver won the singles and was on the winning doubles team with Buchholz, he pocketed $1,770.25.

Jimmy didn't give up after 1965. In his later VASSS tournaments in 1966, 1967, and 1968, he redid the event. The format again was for round robin matches at the start of the week with the four winners who had the most game points competing for the winning purse at the end of the week in semifinal and final elimination matches. Points were again collected by winning two out of three games, and the scoring was again ping-pong style, 1 to 31. But only the points in the winning two games were counted for both the winner and the loser.

However, a big surprise occurred in 1968. Butch Buchholz was playing Cliff Drysdale. As Buchholz remembers, "Jimmy was there and there were…I guess there were 8 of us, 2 groups of 4. And I'm playing Cliff Drysdale, and I'm serving to him, on ad-court. And I serve to his backhand, and he takes the ball and hits it into the stands. And I'm looking at him like, what the heck is going on? Then I serve to him to deuce court, and he hits the next ball… into the stands (again). And then Jimmy comes out onto the court, and says, 'What the heck are you doing?'" Cliff Drysdale had out-maneuvered Jimmy's scoring system.

In Jimmy's scoring system a player had to win two out of three games of 31 points to win the match. At the end of the week the four players with the most cumulative points advanced to the semifinal matches. But only the points from the victor's two winning games were counted for both the winner and the loser. Drysdale had figured out that there were three possible scenarios for his match against Buchholz. In the first, Drysdale could win the first game and lose the second and third. In that case, the 31 points from Drysdale's first game would be lost, and only his lower scores from the second and third games would be counted. The second possible outcome was that Drys-

PRO TENNIS STARS HERE — Mike Davies, left, of Great Britain and Luis Ayala of Chile meet with James H. Van Alen, center, president of Newport Casino, today as 10 of World's top players come here for second annual National Hall of Fame tournament opening tomorrow afternoon. Standing behind them are, from left, Wally Dill, executive director of International Professional Tennis Association, Henry Heffernan, chairman of Casino executive committee, and Winslow (Mike) Blanchard, nationally - known referee.

Tennis Pros Play Tomorrow

Professional tennis and VASSS will hold the Newport spotlight tomorrow through Sunday, when 10 of the world's top players will compete for a pot of gold at the Casino.

nament will play afternoon and night. This schedule will be followed all four days.

In addition, there will be a clinic for young tennis enthusiasts tomorrow and Sat-

Ayala and Davies. In the second flight will be Laver, Gimeno, Buchholtz, McKay and Barnes.

In each flight every player will meet every other player, and the two players with

Newport Daily News article announcing 2nd Annual Hall of Fame Tournament, 1966

dale could win the first two games, in which case his 31 points in both games—a total of 62—would be counted. In the third scenario, Drysdale could lose the first two games to Buchholz, and his losing score in both those games would be counted.

Because Drysdale had no way of knowing who would win any of the games, he decided to purposely lose the first game as soon as he had the number of points—say, 17—that he needed to qualify for the elimination rounds. The strategy ensured that Drysdale would have enough points to qualify for elimination rounds no matter what. If Drysdale lost the second game and Buchholz won the match, then Drysdale's points from both games would still be counted. If Drysdale won the second game and lost in the third, giving Buchholz the win, then the 17 points from the first game (as well as those in the

New York Times sportswriter Allison Danzig

third) would still be counted. And if Drysdale won the second and third games, all his winning points from those two games—a total of 62—would be counted, and the 17 points from the first game would be unnecessary. "There was the flaw," said Buchholz. "And Cliff had figured this all out in advance. And Jimmy was beside himself."

Laver not only won the 1965 VASSS tournament, but also the 1967 tournament in front of fifteen hundred Casino fans. Allison Danzig, who covered both tournaments for the *New York Times*, proclaimed it to be "one of the most entertaining VASSS events so far. The play last night was exciting in the extreme and the spectacular stroke production brought forth thunderous applause."

Danzig, the first journalist to be inducted into Jimmy's International Tennis Hall of Fame, was a celebrated sportswriter for the *New York Times* from 1923 to 1969. Assessing the quality of sports writing during the twentieth century, writer George Plimpton evolved what he called the "Small Ball Theory"—namely, "the smaller the ball, the more formidable the literature. There are superb books about golf, very good books about baseball, not many good books about football, or soccer, very few good books about basketball, and no good books at all about beach balls." Plimpton admitted his theory was "on shaky ground with tennis," where both the ball and the literature are "lighter" and "fuzzy, without much density." In doing so, he evidently forgot about one of the greatest sports writers of the twentieth century—a passionate critic of tennis and a close friend of Jimmy Van Alen's—Allison Danzig.

Although he also covered the gridiron of college football and the Olympic games, his real métier was racquet sports—lawn tennis, court tennis, and squash. His coverage of lawn tennis chronicled the greatest changes to the sport during the twentieth century, beginning with the golden matches of Bill Tilden, Suzanne Lenglen, and Helen Wills, and ending with the dawn of open tennis and live television broadcasts. Throughout his career Danzig maintained such attention to detail and sensitivity toward the sport that Gene Scott, a Davis Cup player who later founded *Tennis Week* magazine, once said that his "opinion on the quality of a match had the imprimatur of a theatre critic." His probing analysis of strategy, spin, placement, and form rivaled that of the coaches and players themselves. In 1963, the Longwood Cricket Club in Boston honored Danzig by establishing the Allison Danzig Award for distinguished tennis writing; Danzig was its first recipient.

Danzig distinguished himself as one of the few sportswriters in the United States who could understand the complexities of court tennis well enough to cover matches. It was during his coverage of court tennis that Danzig first met Jimmy Van Alen, who won the U.S. singles championship in court tennis three times—in 1933, 1938, and 1940. Danzig covered each of these tournaments, praising Jimmy for his artful strokes, expert placement, and deadly spin. Around this time Jimmy began to exchange personal letters with Danzig, a correspondence that increased in the years Jimmy was plugging the tie breaker and his VASSS scoring reforms. In the years that followed, Danzig was the first journalist Jimmy would contact when he wanted press coverage or publicity for his tennis projects.

In the 1960s and 1970s, Danzig continued to support Jimmy's tennis reform efforts, even after he retired as a writer for the *New York Times*. He wrote to Jimmy in 1969 advising him to seek financial assistance from the USLTA for "the maintenance and upkeep" of the Hall of Fame, "a true and lovely cradle of the game." And later, when a twelve-point "lingering death" tie breaker threatened to replace Jimmy's nine-point sudden-death tie breaker, Danzig wrote to voice his support for Jimmy. He criticized the twelve-pointer for its lack of "urgency and crisis," agreeing with Jimmy "that anything that adds drama to the performance should be retained." Besides supporting Jimmy publicly, Danzig and his wife Dorothy often came to Newport to stay with Jimmy and Candy.

Jimmy's VASSS tournaments were taking place just when the status of amateur tennis was breaking down. Since amateur players could not make a living playing, the best had been turning professional. The amateur tournaments like the one at Newport and other country clubs might be attractive to the spectators, but they were less attractive to the players. For one thing, there was the question of money and arrangements. Gardnar Mulloy, who had been ranked No. 1 in the country soon after the Second World War, had his complaints about the way Jimmy Van Alen and others ran these tournaments. The less well-seeded players were put up in sleeping bags in the club's squash courts and as soon as they lost, were no longer given meals. He had a fight with Jimmy, who said, "You'll never play at Newport again." The next year the tournament organizers wanted him as number one to come back but he wanted Jimmy to apologize to him. Everyone said Jimmy wouldn't apologize—and he didn't, but at the same time they really wanted Gardnar. Gardnar refused.

While Jimmy was promoting his tie breaker and VASSS in the 1960s, the fight by the pros for open tennis continued. Open tennis—which would allow the pros to play in the major championships previously only open to amateurs—had been defeated by only 5 votes during a meeting of the International Lawn Tennis Federation in 1960. Its proponents had secured only 134 votes of the required 139 out of 209; a switch of five votes, and open tennis would have come in 1961 instead of 1968. Tennis promoter Jack Kramer believed "It was an absolute fix; one man who had committed to open tennis went to the bathroom when the vote was called. The Big Four [tournaments or "Majors"] all voted for the measure, but it was the United States that brought about its defeat. The USLTA voted one way and lobbied another." For Kramer, this loss was a blow to the future of tennis and essentially prolonged the inevitable. In his mind tennis had to go open. It needed to in order to survive.

In reality most amateur players—if they were good—were paid under the table, which would have been a shock to the naïve tennis public. When tournament directors wanted to attract the very best players, they offered them hundreds of dollars—the better the player, the larger the sum. A little money on the side allowed them to survive playing the sport they loved. Butch Buchholz called the amateur system "crazy. People couldn't support themselves...it was under the table. It was not the right way to do it...They would give you an envelope with 100 dollars and once you lost, that was it." Many amateurs with families and retirement to think about opted to turn professional. But that, too, had its downsides. As professionals they were banned from playing the most prestigious competitions, which were exclusively for amateurs.

Professional players were relegated to playing one-night stands in city after city for small change instead of playing in respectable tournaments. Although the best pros were making $50,000 or more in the late 1950s, many others were not. And it was bad for the amateurs, who were unable to make a living doing what they loved best. Amateurs, as a rule, were only to receive compensation for expenses incidental to the competition itself, such as room, board, and transportation. Even while these professional players were competitive, much of the public did not consider the winners of their closed tournaments to be true champions.

In the 1950s all the good Wimbledon Champions like Gonzalez, Hoad, Rosewall, Trabert, and Segura were forbidden from playing in major tournaments once they turned pro. As Butch Buchholz describes it, "there was this feeling that all the best guys weren't allowed to play. There was a negative stereotype against the pros—they were thought of as dirty old guys." And tennis players playing the amateur circuit knew that this should change and that professional tennis would and should come soon.

Jack Kramer described the amateur system as "a thoroughly rotten arrangement... In the shamateur days, we were only athletic gigolos—which is what Tilden called us— and the system was immoral and evil. I mean to be harsh...Oh, sure, we were kids: we had fun playing clubs and chasing dames, it was nice hanging around country clubs and money, and a few of us like myself even moved up—but overall the system was rotten." The amateur system which had begun in the 1920s and lasted until 1968 had its dark side that the fans never saw. For many amateurs on the circuit it was a dead-end job with no long-term job security. "Players would wake up at the age of thirty with no job and no business background. They were dismissed as tennis bums—and often by the very people who had kept them strait-jacketed."

Kramer also believed the inherent flaws in the system hurt the players' ability to grow. Over the years amateur players played at various East coast tennis clubs. At one point the summer circuit started at the Merion Cricket Club near Philadelphia. Other stops on the tour were Baltimore, Longwood outside of Boston, Seabright on the Jersey coast; Southampton, Long Island; Rye at the Westchester Country Club outside New York; and the Newport Casino; and finishing at Forest Hills. All the tournaments were played on grass, an unfamiliar surface to most of

VASSS Intercollegiate match, Florida State versus Navy, 1965

the young players. "As a consequence," says Kramer, "a kid would come on tour and each week get whipped in the first round. Then he would be denied a chance to practice on grass since he was out of the tournament and the members didn't want losers damaging their courts. By the end of the summer, the kid would have regressed considerably."

Not everyone believed the system was as corrupt as Kramer did. Donald Dell, a three-time all-American tennis player from Yale and former Davis Cup captain, remembers the time of amateur tennis fondly. "In my second or third year—when I was at Yale, either in '58 or '59…I knew a lot of people, because of Yale, and I went to all the debutante parties that week. It was a fun week. But it was truly an amateur tennis week. Nobody

was making money, and it wasn't a big professional deal. And it was a lot of fun."

Many other young players were thrilled to be part of these tournaments. Bill Talbert was always a champion of amateur tennis. It opened up a glamorous and interesting life for this young man from the Middle West and he was well-liked and sought after by those whom he met during his playing days. Talbert would make a great contribution to the sport. What's more, he was able to carry on his business life as an executive of a New York printing company at the same time that he was playing tennis. Two young South African players, Owen Williams and Gordon Forbes, came of age in their tennis travels and matches all over England and Europe and had a wonderful time.

Jimmy's mother, Margaret Bruguiere, at Wakehurst where she entertained players in the VASSS tournament.

Professional tennis, however, would never be as big or as successful as it could be without the support of the old guard—the USLTA and the ILTF. Tired of fighting with USLTA officials, reporters, and players, Kramer decided to call his fight for open tennis quits in 1962. Years went by in what Kramer called "the dark decade for tennis professionals" until finally, in 1967, the open tennis prospect received its biggest breakthrough. In August, Jack Kramer spoke with Herman David, the Chairman of the All England Lawn Tennis and Croquet Club at Wimbledon. The television ratings for the last championship match were low; Herman David was looking for something to boost the popularity. "In essence, what David finally said was: look, we're tired of putting on second-class tennis as 'the championships' and we want a true

champion." What Wimbledon agreed to was an eight-man trial professional event to be staged at Wimbledon the next summer. "The BBC agreed to put up the purse of $35,000 and Wimbledon sprang for the doubles money of $10,000. This total made the tournament the largest purse-money event in history."

As Butch Buchholz describes it, "[Herman David] said that if we filled the stands, that tells him that the British public still wants to see the players. And we filled the stands every day! And that was really the turning point...Wimbledon was first. Before that, everyone thought that if the professionals set foot on the courts at Newport or Wimbledon, the grass would turn brown." The eight who played were Pancho Gonzalez, Rod Laver, Ken Rosewall, Pancho Segura, Andrés Gimeno, Butch Buchholz, Frank Sedgman, and Lew Hoad. "It was an absolute smash. The matches sold out every day and the BBC ratings were high." By March of 1968 the ILTF had signed off on a dozen open tournaments for 1968 and dozens for 1969. To Jack Kramer the situation was more than ironic. "The whole damn thing is that all along we thought we had to convince the whole tennis world but when Herman David decided that open tennis would be good for Wimbledon, the country and the world followed in step."

The year before, in late 1967, New Orleans businessman Dave Dixon had teamed up with Lamar Hunt in forming the World Championship Tennis (WCT). Hunt was a Texas oil millionaire turned pro-football promoter, helping to shape the American Football League (AFL), and is credited with coining the term "Super Bowl." His enlistment into the WCT hastened the dawn of open tennis along with WCT's rival George

McCall's National Tennis League. At the time, McCall had the best players—Laver, Rosewall, Emerson, and Pancho Gonzalez—but Hunt had the organization and the money. In 1968, Dixon and Hunt rounded up John Newcombe, Tony Roche, Cliff Drysdale, Nikola Pilic, Butch Buchholz, Dennis Ralston, Pierre Barthes, and Roger Taylor, who comprised "The Handsome Eight." The old split between amateur tennis and professional tennis was beginning to close in favor of the professionals. Eventually, Hunt's WCT emerged as the dominant tour in signing amateurs under contract. By the 1970s, open tennis had arrived.

Jimmy Van Alen had been all for open tennis. He had invited the pros to Newport in 1965, 1966, and 1967, breaking a longstanding rule that the pros did not play in the venues of the amateur tournaments. He wanted tennis to be as popular as other American sports for fans and players. Going open was the only way.

In 1957, Allison Danzig had seen Jimmy's backing as significant, and he wrote to praise two developments, which had pointed to the improvement in the relations between amateur and professional tennis. The Nassau Country Club at Glen Cove, Long Island, one of the most beautiful grass court venues, had allowed professionals to play a round robin tournament at Forest Hills close to the yearly amateur invitational. Also, "James Van Alen was willing to open the courts of the Casino for an open tournament for both professional and amateurs if the USLTA and the ILTF legalized the event." According to Danzig, Jimmy's invitation was important because of the Casino's "association with conservatism and the old guard of tennis." He also gave a

compliment to Jimmy's mother, Mrs. James Laurens Van Alen Bruguiere, who "ruled for many years as Newport leader of the 400. From her box in the Casino grandstand she has watched the world's greatest amateurs pass in review and she has entertained them in her villa." But now Jimmy, "who makes a practice of defying tradition and [is] seemingly hopelessly at odds in lawn tennis and court tennis and usually carries through to success, has put Newport on record as ready to open its sacrosanct portals to the professionals in competition with amateurs."

As the tennis world was changing, Jimmy in his position would encourage open tournaments as well as running the customary amateur ones at Newport. The traditionalist was all for radical change. He believed in preserving Casino history but he also recognized the future of tennis was open tennis. The amateur tournaments continued until tennis went open in 1968, as the organizers were determined to carry on the traditions of Newport's legendary past. But Jimmy, ahead of the game, had already staged his VASSS tournaments beginning in 1965. And in 1968 a pro tournament was voted in by the Casino board. "Each of the board members expressed his views. The consensus was against attempting to hold an amateur tournament in 1969." Rather, the Newport Casino would recommend that another pro tournament be held the following summer.

Jimmy realized that the sport depended not just on the players but on the fans too and they had to be kept happy. He was big on making the matches' times predictable so they could be televised, and this meant changing the scoring and it meant he could realize his dreams. It seemed the time had truly arrived for VASSS!

*Jimmy and Candy
at Virginia Slims
Tournament, 1972*

Chapter Eight:

The Open Uses the Tiebreaker

Once he had made a splash with his own VASSS tournaments, Jimmy's next challenge was to get VASSS officially accepted for tournament play. He was lucky to convince some key personalities of the importance of his changes, but now the question was—how to get the changes out of Newport and into the tennis world at large.

Beginning in 1958, *Boston Globe* writer Bud Collins joined Jimmy's group of supporters. Outspoken, articulate, amusing Bud Collins felt it was a time for change in the late 1950s and early 1960s, and he was glad to see things shaken up. He had received continuous invitations to come down to Newport to watch the consolation matches at the Invitational. Previously Jimmy hadn't paid much attention to the Bostonian sportswriter because, as Collins says, "Allison Danzig of the *New York Times* was his man." Bud immediately saw that as tournament director Jimmy was fed up with endless, unpredictable matches and he wanted to play his Newport tournaments his new way. "And the USTA were really stuffed shirts at that time. They thought that you couldn't mess with the game. So, as a result Jimmy ran the consolation tournaments with the new scoring. That's one reason I went down. I wanted to see it in action. I remember overhearing two Australians saying, 'Do you understand what we're doing?' And the other said, 'No, but let's just play the game the regular way, and then we'll tell him certain scores—that will do it.' The players were not impressed. And then some of them complained later that he gave

better prizes for the consolation matches. But he was determined! That was the thing about Jimmy—he was a bulldog."

And his humor had helped. As Bud Collins said later, "traumatized and trichotomized, Jimmy had become part-witch doctor, part-revolutionary, part-missionary," intent on saving tennis from deuce sets. It was the endless matches that had gotten Jimmy really going for VASSS: "Such monstrosities are urological torture for players, spectators, and court officials." As Jimmy put it in verse:

You want to know why I won't sit on a line
Or umpire a match, well, I'll tell you.

If it happens to be one which goes on for three
Hours or more, no one ever will spell you.

You're expected to stay on the job come what may,
Though the duties of nature are calling,

And the beating you take, if you get such a break
Urologically speaking's appalling.

Billy Talbert was also fascinated by what he saw at the consolation tournament matches using the new scoring. Talbert had grown up Cincinnati, OH. Stricken by diabetes at the age of ten, he was not allowed to play baseball or the sports he loved. Tennis was thought to be less strenuous and when he was given lessons he excelled quickly. By the 1940s he was at the top—winning match after match with his champion doubles partner, Gardnar Mulloy. Talbert won four of his

VASSS sudden death scoring rules, 1970

nine Grand Slam doubles titles with Mulloy and was said to be the best backhand court player ever. He also played in the Davis Cup for six years, winning nine out of the ten matches he played.

Billy Talbert had come to the Casino tournaments as a young man and stayed in the dormitories like other unknowns. He was in awe of everything at Newport—the beautiful courts, the clubs, the mansions. After a short first marriage, he wed socialite Nancy Pike and was propelled into the society group in which Jimmy moved. Gardnar Mulloy, his partner and friend with whom he traveled the world, would tease Billy by saying, "You didn't marry Nancy, you married the Social Register." He was charming and

pleasant, liked by everyone, and able to stay in the amateur tennis world by the success of his printing company, which often worked for clients he met in his social life—like the Du Ponts and Fords.

Jimmy, who was always looking for court tennis partners, got Billy playing court tennis and they became good friends—friends because they played together and friends because he, like Jimmy, became a tennis manager. After returning from tennis in 1951, he was powerful in the USLTA and became Davis Cup Team Captain, and later was the director for the U.S. Open in 1970, just when the tie breaker was looking for acceptance. He fought on Jimmy's behalf and helped introduce the tie breaker into official tournament scoring.

When Talbert became won over by the tie breaker he reported how "visitors at the Newport Casino rubbed their eyes and indulged in a double-take" when they saw the tiebreak points played. On some of the side courts during the annual Newport Invitational Tournament fans witnessed a strange sight and heard noises hitherto unassociated with championship tennis. They saw the server delivering the ball from an added line three feet behind the regular base line of the court. They heard umpires barking, "Score, 15–13," and, "19–18." Talbert was a big fan of Jimmy's, impressed by how Jimmy was the "overseer of the Tennis Hall of Fame" and "conducts one of the nations' top grass-court tournaments." Talbert said he liked what he saw in the consolation matches—long and exciting rallies and plenty of strategic maneuvering. However, the system, he felt, would favor a particular type of play because it would "put a premium on skill but it would offer little reward for sheer stamina."

Besides tie breaker enthusiasts in America, Jimmy also had a great champion in England. Jimmy (or C.M.) Jones, a British sports editor, published three months worth of pro-VASSS material in his *British Lawn Tennis* magazine. He was getting huge amounts of criticism as the "official journal" for giving so much support to "non-traditional" scoring. "Heaven knows what the I.L.T.F. will say when the March issue has reached all members and been discussed." He reported and then suggested to Jimmy that he extend the coverage to April, May, June issues and even July. "Please let me know soonest…and if I am drummed out of the boy scouts for daring to push VASSS, do you have any vacancies for gardeners, chauffeurs or butlers!!" Two weeks later Jimmy responded tongue-in-cheek, "Strangely enough, I have a place for a third gardener in case things go wrong."

Once tennis went open the big smash for Jimmy would be to have his tie breaker used at Forest Hills, and the fact that his great friend Bill Talbert, the tournament director of the 1970 U.S. Open, favored the tie breaker made a big difference. As Bud Collins remembered, "Bill could see the value of the tie breaker. And he was the one who decided that it would be used at the U.S. Open. And that is where it really got showcased, because Newport was pretty small stuff." The tie breaker had been used at larger tournaments—including the Pennsylvania Grass Championships in 1970 at the Merion Cricket Club and at the Longwood Cricket Club in Boston—just months before the Open, but its true debut was at Forest Hills.

The players, however, didn't like it. As Bud remembered: "In 1970, when they were going to use it for the first year, and at Longwood before, and at the U.S. Pro Championships, the players were furious. They didn't like it. Because they were nervous. And Talbert said, 'Well that is what it's all about.' And they drew up a petition at Longwood to Talbert, asking him not to use it at the U.S. Open. And they came up to me asking me if I would give it to Talbert. I said I'll deliver it, but I don't agree with it at all. And I gave it to Talbert and he said, 'Well, it makes them nervous, and that is what it is all about.'"

Talbert knew the crowds would love it. As Bud says, "Now when you talk to people about the days before the tie breaker, they just think it was always like this. I mean nobody has any historic memory." Thanks to Jimmy, the USTA uses it for every set in the U.S. Open—although the other majors don't use it for the fifth set, or for the third for the women.

Newport doubles match, 1967

Talbert praised this breakthrough change in scoring, citing how the length of matches would now be predictable. The *New York Times*, in its reporting, mentioned how many long matches had exhausted players and fans in the past and noted that of all the long, long matches, the longest on record was a match of 126 games won by British player Roger Taylor, who beat Wieslaw Gasiorek of Poland 27–29, 31–29, 6–4. Talbert said that the tie breaker would have tremendous impact, "artistically and psychologically," and it would "improve the sport's chances of gaining national television exposure," previously impossible because of the unknown length of many matches.

Another key person in the tie breaker's acceptance was Alastair Martin—an old Jimmy Van Alen friend and former court tennis champion. He was President of the USLTA and known as very progressive. He had worked with Robert Kelleher, his predecessor as President of the USLTA, in achieving open tennis in 1968, and it was Martin who authorized Talbert to use the tie breaker at Forest Hills in 1970. Martin was all for true open tennis in tournaments and in the Davis Cup. The ILTF qualified "open" tennis by allowing only pro players who were regis-

Trophy Presentation at the Casino, 1955. Left to right, Kosei Kamo, Vic Seixas, Candy Van Alen, Ham Richardson, and Atsushi Miyagi

tered with their national associations to play in sanctioned events; other pros were still excluded. Martin didn't like the power that the ILTF exerted over American tennis, and at the Federation's meeting that spring in Dubrovnik (in the former Yugoslavia, now Croatia), he introduced an amendment that would allow each country's tennis association independence and the power "to establish rules of play, categories of players, and rules for the conduct, promotion and scheduling of tournaments."

VASSS had been used in other important tournaments too, with some success. As early as March 1966, Allison Danzig noted the increasing popularity of VASSS among fans who had seen the scoring system in action at the Vanderbilt Athletic Club in New York. VASSS was then used at the pro tournament at Forest Hills in June. The aim of the tournament, which boasted a purse of $30,000, was to "build a new image for tennis rivaling golf's." Many of the pros from Jimmy's VASSS invitational tournaments in Newport—including Pancho Gonzalez, Rod Laver, and Ken Rosewall—played at Forest Hills as well. Laver won the Forest Hills tournament, beating Rosewall 31–29 in "a superlatively fought final match that had the 5,000 spectators breaking into prolonged applause repeatedly in appreciation of the electrifying passages of super strokes." Laver's performance earned him a check for $6,070, which he qualified as "the biggest check I

Jimmy with his tiebreaker chicken flag and sign

ever won." Several months later, Laver beat Pancho Segura 31–28 in the $25,000 Don Budge Masters Tennis Tournament in Binghamton, New York, which also used VASSS.

By 1969, the year after tennis went open, VASSS was approved for use in consolation matches at the U.S. Open. The prize money for the matches—$1,500 for the men and $750 for the women—was a "most generous donation" on the part of the National Tennis Hall of Fame. No longer limited to pro tournaments, VASSS was slowly making its way into a major Grand Slam competition. But Jimmy was not content to keep VASSS in the consolation matches. He wanted his scoring system to become the scoring system—and to do that, he would have to get it approved for use in all U.S. Open matches.

In July 1970, the big breakthrough came for Jimmy. Plans were made for the nine-point tie breaker to be used in all of the matches in the $160,000 United States Open Championships held between September 2 and 13 at the West Side Tennis Club in Forest Hills. The International Lawn Tennis Federation had recently approved it for "experimental use." This meant that a lot of money rested on one point. Since the prize money was $20,000 for the men's singles, that much could rest on one shot if the scores reached 6-all in the fifth set and 4-all in the tie breaker. The way the tie breaker worked was that when games reached 6-all, Player A would serve two points and then Player B would do the same. This was repeated if the points remained tied. The ninth point, served by Player B, then decided the match. If the score wasn't tied, the first to five won.

At the 1970 U.S. Open, Ken Rosewall and Tony Roche were in the finals. Roche took the first set 6–2. Rosewall rallied and took the second set 6–4. When the third set went to 6-all it was time for the tie breaker. Rosewall won—in front of a frenzied crowd—taking the third set 7–6, and went on to win the final set 6–3.

The reactions to the tie breaker were mixed. Most players hated it but spectators loved it. The sticking point was that one player got to serve four of the first six points. Pancho Gonzalez was often quoted, "Looks like half-VASSS to me." It also soon became apparent that the tie breaker favored a player with one sort of game—the player with the strong serve. In the 2008 Wimbledon final between Rafael Nadal and Roger Federer, Nadal could not win the two tie breakers because Federer was stronger on the service points. That match, which Nadal finally won at the last set and which didn't have a tie breaker, showed the importance of the tie breaker in the time taken. Even with two tie breaker sets the match lasted more than four hours and forty-eight minutes, longer than any other Wimbledon final. For TV audiences it was even longer, as two separate rain delays stretched the match to an all-day endeavor, barely finishing before dark.

Sports columnist Barry Lorge, writing years after the 1970 U.S. Open said, "One thing was certain: Sudden Death in the Afternoon at Forest Hills was an instant smash. There were 66 tie-break sets in men's singles at the 1970 Open, 52 in men's doubles, 10 in women's singles, seven in women's doubles and 10 in mixed doubles."

So the sudden death tie breaker—nine points and sudden death at 4-all—was approved by the USLTA for use in the 1970 U.S. Open, even after the players complained to Billy Talbert, who famously said, "I never knew a player who bought a ticket." [Although the tiebreak was adopted for the open tournament, the other VASSS scoring was not—not the table-tennis-style scoring (0, 1, 2, 3, and 4 as opposed to love, 15, 30, 40, game) or the pushed back baseline.

After the big breakthrough—the tie breaker being played at the 1970 U.S. Open—Jimmy Jones, Van Alen's English tennis editor friend, responded from England enthusiastically. "Well, it looks as though we have won. First of all, congratulations on your success at the U.S. Open Championships. Maybe the players find the going a bit tough, but from every report I have heard the public just loved it. When Derek Hardwick arrived back in England I specifically asked him how long before it would be applied here and he replied that the I.L.T.F. had to face up to the fact that they must introduce tie-break scoring into the rules. He also thought it would be in use at Wimbledon in the very near future. You and I know that Frank Rostron and *Lawn Tennis*, which means me, were the only ones one hundred percent with you throughout your long campaign."

After the tie breaker was adopted, it was announced with flair at every match. As Bud Collins says, "At Forest Hills, when there was a tie breaker, a red flag would go up on center court. The huge flag would curl, and when people saw these flags, everyone would go, 'Oooh! Tie breaker!' And that's why Jimmy was known as the Newport Bolshevik. But after they moved to Flushing Meadows that was done away with. And

Candy and Jimmy with his Sudden Death Flag

God knows whatever happened to that flag. But they should reinstate it. I have suggested it many times." As Jimmy explained in his correspondence to Jimmy Jones, "What VASSS Sudden Death did to pump new life into tennis in the Pro Championships in Boston and the Open at Forest Hills had to be seen to be believed. People went crazy. Every time the Sudden Death red flag was hoisted on a court, people would flock to have a look. Furthermore, they didn't have any of those ghastly carry-over matches or, at best, one or two, and people went home

between 7 and 7:30. After what I saw, I certainly agree with you that sudden death is well on the way to general adoption. Let's hope so anyway. The game deserves it."

Even with this victory, Jimmy was not content to rest. He wanted all of VASSS accepted. He wrote to Jimmy Jones: "No doubt you will have seen that VASSS NO-AD tiebreak has won through and received acceptance of the USLTA and the ILTF. I can't appreciate it yet...I'm delighted to have won this victory, but I consider that the other two points are just as important—the seven-point game and the 1–2–3 as opposed to the 15–30–40, and 'o' instead of 'Love.' So, it would appear that there is no rest for VASSS yet awhile, so keep banging away at it, if and when you can, and emphasize that we have won the first round in this tortuous contest which started in 1958 in Newport and ended at Longwood in 1970."

Not long after the acceptance of the tie breaker in 1970, a new debate raged: should the tiebreak be determined by nine points or by twelve? The twelve-point tie breaker was first developed by two tennis greats, Rod Laver and John Newcombe, before the U.S. Open in 1970, the first tournament to integrate Jimmy's nine-point tie breaker into the scoring system. Laver and Newcombe felt that Jimmy's nine-point tie breaker "raised the element of luck to an unnecessary and perhaps dangerous degree," as the entire match hinged on a single point. If a player with a particularly powerful serve held service on the last point of the tie breaker, entire tennis matches could be won on serves alone, rather than all-around play. Or a match might be won on a lucky shot that strikes the net and falls over. As tennis historian Steve Flink argues, "the strength of the scoring system has always been separating the winner from the loser in a game, set, or match by two points. The concept of allowing two players to reach simultaneous set or match point was too extreme." Acknowledging the need for a tie breaker to prevent endless matches, Laver and Newcombe instead experimented with a twelve-point tie breaker, "which required the winner to take seven points by at least a margin of two." Such a system, which Jimmy called "lingering death," would allow a player to win by only one set, but would not

allow a player to win a set or match by only one point. Laver and Newcombe hoped that a twelve-point tie breaker would reconcile the much-needed innovation and excitement of the tie breaker with the more traditional scoring rules of tennis.

Jimmy successfully pushed his nine-point tie breaker into the scoring system at the U.S. Open with support of the President of the USLTA and the faint-hearted ILTF (for "experimental use") in 1970. But later that year, Ed and Marilyn Fernberger, then-co-chairmen of the U.S. Pro Indoor in Philadelphia, broke with both the International Lawn Tennis Federation (ILTF) and the new scoring system of the U.S. Open by introducing Laver and Newcombe's twelve-point tie breaker into their winter tournament in Philadelphia. According to British author and critic David Gray, the USLTA, which had just begun its efforts to persuade the ILTF and the rest of the tennis world to accept Jimmy's tie breaker, "benevolently turned a deaf ear and blind eye" on the Philadelphia tournament. On the third day, however, "a cable arrived from the ILTF in London, saying that the tournament must revert to normal scoring at once. Apparently, no one on the ILTF's management committee could understand why sets kept ending at 7–6."

Ed Fernberger patiently explained to the ILTF why the tie breaker was necessary to keep the tournament on schedule, but the ILTF continued to insist that the Philadelphia tournament revert to normal scoring. By that time, however, the tournament was almost over. Both the men's and women's finals had already been decided by the new twelve-point tie breaker: Rod Laver beat Tony Roche 6–3, 7–6, 6–2, and Margaret Court beat Billie Jean King in a smaller women's event 6–3, 7–6. The tie breaker between Court and King proved that a twelve-point "lingering death" would not extend matches indefinitely, as Jimmy had feared: in the women's final, Court overcame King 14–12.

Jimmy felt strongly the tiebreak should only be played to nine points but the ILTF would never accept the nine-point so the twelve-point was adopted in 1974. In a letter to C.M. Jones, he highlights the flaws. "This is also a weakness in the twelve-point if the score shall be tied at 6 points. For instance, in the Rosewall-Roche key 3rd set sudden-death, the server lost 3 of the first points played. Also, if the service holds at the end of 6 points, the first server will have served 4 out of the 6 and leads 4–2, the pressure on the server of the final 3 points is tremendous. He must win them all. It's curious how seldom the play reaches the ninth point. The pressure in sudden death has produced a new dimension—none of the old estimates hold true. Anything can and does happen—it divides men from the boys as in the Colosseum in Rome. Anyway the way I see it, sudden death is best, 5 out of 8 as played in the PRO VASSS at Newport. Prior to 1969 is the next best. Both required only one change of court, but, of course, 5 out of 8 can and has carried on as many as 4 times which is why I devised sudden death. Sudden death is like being pregnant. You can't be just a little bit in the family. You either 'is or you ain't.'"

Jones replied again, "I feel strongly, namely, 'you have won.' Whether your nine point system or the 12 point method which the L.T.A. are pushing becomes standard, the inescapable fact is that your energy and drive have banished boring, marathon matches from the tennis scene. There are some who regret this entirely and I cannot help feeling that at Wimbledon, Forest Hills, etc. some neo-Nero should sit in the stand and at the appropriate moment give either a thumbs up signal for the match to continue under traditional scoring or thumbs down for a tie break termination."

Jones was in a precarious position—his readers and even his magazine editors had had enough—and he asked Jimmy, "Now, how strenuously do you wish to campaign for nine points versus 12 points? Can you brief me? Should I now take up cudgels on your behalf? Having rested for a set after winning the first two, am I to attack like a fury in the fourth? You must spark me off once more because the overall win brought me a great deal of unjustified criticism and I confess that it temporarily damaged my spirit. Tell me, James, why is it that those of us who have sufficient vision to see needs for reform and the way it should be brought about are always reviled by so many of our contemporaries? It seems to me that in this life those who try to help their fellow men are always suspect."

The debate over the tie breaker continued into 1971. The Fernbergers, who had introduced the twelve-point tie breaker at their 1970 tournament in Philadelphia, were ultimately fined by the ILTF for violating traditional scoring rules. But their conscious disobedience helped change the minds of many opponents. At the annual meeting of the ILTF in 1971, even the "conservative members of that organization came around to the cause and voted in favor" of adopting the twelve-point tie breaker. The Grand Slam tournaments—including the

U.S. Open, which had introduced Jimmy's nine-point tie breaker just a year earlier—began implementing the new twelve-point tie breaker later that year. Actually, the U.S. Open declared that either the nine-point or the twelve-point tie breaker could be used in tournament play, but continued to use Jimmy's "sudden death" tie breaker in competition. By 1973, the Australian Open and the French Open had integrated the twelve-point tie breaker into their tournament scoring. The only holdout was Wimbledon, which elected to wait until a set was tied at 8-all before introducing the tie breaker. It was not until 1979 that Wimbledon began using the tie breaker at 6-all, just as the other Grand Slam tournaments had done years earlier. The U.S. Open continued to use Jimmy's nine-point tie breaker until 1974, when the tournament "buried sudden death and went with the world"—that is, with the twelve-point tie breaker exclusively.

For Jimmy, the twelve-point tie breaker was a disappointment. Forcing players to win a tie breaker by two points was what Jimmy called "lingering death," a solution he regretted. As his brother Sammy said about Jimmy's tie breaker being changed, "they really took the teeth out of it." There were other reasons that Jimmy didn't like the twelve-point tie breaker. As he explained to Lamar Hunt in December 1970, expressing how disappointed he was that the WTC had elected to use only a twelve-point half-break instead of sudden death, "It doesn't work equitably out-of-doors. It means changing ends on odd point, 1,3,5,7, and there is no assurance that the players might not hold serve for 40 points or more requiring changing ends (N-S) 20 times! Which is ridiculous."

A further disappointment came several years later. Before Walter Elcock took over as president of the ILTF he passed a resolution saying "The USLTA may carry out experiments with the No-Ad system. However, after December 31, 1974, the nine-point system (which has been used with complete success from 1970–1974) cannot be used." Only the twelve-point break can be used. In the nine- and thirteen-point tie breaker the player didn't have to win by two points—hence it was much more exciting and suspenseful—the last point which wasn't two more than the other player's score was clearly "sudden death."

According to Van Alen, at that time, in 1975, the sudden death tie breaker was being used by the NCAA (the National Collegiate Athletic Association), WTT (World Team Tennis), WTA (the Women's Tennis Association), WCT (World Championship Tennis), Virginia Slims, and handicap events. "Only ATP [the Association of Tennis Professionals] is out of step."

He raised the challenge again: "For five years the Sudden Death flag has flown at the U.S. Open, Forest Hills. LONG MAY IT WAVE. Let the voice of 34,000,000 U.S. Tennis players be heard, and double that many in T.V. audience."

Even though Jimmy didn't get his way with the sudden death tie breaker, his other tennis endeavors were going along well. The annual July tournament drew enthusiastic spectators and good players in the Casino, and tennis greats were regularly honored at the Tennis Hall of Fame.

*30th July, 1937, The victorious US Davis Cup team
aboard the liner 'Manhattan' prior to leaving
Southampton for home, They are L-R: Frank Parker,
Gene Make, Don Budge, holding the trophy with
Walter Pate and Bitsy Grant.*

Chapter Nine:
The 1970s—Tennis and Jimmy After the Tiebreaker

Jimmy now had a number of victories on his score sheet and he was looking for more. The tie breaker was accepted and used at the 1970 U.S. Open and for many other tournaments and matches. He wanted his tie breaker to stay at "sudden death"—that is, when the first player to win five points wins the tie breaker and the set, instead of "lingering death," when the player has to win by two points. The Casino finally managed to merge with the Hall of Fame so that it was a tax-exempt entity. The '70s would see a new team, led by Jimmy's friend Alastair Martin, take over at the Hall of Fame and update the exhibits and refurbish the plant. Staring from the mid-1970s, Jimmy relinquished many of the business duties he had performed for the Casino and became an enthusiastic presence, but not the one who ran things. In their personal life Jimmy and Candy had some jolts but Jimmy's hunger for new adventurous projects took him, as usual, in new directions. At the Hall of Fame, the transfer of stock was successful in 1975, but the plant had continued to deteriorate. In the mid-70s a powerful new group became involved. Things began to change when John Davis, grandson of Dwight Filley Davis, founder of the Davis Cup in 1900, was asked by his uncle William McChesney Martin to help with an exhibit at the Hall of Fame on the Davis Cup. Martin was married to Cynthia Davis, daughter of Dwight Davis. He was the former president of the New York Stock Exchange and the longest serving chairman of the Federal Reserve Board, and

was now on the Hall's Board of Directors and had wonderful business connections.

The Davis family was the ideal family to become involved in Jimmy's International Tennis Hall of Fame. They had begun the Davis Cup competition—one of the most important and long-lasting series of matches in sports history—beginning in 1899 while Dwight was an undergraduate at Harvard. Davis came from a well-to-do family from St. Louis, Missouri, where he and his brothers attended the Smith Academy. For Dwight, Harvard was a logical sequel to Smith, as both of his older brothers and his uncle Samuel were all Harvard graduates. His grades at Harvard, however, were less than perfect—in fact, they were so poor by the end of his sophomore year that Harvard dropped Davis to the class of 1901 and demanded that he repeat his sophomore year altogether. Still, Davis was an active member of the undergraduate community, joining clubs—such as the highly selective Institute of 1770, Delta Kappa Epsilon, the Hasty Pudding Theatricals, and Alpha Delta Phi—and playing sports, including baseball, football, and most of all, tennis.

In 1897 during his freshman year, Davis honed his tennis skills with a fellow classmate and close friend, Holcombe Ward, at the Longwood Cricket Club. A year later, after losing the championship match at the Newport Casino to Malcolm Whitman, Davis continued to play, ultimately attaining the No. 2 rank among American players in 1899 and 1900. But during 1900, Davis and several of his Harvard classmates decided

Troy Gowen Hall (Hall of Fame)

The Davis Cup—both tournament and trophy—has had a long and prestigious life. By 2009, 125 nations were competing for the Cup, and the trophy now stands over three feet higher than it did in 1900. Plinths have been gradually added to accommodate more than a century of champions. It is as though the original cup has been placed atop a three-tiered wedding cake of tennis history, and by the 1970s, there was more than enough history behind the Cup for John Davis to create a stunning exhibit at the Newport Casino's International Tennis Hall of Fame.

When John Davis got a call from his uncle Bill Martin in the early '70s, he knew almost nothing about the Hall of Fame. He remembers it having little national visibility then. Davis went up to Newport and found that the old Casino Club rooms on the second floor—the site for the exhibits—were practically empty. Robert S. (Bob) Day, the Casino's Executive Director, showed him around. As Davis remembers, "What I saw was an enormous 12,000-square-foot space with nothing in it." The Casino was in another period of disrepair. "The court tennis court and the theatre had been condemned. There were ropes around the Horseshoe Piazza. Its floor boards were rotten." A graphic designer, he didn't like the proposed plans for the Davis Cup room, so he created three exhibits himself: one on the Davis Cup, one on women in tennis, and one on the four tournaments that compose the Grand Slam—the Australian Open, the French Open, Wimbledon, and the U.S. Open. In the Davis Cup room he installed eight enormous 8'10 glass panels. "They weighed 500 pounds. I had silk-screened figures—of my grandfather, the early years of tennis, the Doherty brothers, the Age of Tilden, etc. I followed the devel-

to host their own competition, the International Lawn Tennis Challenge, between the United States and Great Britain. Davis commissioned the William B. Durgin Company, a Concord, New Hampshire-based silversmith, to design and forge a solid silver cup for his tournament. Rowland Rhodes, a decorated English sculptor who worked at Durgin, created an elegant, classical design for a bowl that Davis purchased for $750—part of the petty cash allowance he received from his family. Cast in sterling silver, it is wreathed with Georgian primroses and acanthus leaves swirling from the rim. Neither Davis nor Rhodes would have guessed that this trophy would become one of Durgin's most famous pieces, and the only major cup in worldwide sports to survive the twentieth century and beyond.

Ted Tinling Exhibit—
Hall of Fame Museum

WTA Gallery—Hall
of Fame Museum

Court Tennis
Exhibit—Hall of
Fame Museum

Ken Rosewall and Joe Cullman, U.S. Open Championship, Forest Hills

with 18 Grand Slam titles) and Peggy Woolard. Jimmy was made an Honorary Director and was now on the Board of Directors but not on the Executive Committee.

Next thing Davis knew Bob Day called and said, "We have a big problem." There was a sag in the south wing. A contractor was called in and found that the foundation by the entrance way was rotten. It would cost $3 million to restore. This included the court tennis court and the horseshoe piazza. Now big money was needed.

In 1982 or '83, a New York office was created and it was located in the Philip Morris building where Joe Cullman was the Chairman.

Joe Cullman was a staunch defender of the tobacco industry, and of smoking, but also a lifelong lover of tennis, and had been essential in getting the first U.S. Open televised in 1968. Alastair Martin, USLTA President, appointed him Chairman of the U.S. Open at Forest Hills in 1968 and 1969. Through Cullman's donations and the efforts of professional fundraisers, millions were raised and the plant was put back together. Joe Cullman now became the force behind the restoration of the Casino, and the Board began to run it in a much more corporate fashion.

The donors, however, were not from Newport. "It was not a great success in Newport." John Winslow explains that in Newport in the '70s there was not a lot of money for non-profit organizations. Even though Newporters wanted to maintain their old

opment of tennis, while featuring the Davis Cup." The new exhibits and new renovation were finished in the mid-70s, and his rooms were opened during 1975 and 1976.

Current Tennis Hall of Fame head Alastair Martin decided that another shot in the arm for the Casino and the Hall of Fame would be to merge with the National Tennis Foundation. The merger was rife with politics. Alastair Martin asked Davis to come to the annual meeting of the new organization in California and he refused. A month later Davis got the minutes of the meeting and, to his surprise, saw he had been elected Vice President of an eight-member board. This appointment would associate him with the Hall of Fame for years to come.

At the first meeting he was put in charge of all the operations. The executive committee was made up of William McChesney Martin (President), Joseph F. Cullman 3rd (Vice President), John G. Davis (Vice President), William H. G. FitzGerald, William F. Talbert, William J. Clothier, Allison Danzig, Sarah Palfrey (a tennis player from the 1930s

landmarks, they didn't have the big money to make much of a difference. The supporters of the Hall now came from other parts of the country.

Joe Cullman and Bill Martin poured money into the Hall of Fame. Cullman began a longstanding relationship with the Hall of Fame in the early 1970s, when he provided much-needed financial backing—donating millions of dollars from his personal funds—for the struggling Casino. He eventually served as the President and Chairman of the Hall of Fame from 1982 to 1988, a period during which the Casino recovered from years of steady decline. He was inducted into the Hall of Fame in 1990.

In the late '80s Davis's exhibits needed updating again. A professional designer was called in—and board member Marilyn Fernberger helped to create contemporary, interactive audiovisual exhibits to attract more visitors. Another fundraising drive was started. A total of $4 million was spent on creating and updating the exhibits.

At the time power was shifting at the Casino, things had become very different in the tennis world as a whole. Now that tennis was open, where it was played, for what sort of money it was played—everything was up for grabs. And the power had shifted from the tennis associations to the players. It would be different for the fans, too, with well-televised tournaments that were as exciting to watch as televised football or baseball games—which made the champion tennis players into celebrities.

The opening up of tennis couldn't come fast enough for most players, and some who were starting out their careers in the 1960s and '70s played a big part in what was to come next. These recent converts from the ama-

teur to the professional circuit were young, ambitious, and passionate about playing and they took full advantage of open tennis to build a successful future in the tennis world as agents or tournament promoters. Most of the good players turned pro and now could play in all the important events.

Donald Dell was one player who had come of age in the '50s, and now would use his influence as things changed. He was ranked No.1 in doubles in 1961, number four in singles, and in the top ten in America four times. He finished Yale in 1960 and then played a full year on the amateur circuit. After graduating from law school at the University of Virginia in 1964 he played another full year, and then went to work. "I was a lawyer by then and I wanted to work in Washington. I retired from tennis in about October of '66 and went to work for a big firm called Hogan & Hartson."

His success as a player and his later law work put him in a key position when tennis went open. In March of 1968 he was named Davis Cup Captain. His experience as captain showed him that players needed to make money and he used his passion for tennis to help achieve that. "In 1970 I got out and I started managing athletes. I was the first agent or lawyer to represent a tennis player anywhere in the world. Mark McCormack of the International Management Group (IMG) had led the way with golfer Arnold Palmer. Over the next twenty years, IMG would become one of the biggest names in tennis and sports marketing.

Much of the money for tournaments nowadays comes from such sponsorships, in which a business provides branded goods to a player—such as equipment or apparel. The player then uses these products during (often

Margret Smith Court,
Billy Jean King, and
Jimmy

Doubles match at
the Virginia Slims
Tournament, 1972

televised) game time. This effectively makes the player an advertisement for that business. For example, Andy Roddick has a sponsorship with Lacoste, which provides the tennis polos, shorts, and caps he wears during games. Previously, his sponsor was Reebok. Russian tennis player Maria Sharapova has taken sponsorship to entirely new level with several custom-designed tennis dresses by Nike, which she wore at three of the Grand Slam tournaments in 2008. And at the U.S. Open, the world not only saw Sharapova on the court in her rose-colored, sequined tennis dress, but also in television ads for Motorola, Canon, and Powerade, broadcast during the game.

Donald Dell was not reappointed Davis Cup captain because of the conflict of interest if he was to represent players selected for the team. Arthur Ashe and Stan Smith wanted him to manage them. "I left Hogan & Hartson and started my own firm: The Law Offices of Donald Dell," and he worked in sports law—first tennis, then basketball. He incorporated as ProServ (for "Professional Services") in 1976 and his first two clients were Arthur Ashe and Stan Smith. "I was Arthur and Stan's lawyer—Arthur for 23 years, before he died." Arthur Ashe had earned national attention in 1963, when he became the first African-American ever selected to play for the United States in the Davis Cup. He went on to win three Grand Slam titles. Stan Smith, born in 1946, was the No. 1 ranked singles player in 1972, and, along with his partner Bob Lutz, was one of the best doubles teams of all time.

The money for tennis today also comes from endorsements, which had existed somewhat before open tennis but became much more prevalent during the 1970s. An endorsement means a tennis player becomes a spokesperson for a particular product. While sponsorships for players tend to be from companies that specialize in athletic gear and apparel, players can endorse all kinds of products. Arthur Ashe famously endorsed Coca-Cola during his career. Today Andy Roddick has endorsed American Express. As a result, American Express has the right to use his likeness, name, or photo in commercials and print advertisements. Nowadays, many players make the bulk of their income from endorsements rather than prize money. In 2006, Maria Sharapova earned the title of the world's highest-paid female athlete due to her extensive commercial endorsements. Sharapova's contracts with companies as diverse as Pepsi, Colgate-Palmolive, Nike, Motorola, TAG Heuer, Canon, Honda, and Lady Speed Stick have earned her an estimated annual income of $23 million as of 2008.

Today Donald Dell runs a Washington, D.C. tournament on the tour called the "Legg Mason Tennis Classic" which is sponsored by Legg Mason, the Baltimore-based global asset management firm. It contributes about $1 million each year to name the tournament. In Newport today, the endorsing company for the Casino's July tournament for the Van Alen Cup is Campbell's Soup, which puts up about $400,000.

There is a third source of revenue for a tournament besides sponsorships and ticket sales. It is television. "Now TV stations are going to pay 25 times more for Wimbledon than they are for Washington, because it is a bigger tournament."

Jimmy insisted—quite correctly—that live television was impractical under the traditional scoring system. In June of 1966, Jimmy wrote to Roone Arledge, the Vice Presi-

1984 Virginia Slims Tournament, Martina Navratilova, George Graboys, Joe Cullman, and Gigi Fernandez

dent of Sports Programs at ABC, in response to an article written by Arledge and his colleague Gilbert Rogin in *Sports Illustrated*. In the article, Arledge and Rogin had asserted that "Tennis is perfect for television." Jimmy sharply disagreed in his letter, claiming that "not even 2% of the general public understands the scoring, which certainly dampens interest and enthusiasm" for the audience, while a potentially endless deuce set game "makes a farce of live television" scheduling for network executives.

He received a reply a few weeks later from Arledge, who clarified what he had meant by tennis being "perfect" for television—that "the physical ease of coverage and the readily understandable battle between two main protagonists" made it ideal for a TV audience. But he also admitted that "the standard scoring system of tennis is difficult for the uninitiated to understand, and from what I have seen and heard of the VASSS rules, they considerably alleviate this problem." Jimmy thanked him for his support in a reply, further stressing "the question of timing, which is even more important and for television most costly." Timing, Jimmy reminded Arledge, "is vital for live television." If matches were allowed to continue indefinitely, Jimmy contended, few television stations would risk a live broadcast that could potentially swallow the timeslots of other programs and their paying advertisers.

In 1963, Bud Collins, then a young sportscaster, had begun covering tennis matches in the Boston area for the local public television station, WGBH-TV. At that time, Collins recalls, WGBH was hardly the "justly celebrated bulwark of PBS" that it is today; rather, it was a "learn-as-we-go, slightly advanced crystal set operating from a Cambridge garage, having been burned out of its room-above-a-drugstore."

The first televised tennis match to air on WGBH was the 1963 U.S. National Doubles at the Longwood Cricket Club in Brookline. "Luckily," Collins recalls, "the station couldn't afford to air the 1963 National Doubles live. A weekday afternoon audience would have been sparse." Instead, WGBH taped the matches and aired them later the same day—a common practice with television stations for years, as there was no way to predict how long a tennis match would last. Collins' program became known as the "Tennis Late Show," and would record the matches from 1:00 PM until dusk—there were no floodlights at Longwood to extend competition past sundown—and then air them later that evening, at 8:00 PM. Despite Jimmy's warnings that the traditional scoring system and pre-recorded footage would frustrate TV audiences, the matches at Longwood did become a sleeper hit in the Boston area, with viewers tuning in wherever they could pick up the WGBH broadcast. Several shows lasted as long as six and a half hours, and many viewers tuned in from primetime until two or three o'clock in the morning.

The Boston matches proved that tennis, like baseball and football, could attract a wide and diverse television audience. PBS affiliates like WGBH quickly became the home for tennis on television around the country. By 1974—three years after the tie breaker

was adopted at most tournaments—PBS was broadcasting tennis coast-to-coast and even abroad, with Greg Harney overseeing the production and Donald Dell raising the necessary funds. Collins remembers how their "usual tournament televising encompassed play on Saturday and Sunday afternoons and Monday night finals. The mail told us people were watching, gratefully, and for a while most of the consequential men—Connors, Borg, Guillermo Vilas, Wojtek Fibak, Arthur Ashe, Stan Smith, Manolo Orantes, Harold Solomon, Eddie Dibbs, Bob Lutz, Vijay Amritraj among them—were first seen by Americans on PBS."

Once the tie breaker became part of the scoring system the length of matches became much more predictable, and other networks were able to broadcast tennis tournaments without worrying that an extended set might prove too long to air in full. NBC had begun broadcasting matches, including Wimbledon, by the late 1960s. But many of these matches were still broadcast with a tape delay; by the time the games were aired, potential viewers could already know the results via newspapers or radio. If networks were going to attract the largest possible audience, they would have to find a way to broadcast the matches live—a suggestion Jimmy had made a decade earlier. Live tennis promised to add more suspense to the game for spectators watching at home and would eliminate any chance of a media spoiler.

In 1979, NBC decided to broadcast the Wimbledon Final live. The finals at Wimbledon invariably and religiously began on Saturday at 2:00 PM sharp in England, which meant that a live broadcast would air at 9:00 AM on the East Coast and—to the network executives' chagrin—6:00 AM on the West

Coast. The network executives were worried "that no seriously consuming adult would face up to a TV set at nine, or earlier, on a Saturday morning for tennis. The only household viewers at that hour would be the 'Sesame' set, tenaciously guarding the cartoon channels." NBC's marketing solution, spearheaded by their Executive Sports Producer Don Ohlmeyer, was to aggressively advertise the broadcast in the United States as "Breakfast at Wimbledon."

Unfortunately for NBC, the hometown favorites—John McEnroe and Jimmy Connors—had been knocked out of the competition, leaving Roscoe Tanner to face Björn Borg in the final. NBC was worried that Tanner, although an American, had considerably less appeal for viewers than the "Brash Basher" Jimmy Connors or the notoriously hot-tempered John McEnroe. To make matters worse, NBC had also wanted to begin the match five minutes later, in order to introduce the competitors and provide audiences with a prelude to the match that would convince them to watch. But tradition ruled at Wimbledon, and their request was denied. Donald Dell, who was Tanner's agent at the time, took matters into his own hands. As the clock ticked closer and closer to 2:00, there was still no sign of either Tanner or Borg. When the hour finally came with Borg and Tanner nowhere to be found, NBC was able to proceed with its introduction to Wimbledon and fire off some preliminary commentary. By 2:06, Collins recalls, "with everyone in the production truck feeling a lot better, Björn and Roscoe were sighted at last emerging from the doorway below the Royal Box." Dell had told Tanner of the bind NBC was in and asked him to stall somehow—which he did, by locking himself in the bathroom for five minutes just as the match was supposed to begin.

The match was a success for NBC, and "Breakfast at Wimbledon" went on to become a highlight of the network's sports programming. The advent of live televised tennis opened the door for a litany of changes, including increased commercial visibility and celebrity for the players, both of which have made the sport what it is today. And tennis has become a very popular spectator sport both at the stadium and at home on the TV—it is one of the few exciting sports in which one competitor takes on another.

Many changes to the game were already in the works before tennis hit the airwaves. For one, the court surface changed. After the sport went open in 1968, grass was no longer the surface used for important tournaments, and clubs receded into the background. The Open at Forest Hills changed its surface from grass to clay for two years. In 1978, the location of the tournament changed to its current home, the National Tennis Center in Flushing Meadows Corona Park, Queens, New York where the surface is hard court.

In the late 60s, tennis was an amateur grass court country club sport. In the '70s it moved out of the clubs into bigger facilities, into sponsorship, and onto hard courts, and the Association of Tennis Professionals (ATP) started a computer ranking system. The ATP, is a union of male pro tennis players. Both the ATP and its counterpart, The Women's Tennis Association or WTA (formerly Women's International Tennis Association, or WITA) were instrumental in making tennis what it is today after the sport opened in 1968. In particular, the ATP negotiated increases in prize purses and in tournament playing opportunities for its members. The ATP provides weekly rankings of professional male tennis players worldwide. The two rankings published by the ATP are the ATP Entry Ranking, a 52-week rolling ranking, and the ATP Race, a year-to-date ranking. A player's Entry Ranking is used to determine his qualification for entry and seeding in tournaments. The Race Ranking is exclusively used to determine which players—the top eight singles and the top four doubles—qualify for the Tennis Masters Cup at the end of the season. Rankings are given for players from every country, so that "the Croatians and the Serbians, and the French, or the Germans, can be ranked just as much as the Americans, the British, and the Australians, who dominated the sport in the past." Tennis has become an increasingly global game. Today, if you looked at the top 50 ATP rankings to see how many players are American, you'd be lucky to find 7 or 8.

Another important change in the 1970s was the gains that women's tennis made. Leading women players created a circuit for themselves, the Virginia Slims tournaments, which started in Houston and came to the Casino in 1972. Men's earnings were growing—Rod Laver won $201,453 in 1969—but women's earnings were not keeping pace. Their winnings were usually about a quarter of men's. A showdown took place in Los Angeles at the Pacific Southwest Open in 1970. The men's winnings were going to be eight times what the women's were. Gladys Heldman, a top player and a shrewd businesswoman who started *World Tennis Magazine* in 1953, wanted to get Jack Kramer to sweeten the prize money, but he refused. The star women boycotted the tournament. They played instead in a $7,500 tournament in Houston even though the USLTA threat-

Lew Hoad speaking at his Hall of Fame Induction, 1980

ened to suspend them. "The Houston Nine," as they called themselves—Heldman, Billie Jean King, Rosie Casals, Kerry Melville, Judy Dalton, Nancy Richey, Kristy Pigeon, Peaches Bartkowicz, and Valerie Ziegenfuss—started with these matches a competition which would become the Virginia Slims circuit the following year. They had signed a contract with Heldman for one dollar apiece.

Gladys Heldman was a good friend of Joe Cullman and according to Bud Collins, she called him up and said, "A club in Houston will take us and I have to get a tournament. Will you underwrite it?" and Cullman said "sure." Cullman "saw the Houston tournament as a chance to support the women's game and as a unique sponsorship opportunity for Philip Morris. So we put up $2,500

Jimmy playing golf

and had the name of the event changed to the Virginia Slims Invitational." Rosie Casals won the first tournament and a total prize of $7500. It was the beginning of a women's professional tennis tour. Cullman writes that "within a week after the first Virginia Slims Invitational in November 1970, we were able to announce that Virginia Slims would sponsor eight women's tournaments, each in a sixteen-draw format, beginning in January 1971. And the rest is tennis history." Women's tennis no longer had to play second fiddle. In 1972 Billie Jean King earned $100,000 in prize money.

Without a doubt, the most famous match during this era, and a match that emphasized the growing prestige of women's tennis, was the Riggs-King match, better known as the "Battle of the Sexes." The whole affair began when Bobby Riggs, whose claim to fame before this match was his 1939 Wimbledon and U.S. Championships wins, decided to create some buzz to promote men's senior tennis by challenging a prominent female tennis player to a winner-takes-all match. Riggs originally aimed to goad the outspoken leading voice of women's liberation in sports, Billie Jean King, to take up his challenge, but King, who made headlines by becoming the first female to win over $100,000 in prize money and an infamous ringleader of the Virginia Slims Tournaments, refused, saying, "If we played and I won, so what? I beat someone twenty-five years older than me. If I lost, Bobby would carry that Male Chauvinist Pig thing on forever." Unperturbed by King's refusal, Riggs then offered the challenge to his second choice, Margaret Court—the reigning player of the season who had won the Australian, French, and U.S. Opens and who was said to be able to beat King in three of four meetings. Riggs trounced Court 6–2, 6–1 in what was dubbed The Mother's Day Massacre. And now, with the weight of the hopes of all female tennis players and, some would say, of all womankind, King accepted the challenge. The "Battle of the Sexes" match was born.

On September 20, 1973, the chosen day for the match, an estimated thirty-seven to fifty million people all around the world tuned in to ABC, who paid an exorbitant $750,000 for the rights to televise it live on prime time (in contrast, NBC had paid a mere $50,000 that year to show Wimbledon). A crowd of 30,472 spectators filled the seats of the Houston Astrodome in Texas, paying more than at any other match. Tickets went for as high as $100 a piece.

The twenty-nine year-old King arrived "in Cleopatra style," carried on a loft chair by four ruggedly handsome men dressed as Egyptian slaves. She presented Riggs, who entered the stadium in a rickshaw pulled by five scantily clad women, a live baby pig which corresponded with the "Pigs for Riggs" buttons that some of the men displayed on their shirts.

Whether it was from over consciousness or having learned from Margaret Court's mistakes, King abandoned her usual combative style and tailored her game to use her speed to exhaust Riggs. To her surprise, her method worked. "I couldn't believe how slow he was…I thought he was faking it," King recalled. King defeated Riggs 6–4, 6–3, 6–3. The stadium erupted into cheers when King, victorious, stooped to give a red-faced Riggs a kiss. King's victory not only redeemed all female tennis players, but women from all over the country sent in letters telling of husbands washing dishes and bosses making coffee for their secretaries because of her triumph. Yet the real victory won that day was not one of gender conflict, but that "tennis can be a big-time sport in the hands of people who know how to promote it."

The growing awareness of tennis, from high-profile matches to greater television coverage to the Riggs-King media frenzy, was heartening to Jimmy. He continued to fight for his sudden death tie breaker and his VASSS scoring changes in the 1970s but he also had other tricks up his sleeve. Since 1966 he had been getting publicity for his VAAGG and now he continued to push it. VAAGG was "Van Alen's Answer to Grief in Golf." It had been featured in an article written by him in *Sports Illustrated* with a subtitle "Having Invented VASSS, the scoring system that takes the love out of tennis, the author now turns to greener pastures by advancing proposals that take the hate out of golf."

Jimmy had always played golf but was never a top player. The golf club was close at hand, however, as the Newport Country Club adjoined the Van Alen's Avalon property. In 1995 when the Club needed more space to qualify as a host for the U.S. Amateur Championships in golf (the year Tiger Woods beat Buddy Marucci), the Van Alens

VAAGG or Van Alen's Answer to Grief in Golf

WHO PLAY VAAGG

Having invented VASSS, the scoring system that takes the love out of tennis, the author now turns to greener pastures by advancing outrageous proposals that take the hate out of golf

by JAMES VAN ALEN

let them use the needed land. In exchange, Candy got a promise that no Avalon guests would be required to pay greens fees. When Jimmy used his VAAGG method he could beat players with small handicaps. This spurred him into promoting his new scoring system.

His theory was that 90% of golfers were "hackers," that is players who cannot break one hundred without cheating, which "includes conceding yourself three-foot putts, improving your lie in the rough, grounding your club in the bunker and playing winter rules when the sign by the first tee says SUMMER just as plain as your reflection in the water hazard." It is a lucky thing, he felt, that golfers did not think about or analyze their situation; otherwise, they would "be queued up by the thousands around the George Washington Bridge waiting for their turn to jump into that big lateral water hazard that borders Manhattan."

Jimmy's aim was to take the torture out of golf. He would address four problems that golfers experience: A round of golf takes too long. There is not enough exercise involved. There is not enough club action. There are too many clubs in the bag to carry it easily. What he suggested was a method by which a round takes less time, so you can get real exercise with the time you have saved, to hit and putt the ball twice as many times as you traditionally would, and to hit the ball straight so you don't have to waste time looking for the ball.

His changes were therefore to play nine holes instead of eighteen and to take a mulligan on each shot. You would then choose the better lie of the two shots for the next shot. You then hit two more shots and select the better lie for the third, and so on. You use only two clubs—a "mashie" or 5-iron for all shots before the green and then a putter on the green.

The benefits of Jimmy's new system according to him: For starters, it takes less time to make second shots than to hunt for a lost ball in some grassy or woody or watery spot. "A firm friendship is established with one club instead of a nodding acquaintance with 14." You learn how to use your one club in many different situations. You need no caddy—a necessary part of golf games in those days—no "downy-faced juvenile who quite possibly has severe myopia."

"When you travel, two clubs wrapped in a Navy officer's sword cover are far handier and lighter than a voluminous bag containing fourteen." The course loses its terror for you and you can forget the bad first shot and focus on the good second one. It evens up the playing field. The good golfer can only take one of his two good shots and hopefully the bad player will make one of two good ones. When you repair to the nineteenth hole, you can "gloat over hitting more good shots in nine holes than you normally hit in a hundred and nine."

When the article came out in *Sports Illustrated*, readers—mostly irate, but some amused—responded in heated letters to the editor. A fuming female player from Montreal penned four handwritten pages in reaction to a local piece on the subject, expressing her annoyance at "the Gazette in Montreal for printing such nonsense."

She wrote, "I have just read an article which is presumably written or dictated by you. I do not believe it!!!!! *Nobody*, having been interested in sports, could write such nonsense, and so much of it, and still hope to have friends in either tennis or other sports. As a former tennis player and I think I was quite good as an amateur, and now a lady of 61 with a 12 handicap in golf, I feel that your insulting remarks about golf is not only unkind, but would like to know on *what* you form your opinion."

"Toppity Tom" told *Sports Illustrated* that he was "incensed." He had worked for twenty years slaving on the practice tee and had earned a handicap of six. He resented Jimmy's suggestion "to change the game to suit his inability to master it." "Let Van Alen run through the woods hitting acorns with his shooting stick to get his exercise."

Paul Kaplan from Brooklyn, New York called the ideas "absurd" and guaranteed to "set all organized sports back to the Dark Ages. Imagine in football a quarterback throws an intercepted pass. Then he requests another attempt to hit his receiver and he completes his pass. He then has the option of choosing either play. I wonder which one he would take. The VAAGG system looks to protect the average poor slob golfer. Let them help themselves by practicing more… Van Alen, stick to tennis and you'll be doing us all a favor."

Not every letter, however, condemned VAAGG. F.P. Sherry cheerfully noted that it "would convert golf from a cross to a crown… and might inspire honesty on the scorecards." Although the article came out in 1965, Jimmy was still plugging VAAGG in the '70s.

Towards the end of the seventies, the Van Alens suffered a big blow. In early December of 1976, when Jimmy and Candy were about to return from a vacation in Madrid, a fire started at Avalon. Much of the 70-year-old "Mediterranean Villa"-style summer home, built by the architect Grosvenore Atterbury, became an unrecognizable smoldering heap on December 7, 1976.

Sandy Rodrigues, the estate's caretaker's wife, saw lights flickering off and on around in the big house around 4:30 PM and figured that a burglar had tripped a switch in the mansion. When smoke began to billow from the garage, she grabbed her two-year old daughter and ran to a neighbor's house to call for help. Her husband, James Rodrigues, who had been shopping, arrived at the mansion minutes after the fire engine pulled up and the firefighters began to combat the blaze. Eileen Slocum, one of the Van Alens' close personal friends and a neighbor in Newport, was on her way back from Providence when she heard of a three-alarm fire. She telephoned the Fire Department and asked what was on fire, only to be told that the Van Alen house was burning. Knowing that many of the Van Alens' prized possessions—including an extensive art collection and a set of priceless china—were inside the house, Slocum immediately drove over to the Fire Department. "I got into the fire engine and said, 'Take me to the front door—there is a beautiful set of china just inside!'" By the time she arrived, flames were raging from the basement and the first floor as the firemen ran in and out of the building salvaging what furniture and artifacts they could. About an hour and a half later, the roof collapsed, making it hard to save the mansion. Fire Chief William H. Connerton Jr. blamed Newport's poor supply of water from the street main as a contributor to the

firefighters' defeat. He said, "The lone, eight-inch main that supplies the rocky coastal area simply did not deliver enough water to extinguish the blaze…you need more water."

Luckily, the fire did not cause any serious injuries to any of the firemen, although one narrowly escaped, becoming a casualty by jumping out a basement window when the stucco wall fell. However, Miss Grace Watson, the loyal 71-year-old woman who had been the Van Alen's personal secretary of 25 years, died from a fatal heart attack shortly after learning of the fire. A spokesman for the office of the state medical examiner, however, did not cite the fire as a cause for her death. She was known to be Jimmy's right hand and Jimmy would definitely be in a bind without her. The bewildered Rodrigues added that Jimmy would be greatly "distraught over the destruction of his art, china and gun collection." At the end of the day, an approximated $900,000 from the value of Avalon and the Van Alen's personal property was lost in damages. However, all was not lost, as part of the first floor was unscathed, and the Van Alens would rebuild the rooms around it, making a spacious—albeit much less attractive—house.

Still, Jimmy appeared in the *Newport Daily News* just over a week later standing outside his dilapidated property of Wrenthurst, which bordered Avalon, excitedly describing his plans to convert the mansion into the Clement Moore museum he had been trying to establish in Newport for decades. When asked if the fire would interfere with his annual Christmas reading of Moore's famous poem, he dismissed the notion entirely: "I wouldn't give it up for the world. Despite all that has happened, we have a lot to be thankful for."

Jimmy with court tennis players from Yale, Princeton, and Harvard preparing to compete for the matches in the Van Alen Cup against Oxford and Cambridge. The matches are still held today.

Chapter Ten:
Last Years and a Lasting Legacy

Although Jimmy nearly always sat in the royal box at Wimbledon, he made an exception during the summer of 1980, when he decided to take his eleven year-old granddaughter, Lee, on a five-week vacation to Europe. Along with Candy, Jimmy and Lee first traveled to England, stopping at the Tower of London and Westminster Abbey before heading to Cambridge. The three then visited the Gerald Durrell Zoo on the island of Jersey in the English Channel. From Jersey, they traveled a short distance to the rocky tidal island of Mont Saint-Michel, with its towering abbey, just off the northern coast of Normandy. They ordered big fluffy omelets and took a walk around the island as the tide went out. From the Mont they headed to Paris. As Lee recalls, "We had a great time in Paris. He [Jimmy] loved to eat. We ordered an *amuse-bouche*, but they did not have escargot. He and I both loved them. So we had them go into the kitchen and they made up a big bowl of them for each of us—much more than we would have gotten. So that was fun."

Jimmy, Candy, and Lee spent the last leg of their European vacation at the Van Alens' flat in Madrid. Wimbledon was in full swing during their stay in Spain, and Lee remembers watching the final in men's singles with Jimmy and Candy. That final, called by many "the most memorable match in Wimbledon history," pitted the cool, unemotional Björn Borg of Sweden—who was playing in his fifth consecutive Wimbledon final, having won the previous four—against a hotheaded

and mercurial John McEnroe of the United States, who was playing in his first-ever Wimbledon final after beating former champion Jimmy Connors in the semifinal match.

On July 5, 1980, Borg and McEnroe stepped onto the All England Lawn Tennis and Croquet Club's prestigious Centre Court to a roaring, sold-out crowd. McEnroe's infamous left-hand serve gained him a speedy advantage in the first set, which he easily won 6–1. Speculation that he would easily defeat Borg was quickly put to rest in the second set, however, when Borg came back to win 7–5. Borg maintained his momentum through the third set, reaching a score of 5–2, and despite McEnroe's fierce rally in the eighth game, which he won, Borg ultimately triumphed 6–3. With two sets to McEnroe's one, a fifth consecutive Wimbledon title seemed inevitable for Borg. He needed only one more set to win the match and the Championships.

But McEnroe was about to teach him how difficult winning one set could be. Borg had taken an early lead in the fourth set, but McEnroe managed to stave off double match point with a ferocious, cross-court, backhand service return to tie the set at 5-all. Borg would need at least two more games to win the match, but McEnroe was careful not to let that happen. After two games, the score was tied at 6-all. The tension was palpable as the crowd realized that history was in the making. Wimbledon had previously approved the twelve-point tie breaker for use only when a set had reached 8-all, but in 1979,

just one year earlier, the tournament agreed to introduce the tie breaker at 6-all instead. With McEnroe and Borg tied at six each, one of the most famous and grueling tie breakers in tennis history began. After twenty-two minutes and a record thirty-four contested points—including five match points and six set points—McEnroe won the tie breaker (18–16) and the fourth set.

Borg was crushed and began to worry that he would lose the fifth and final set, as well as his Wimbledon title, to McEnroe: "… watching myself losing that last point, 18–16, I can feel that walk back to the chair now as if it was yesterday. That was the toughest moment in my tennis career, that walk. I knew John thought he would win the match. I thought he would win the match." Still, Borg managed to keep his anxiety from affecting his game. In the final, deciding set, an inexhaustible Borg scored 19 straight points on serve against McEnroe. And after three hours and fifty-three minutes, Borg finally claimed his fifth consecutive Wimbledon championship by winning the final set and the match, winning 1–6, 7–5, 6–3, 6–7(16), 8–6. "I don't know how I regrouped. If he [McEnroe] had broken me in the first game

*"Fire and Ice": Wimbledon Final 1980; Borg
defeats McEnroe 1–6, 7–5, 6–3, 6–7, 8–6 after
the famous 22-minute tiebreaker*

of the fifth set I would have lost, but I won from love-30 and then I played just unbelievably well, hardly lost a point on serve and won the match. That was the strongest set, mentally, in my tennis career."

Lee remembers how she, Jimmy, and Candy "watched the Borg-McEnroe tie breaker together at the lobby of the Ritz in Spain, the one that went on forever." Of course it wasn't the tie breaker Jimmy had invented— the "sudden death" round played to nine points—but it was a victory for him nonetheless; Jimmy was instrumental in changing tennis scoring rules to allow a tie breaker in the first place. Without Jimmy, Borg and McEnroe might have played dozens more games, and the match would have lost its terrific suspense for spectators in the stadium and at home watching it on television. Jimmy may have been invested in the nine-point tie breaker, but as Lee recalls, "it was probably one of the most iconic moments in tennis history. … Had it been, whoever gets to nine wins, you wouldn't have had the suspense." That the match continued to be played, but not indefinitely, "had everyone on the edge of their seats going crazy." For Jimmy, the tie breaker had always been about making the game more enjoyable for fans and spectators. With the Wimbledon final in 1980, he certainly got his wish.

The Borg-McEnroe final at Wimbledon also highlighted an important change in tennis that has continued ever since the sport went open—the celebrity player. In addition to his innovations on the court and in training, Björn Borg was arguably the first "pop star" of tennis. His slender physique and angular good looks served him off the court as well as on: Borg was known for attracting dozens of screaming, miniskirt-wearing teenage girls, who would storm the court and surround the champion after a hard-fought victory. Fans were interested in Björn Borg as a person and not just as a tennis player. Borg may have been a bit overwhelmed by so much attention, but he rarely let it affect his game or his attitude. His cool, emotionless demeanor earned him nicknames like "Ice Man," or more popularly, "Ice-Borg." At the same time, there was a superstitious streak in his attitude toward competitions. He was suspicious about the effect shaving might have on his game, so he refused to do so and grew his beard during matches and tournaments. And though his racquet, shoes, and dress changed depending on the tournament, he invariably reverted to a traditional green pinstripe shirt at Wimbledon. These and other peculiarities became well known to tennis audiences.

Borg's career marks a turning point in tennis history as well. He turned professional just after the sport opened, and his skyrocketing success encapsulates many of the changes that happened to tennis once pros and amateurs were allowed to play alongside one another. Indeed, many of Borg's accomplishments as a player could be called "firsts" in tennis. Borg helped transform tennis into a sport with enormous prizes for players— enough to make a more than comfortable living. His frequent endorsements procured by Mark McCormick's IMG—including ones for Formula One and Saab—and his coveted sponsorship arrangements were both a product and a producer of his celebrity as well as a lucrative source of income. His annual income from commercial endorsements was around $4 million, more than the amount he made in prize money during his entire career. Borg set a record, which has since been

Jimmy, at left, at exhibition match between Nick Ludington and the British champion in Manchester, England

Jimmy with U.S. Van Alen Cup Team. Their matches were played all over England and in France, and included a gala evening with the Duke and Duchess of Windsor at their Paris house in the Bois de Boulogne. The players danced with the Duchess and found her charming.

Jimmy in middle row with his U.S. Van Alen Cup Team members and British court tennis officials and players

surpassed, for his off-the-court commercial appearances, having had more than forty simultaneous contracts for endorsements at any given time during his career. Before he turned professional—in 1971, at the early age of fourteen—male professional tennis players usually made just under $100,000. By the time he retired, with a record $3.6 million in career prize money, that ceiling was adjusted to just under $1 million. When he announced his retirement from the tennis circuit in 1983 at the age of twenty-six, he shocked players, fans, and the press alike. Nowadays, however, few would be shocked to hear of a professional athlete retiring at a very early age. In short, few tennis players before Borg achieved anything close to his level of fame, and those who came after him and rose to stardom have invariably followed in his footsteps in some way or another. The Borg-McEnroe tie breaker made history, but not in the way Jimmy would have liked; even in his eighties, he still had hope for his sudden-death tie breaker.

Jimmy continued to pursue his lifelong passions, even toward the end of his life. He was attempting to elevate court tennis to a "blue sport" at Cambridge, and his love of that sport was illustrated by a slightly out-of-order toast he made at Sammy's 75th birthday party. Jimmy had brought custom-made ties to the party for his nephews, Billy Van Alen and Jimbo Van Alen, to commemorate their 1956 trip to England to play Oxford and Cambridge in court tennis. When he stood up to give a toast, he began retelling the events of the trip, recalling how Nick Ludington, Jimbo and Billy's teammate, and a family member, too, had played number one. He continued to go on and on, recapitulating all the details with no mention of his brother, as the other guests became increasingly uncomfortable. Finally, Candy tried to stop him, saying, "Jimmy, it's Sammy's birthday!" Jimmy, unfazed, simply replied, "But Sammy wasn't on the team!"

The court tennis trip Jimmy was remembering was the matches played by the team he had organized in the 1950s. Jimmy had been disappointed with the dominance of lawn tennis in collegiate sports. After all, he had given up playing lawn tennis competitively in the 1930s to take up court tennis—a sport in which he excelled, winning the national amateur championships three times. But court tennis was relatively unknown, especially to the general public, and only became more obscure during the 1940s and '50s. As Bill Wister, a Van Alen family friend and court tennis player, recalls, Jimmy "decided that court tennis was in danger of dying." In order to keep the sport alive, Jimmy had established his own international, intercollegiate court tennis competition in 1952, after purchasing a large silver cup to be given to the winners. He called the tournament the Van Alen Challenge.

But Jimmy was not content to simply establish his own tournament; he was also determined to involve other American universities. He remembered how, when he was playing lawn tennis in the Prentice Cup for Cambridge, he invariably felt disappointed that he had to compete against the same two American universities each year—Harvard and Yale. With the Van Alen Challenge, Jimmy decided, competition would be open to other American universities. When he began to organize teams for the inaugural tournament, he went to England—to Oxford and Cambridge—and to the Eastern United States, drafting potential players from Harvard and Yale as well as from Princeton, Cornell, the University of Pennsylvania, and other top schools. Dan Gardiner, who played on the squash team at Princeton in 1954, recalls how Jimmy recruited the "top 5 or 6 players" from his team to play court tennis that year. "He was a very jovial, caring person, obviously dedicated to the sport and dedicated to promoting the sport among racquet players." Gardiner and several of his teammates went up to New York during Christmas vacation that year to play court tennis with Jimmy at the Racquet Club.

Jimmy's legacy as a lawn tennis player at Cambridge made it easy to convince the athletic authorities in England to enter a combined Oxford-Cambridge team. And according to Bill Wister, whom he asked to join the Van Alen Challenge Team, Jimmy had several advantages as he assembled American teams to play in his tournament. He had numerous contacts who were involved with the squash and lawn tennis teams at Harvard and provided him with potential players as well as practice facilities in Boston, since Harvard had "easy access to the Boston Racquet Club," which had a world-class court tennis facility at the time. In addition, Jimmy's nephew Jimbo Van Alen was an undergraduate at Yale, and his nephew, Billy Van Alen, was attending the University of Pennsylvania. Both of them played in the earliest Van Alen Challenge matches, adding to the number of American universities on

Jimmy and Candy

Jimmy playing his ukulele

the roster. Going to England and Paris to play was an eye-opener for many members of the team, with an exhibition match at Hampton Court and dinner with the Duke and Duchess of Windsor in France. The competitions between the American and English teams, now called the Van Alen Cup, still go on today.

Aside from court tennis, Jimmy kept his ties to England throughout the 1960s and 1970s by making regular excursions to Cambridge and other parts of the U.K. In London in the late fall, Jimmy always made sure to attend the annual Hawks Club dinner for distinguished sportsmen who were members of the club. In 1960 Jimmy wrote a song "Hawking Weather" which related to the life of Cambridge where sports were very important. Hawking was an old-fashioned hunting sport for gentleman.

"There's a hawk in the sky
Pay heed feathered folk
If you needs must fly
If you take to the wing
You may cruelly die
For 'it's hawking weather today'.

The sky's clear and blue
There's no cloud or haze
To impair the view
The 'stoop', will be steep
And the 'strike' be true
For 'it's hawking weather today'.

Hurtling down like a bolt of light
Talons outstretched for the kill
The prey brought to earth
In the midst of flight
The chicks in the eyrie to fill.

So beware of the hawk
He's sharp and keen
As a lightning fork
For a hawk means death
And a death means "hawk"
And 'it's hawking weather today'.

A Hawk's always tough
He'll fight to the end
Never cry 'enough'
And his battle chant
When the going's rough
Is 'it's hawking weather today'.

At whatever the sport
If a goal's to be made
Or a ball be caught
If a Hawk's on the team
Every point is fought
He's never out of the play.

Big or small he's as hard as nails

Size doesn't matter a jot
If the score's tied or close
He will tip the scales
He has what the others have not.

So beware of the guy
With a gleam in his eye
And the old Hawk tie
No matter the odds
Still you'll hear him cry
'IT'S HAWKING WEATHER TODAY!!!'

Ov'r the years passing by
A hawk still will thrill
When he ties a tie
For it brings back the days
When he used to cry
'It's hawking weather today.'

And no matter how far
Whether Hong Kong, Melbourne, or
   Zanzibar
The tie make good friends
Wherever you are
In the very best sort of a way.

Hawking style of a special kind
The game played fairly and clean
The best of Cambridge there is to find
A sportsman, a gentleman, mean.

Yes, a tie is a guy
Is worn by hawks with a sense of pride
As they think of the first time they ever
   cried
'It's Hawking weather today.'

As they think of the first time they ever
   cried
'It's Hawking weather today.'

'Hawking weather today.'

In Scotland, Jimmy visited Gavin Reed, son of his friend Edward Reed, a classmate of his at Cambridge, to go shooting. And he always made sure to attend the May Week crew races on the River Cam against Oxford, bringing enough champagne to either celebrate or console a Cambridge boat he would adopt.

Candy joined all these trips to England with great enthusiasm, and she even seriously supported some of Jimmy's British causes. On one visit to England she learned from Lord Butterfield, Chairman of the Hawks Club, that the Club mortgage was over a 100,000 pounds, to which Candy replied: "Is that all?!" and wrote out a check then and there. As a result, there is a room at the Hawks Club called the Van Alen Room. The newly redeveloped club was officially opened on October 30th 1992 by HRH The Duke of Edinburgh who was Chancellor of Cambridge University.

Jimmy continued to see his good British friend Anthony Bevan and Anthony's parents. There was always an adventure, like the one in 1960 when Jimmy flew across the Atlantic for the Rome Olympics. Anthony Bevan recalls staying with the Ruspoli family outside Rome along with the Van Alens and their guests Bing Crosby and his wife. They went to an Olympic event in the days and barhopping every night. On the last day of the games Jimmy organized a shoot outside Rome for which he flew in 1000 pheasants—many of which died on the airplane!

In his last years, Jimmy did not neglect his passion for music. In the spring of 1986, he wrote to Irving Berlin, confessing that he owed Berlin credit for his musical expertise. Although he wrote the letter in 1986 he waited to send it until April 1988, after learning of Berlin's 99th birthday celebration that year.

In the letter he confesses, "I happen to be a Christmas buff, as you can see by my booklet, but I am also a Berlin buff. If it hadn't been for you I wouldn't have gotten around to playing the piano by ear and making up songs in G-flat, which I understand is your key too… Your example has given me great pleasure and interest, starting off when I was 15 and continuing to this day. I am now 83 so you see I owe you a very long debt of gratitude."

The "booklet" to which Jimmy refers was a collection of poems and songs he sent to Berlin, which included "Christmas Stockings," inspired by Berlin's "White Christmas." He described his mission to bring the Christmas Eve spirit to all, and confessed that as a child he "would send notes up the chimney to Santa Claus telling him of the presents I had hoped for." He also asked Berlin "a great favor, namely, to meet you face-to-face, shake your hand and thank you for all the happiness you have quite unconsciously given me through the years."

The letterhead on which Jimmy sent his request to Irving Berlin gave a lengthy return address. Ten years after he was eased out of power at the Hall of Fame he still identified himself with his achievements there (by this time he had changed the acronym VASSS to stand for Streamlined Scoring System):

HEADQUARTERS
INTERNATIONAL TENNIS HALL OF FAME
NEWPORT, RHODE ISLAND USA 02840
JAMES H. VAN ALEN
FOUNDER AND CHAIRMAN EMERITUS
ORIGINATOR OF THE TIEBREAK GAME
AND THE
VASSS NO-AD STREAMLINED SCORING SYSTEM

The letterhead also included a poem invoking his favorite subject—VASSS:

VASSS ultimate's the drama
Introduces Sudden Death
Which tests the players' courage
Makes the gall'ry catch its breath
It simplifys the scoring terms
Its matches start on time
Where LAWN'S rules are ridiculous
VASS No-Ads are sublime.

The 1980s were good years for Jimmy's political passions. Rightly described as "a political conservative and a tennis radical," he took a position on politics that was diametrically opposed to his liberal views on changing tennis traditions. He was pleased with the relative stronghold the Republican Party maintained in the executive branch during the 1970s and 1980s—especially after the election of Ronald Reagan in 1980. In 1984, he honored President Reagan with one of his campaign songs, "Ode to the President":

Believe me Mister President
We're glad to have you here
You speak the sort of freedom talk
America wants to hear
Straight from the shoulder
No holds barred
You don't beguile our youth
With sugar coated fairy tales
You tell the honest truth
We've had a surfeit of Carter-Mondale-Hart
In four short years
These three had ripped
Our fighting force apart
There's little more
They could have done
To aid the K.G.B.
In trying to block
Our Country's fight
To save DEMOCRACEE!

Candy with H.R.H. Prince Philip, Duke of Edinburgh, at Hawks Club dinner for the dedication of the Van Alen Room, 1992

This was a usual practice for Jimmy—to serenade a Republican commander-in-chief with an original song. His songs were met with varying approval over the years, however. In November 1972, the *Providence Evening Bulletin* reported on a political dinner saluting President Richard Nixon in his re-election bid, noting that the "entertainment section" of the evening was to begin with "James Van Alen's campaign song." Jimmy had originally composed a song for Richard Nixon (with a short coda for Vice President Spiro Agnew) to celebrate his imminent re-election over Democrat George McGovern and arranged for "a dozen busty, short skirted 'Nixon Volunteers' to sing his song as 6,000 diners tarried over the coffee." Un-

fortunately, White House officials deemed the lyrics "too controversial" for the dinner, which was held less than a week before the election. Jimmy's original verses had included praise of President Nixon that usually came at the expense of one of his Democratic opponents, both past and present:

…George McGovern's all mixed up, in fact is far from bright,
Thinks "profit" means the same as "loss," and left the same as right
We need a leader wise and cool not wet behind the ears
McGovern brands himself a fool with the zig-zag course he steers.
God bless you, Mr. President, I want to shake your hand,

You've fought a balky Congress four
    long years to save our land.
From the cockeyed Socialistic schemes
    of Kennedy and Lyn,
McGovern's plan would triple the
    welfare mess they left us in.

Thwarted by White House censorship
but determined to have his song performed,
Jimmy "doctored up the final verses to make
it a salute to First Lady Pat Nixon" instead of
the President:

God bless you, dear Pat Nixon, and we
    all bless you, too,
You've shown the whole wide world
    what perfect partnership can do.
You and the President make up the
    nation's greatest team.
We're proud of everything you do;
    you're always on the beam.

Jimmy's ode to the First Lady was, alas,
"less than a rousing success." Besides the
relatively jejune lyrics, there was the issue of the performers. The group of young
women who were selected to perform the
song in front of President Nixon and his wife
"tried hard," as Jimmy put it, but had not had
enough practice. The White House had denied valuable rehearsal time to Jimmy's chorus even though, according to Jimmy, they
let Ethel Merman "rehearse some song she
has sung 400 times."

Jimmy had been more successful with
the last Republican president before Nixon,
Dwight D. Eisenhower. His song "Good
Evening, Mr. President," which he "respect-
fully dedicated" to Eisenhower in honor of
his election, was performed at the President's
Inaugural Ball on January 20, 1953. The song,
written in the traditionally "heroic" key of E-

flat major and set to a brisk *tempo di marcia*,
painted Eisenhower as the wise and fearless
leader of the American people:

Good Evening, Mister President! I tip
    my hat to you,
For you've got the big assignment, and
    you know just what to do.
The country, Mister President, is sure
    that you will keep
Our people freedom-minded, and not
    governmental sheep.

"Bang!" goes inflation; corruption's on
    the run.
Before you've really started, the whole
    free world is shouting, "well done!"
So, Good Evening, Mister President! I
    tip my hat to you,
For you've got the big assignment and
    you know just what to do.

Aside from his interest in writing, music,
and politics, Jimmy continued to plug his reforms for competitive sports. Having already
made a case for changes in tennis and golf,
Jimmy turned his attention to what was perhaps one of the last aristocratic sports during the end of his life—sailing. During the
1970s he had begun devising reforms for the
America's Cup, the most prestigious regatta
in the world and the oldest active trophy in
the sport of sailing, dating back to 1851. Newport played host to the Cup from 1930 to 1983,
allowing Jimmy to see the race firsthand on
more than one occasion. He was less than enthusiastic as a spectator. Never one to let tradition get in the way of excitement, Jimmy
wrote a lengthy unpublished critique of the
famous race: "Let's face it, in terms of red-
blooded action and a sporting spectacular,
the America's Cup Yacht Races make a turtle

Andre Agassi with wife Steffi Graf at her induction into Hall of Fame, 2004

Pete Sampras inducted into the Hall of Fame, 2007

derby look like the Grand National Steeple Chase or the Indiana 500. Except when jockeying for position at the start and a very occasional bump or near-bump, the contests have all too often degenerated into a follow-the-leader type of procession—deader than mutton or Admiral Nelson's left arm."

Aside from the sheer monotony of the race, Jimmy felt that there was no way to determine the real "winner," of the Cup, as individual nations had more or less resources at their disposal, making it impossible to know "how much of the win was attributable to the crews' ability and how much to having cornered the Hood sailcloth and/or titanium markets," which most United States teams had done. Jimmy's proposed solution to "equate this lopsided situation" had each team "swapping boats after each race" with another team and made sure there was "an even number of races—4, 6, or 8" in the Cup. Under this system, "the winner of the contest would be the nation or yacht club whose crew, *not boat*, had racked up the *lowest cumulative* time score by the end of the last race."

The benefits to such a system extended beyond fairness, however. Jimmy saw the potential for publicity as well. "With a committee boat, on which was mounted a gigantic electric scoreboard, surging up and down in front of the spectator fleet, counting out the seconds, it is hard to believe that a fresh and exciting dimension would not be added to this most expensive and passive of contests. The time situation would be kept up to the second and off-course betting would boom." Such a move, which had worked quite well for tennis at Newport, met with considerably less enthusiasm in the sailing world.

Throughout the decade Jimmy continued to attend the championship tennis matches and wave his sudden death flag. But his eyesight was failing and he was slowing down. When Jimmy died on July 3, 1991 it was the day of the semifinal matches at Wimbledon. Bud Collins, as the announcer for the match, felt he must tell the fans assembled in the most dignified and historic of tennis stadiums that the sport had lost one of its great enthusiasts. Bud knew that Jimmy had a wonderful sense of humor so he reported how the great proponent of sudden death in tennis tie breaker scoring had himself endured a "sudden death." The story was that Jimmy had fallen off the porch of his Newport mansion, Avalon, broken his neck, and died instantly. But it turned out, ironically, that Jimmy had died at the hospital an hour after his fall—so that Jimmy's was, in the end, a "lingering death."

It was a sunny day and Jimmy, whose health wasn't good, was sitting on the porch, which was about three feet off the ground and overlooked the Rhode Island Sound. He had his straw hat on and his ukulele in his hand. The gardener was working nearby in the Rose Garden and two young girls were supposed to be watching Jimmy as his eyesight was poor. A young man named Brian Stinson was pulling weeds around the other side of the house. Stinson heard yells from the gardener, "Stints! Stints!" He ran around the house, saw Jimmy on the ground, and the two of them began calling for help. Brian was a lifeguard with emergency training, and when he saw Jimmy was in distress, he administered CPR. The fire department arrived and took Jimmy by ambulance to the hospital, where he died about an hour later.

Two months later, Donna Doherty remembered Jimmy's contributions to tennis, which "forever changed the face of the game," in a retrospective for *Tennis* magazine, where she was a senior editor. The last time she had seen Van Alen was at the U.S. Open the year before he died. Jimmy's box was behind the baseline where he was often seen waving his red flag. On the day, he was sitting in front of her, "snoozing off and on under the sweltering August afternoon sun during the Michael Chang-Jimmy Arias match. The first set was close but uninspiring tennis. But when the score reached 6-all, Van Alen's wife, Candace, poked him hard: 'Tie-break time, Jimmy. Tie-break, Jimmy,' she said loudly. With that, up popped Van Alen, resplendent in pink pants and checkered shirt. He grabbed the little red flag with the symbols 'S–X–D'—'Sudden-Death Tie-break,' stood up and proudly waved it on high." Doherty remembered how hard Jimmy fought for reforms to the scoring system so that fans could enjoy tennis on television and in stadiums alike, contrasting his attitude with the attitude of "celebrity" players who had begun to demand more and more money, publicity, and attention. "In these times of greed and selfishness, it's especially sad for the game to lose a true friend who lived his life to tell other people about the joys of tennis."

Over the course of his life, Jimmy witnessed many changes in tennis starting with his early playing as a boy at Newport at the Casino before the First World War. Then, one entered the interior of the Casino and found "a strange vanished world," what one writer called "a placid world of blue and white hydrangeas, English elms and copper beeches, and in particular, old wooden buildings faced with weather-beaten, ornately patterned shingles and trimmed in old-fashioned New England colors like dark green and raspberry." It was a placid world, too, of white-clothed players, beautifully chalked green grass courts, and matches that proceeded with grace and elegance. And of course also there, facing the entrance, was the famous horseshoe piazza. Jimmy knew the Casino as a boy and later as its President. Through his VASSS efforts, Jimmy was part of tournament tennis in the '60s and '70s and an agitating spectator in the last decade of his life. Jimmy's spirit and legacy still continues on both in collegiate tennis and in World Team Tennis, where no-ad scoring (played 1–2–3–4 with a sudden death point at 3-all) is being used to speed up match play and allow spectators more chance to see more match play.

While many of the changes to tennis over the twentieth century delighted Jimmy—the opening of the sport to professionals and amateurs alike, the addition of the tie breaker, the ability to broadcast matches on live television—there were other changes that he found less desirable. Years before he died, Jimmy spoke out on occasion against prima donna players who valued their careers more than their fans, or even the game itself. For Jimmy, "Newport in 1916 was heaven" compared to the rampant commercialism and celebrity of the sport today. "The Casino was alive with marvelous people playing tennis. It was the hub of the game in America then. And I can't tell you what tennis has meant to my life—the friends, the times, the feeling of well being through playing. That's why it's important that more people play—for the healthful recreation. It's the people who are important, not a few players at the top."

Young Jimmy Van Alen, great-nephew of Jimmy, presenting the trophy to Mark Philipoussis and Justin Gimelstob at the Invitational Tournament, 2006

Epilogue

Fans and players alike did not need time to recognize that tennis was changing rapidly during the 1970s and 1980s. Gordon Forbes, a famous South African player during the 1950s, remembers what it was like to watch the 1976 Wimbledon final between Björn Borg and Ilie Năstase of Romania and feel the game was somehow different than when he had played almost three decades earlier: "I sat there, engrossed in the tennis—this new tennis with its indefinable air of style and grandeur. I sensed the hero-worship for the young Swede and the pure glamour of Năstase. The aura of theatre! And I found myself thinking of the older days when tennis tournaments had been simpler and more personal things; when there were no Las Vegas Spectaculars, no money prizes, nor the fascinations created by money, nor of its motivations; when the spirit of the game had been much more the thing, and getting into the next round meant no increased winnings, but only the excitement of victory and a small step nearer to some private and much-beloved ambition, longed for with unimagined longings."

Jimmy also yearned for the "older days" of tennis, but when he did agitate for change, he always had the many fans and recreational players in mind. He once said that "the pros don't give a darn about the welfare of the game. Have you ever known a tennis player to buy a ticket? No." The welfare of the game was Jimmy's top priority. Tennis had given him years of joy and he wanted others to share that joy, to experience it for themselves by playing and watching tennis. Jimmy's concern was with the average, everyday tennis enthusiast, not the millionaire Grand Slam champion: "I've devised a system for 10 million ordinary players, the backbone of the game—not a handful of pros."

Whether Jimmy would approve or not, the "handful of pros" are the face of tennis today. American sociologist and author E. Digby Baltzell describes the rise of the celebrity player as the result of a "radical change from a provincial amateur game dominated by the ideals of an Anglo-American upper class and its British Commonwealth counterparts to a new world tennis game with no common sporting ideals held together by the common pursuit of money." More than ever before in the world of tennis, emerging champions begin their training at a very young age, winning prestigious scholarships or simply paying—sometimes in the millions of dollars over the course of their training—to attend rigorous "tennis camps" all over the world, one of the most famous being the Bollettieri Tennis Academy in Florida, which has produced many of today's top players.

Bollettieri launched the careers of past champions like Monica Seles and Andre Agassi as well as present superstars like Maria Sharapova. The idea of "tennis training—when it begins, what it entails, and its pressures for both parents and children—has evolved every bit as much as the serves, forehands, and backhands of the modern game." Students of tennis training facilities not only receive instruction in the game, but also top-

Maria Sharapova at U.S. Open in her Nike dress

more. Maria Sharapova launched her career with Bollettieri when she moved to Florida from Russia with her father, but because of visa restrictions, Sharapova's mother was unable to move with them for two years. Since neither Sharapova nor her father spoke English, he took a number of odd jobs to pay for her training, driving her to practice each day on the handlebars of his bicycle. Jan Silva, age 6, and his family relocated to Thiverval-Grignon, France, so that he could attend the renowned Mouratoglou Tennis Academy. By the end of his training—if he remains there until he turns pro—his parents will have spent 2 to 3 million dollars on his training. No longer just a leisure sport, many parents have staked everything they have on their child's future as a tennis player.

Tennis may be different today than it was on the fresh green lawns of the Newport Casino during Jimmy's childhood, but some of the more recent developments in the sport suggest the players' nostalgia for the old days. Perhaps harking back to the more glamorous days of lawn tennis, "one emerging trend" is for players "to incorporate a cocktail-attire look into their performance clothes, especially if they're playing under the lights at night." Female tennis players, such as Maria Sharapova and the sisters Venus and Serena Williams, were pioneers of this trend. When Sharapova won the U.S. Open in 2006, she did so in a custom-designed black cocktail dress by Nike, inspired by the famous black dress worn by Audrey Hepburn in *Breakfast at Tiffany's*. The dress, complete with "a sparkly neckline, satin-bow waistline and keyhole openings down the back," provided both fans and fashionistas with something to talk about. Tiffany & Co., perhaps flattered by the reference Sharapova made with her

notch coaching, nutritional counseling, and medical care. Comprehensive tennis instruction camps like the Bollettieri Tennis Academy do not come without a considerable price—and not just a monetary one. In addition to putting thousands, sometimes millions, of dollars into these training facilities, hoping to produce a Grand Slam champion of their child, parents often give up much

dress, now provides the tennis star with jewelry for off-the-court events, as well as a line of earrings called "Tiffany for Maria Sharapova," which is sold in stores around the world.

Women aren't the only players dressing for success on the court. In 2007, Roger Federer alternated between a blue-and-white ensemble during the day and a tuxedo-style ensemble for night matches. And not all tennis players are aching with nostalgia for the bygone days of tennis. Serena Williams, who has played some of her best matches in white cocktail dresses at Wimbledon, is also known for her less conventional fashion decisions. She played in the 2002 U.S. Open in a black leather-looking cat suit, and wore a denim skirt and athletic boots to the same tournament two years later. But regardless of how conservative or innovative the fashion choices of modern players may be, the attention paid to the players' ensembles is a far cry from the early twentieth century, when the only attention female players would receive for their dress was usually negative—if a dress was cut too high above the calf or exposed too much of her arms.

Other fashion changes in tennis have gone largely unnoticed or at least unannounced. The most significant of these for the sport was the change in racquets and grips during the twentieth century. After 1874, nearly all tennis racquets had been constructed of wood—layers of laminated wood—with strings woven between the edges of the racquet head, and a leather grip. At 13 or 14 ounces, wooden racquets were considerably heavier than modern racquets, which can weigh as little as 7 or 8 ounces, and quite a bit smaller in terms of hitting area. Metal racquets did not gain popularity until nearly a century later, in 1967, when Wilson

Serena Williams, fashionable champion

introduced its first metal racquet, the steel-framed T2000. Jimmy Connors was a well-known user of the racquet, which helped to boost its popularity. The "light weight, huge sweet spot, and greatly increased power of these first oversized racquets made tennis much easier for non-advanced players," which helped begin the "tennis boom" of new recreational and amateur players during the 1970s. Advanced and professional players, on the other hand, demanded a stiffer frame material than aluminum or steel could offer, and so companies like Prince and Wilson began experimenting with a mixture of carbon fibers bound together with a plastic resin. These new racquets became known as "graphite" racquets, even though the material used to make the frame was a synthetic mixture and not genuine graphite. Still, by 1980, "racquets could pretty much be divided into two classes: inexpensive racquets made of aluminum and expensive ones made of graphite or a composite. Wood no longer offered anything that another material couldn't provide better—except for antique and collectible value." The grips changed, too, from leather to synthetic materials.

The style of play has changed over the years as well. Nick Bollettieri, whose famous tennis training camp in Florida has produced many champions, was also responsible for the changes in style of championship play. It was he who encouraged greater overall physical fitness for his students, emphasizing long groundstroke rallies between opponents—a style which would make Jimmy's VASSS rule to move the baseline back in order to mute the power serve less important. As Bollettieri's students became champions and new rising stars began to imitate their playing style, tennis became less focused on powerful serves and more focused on placement, spin, and stamina.

Regardless of his own feelings about the changes to tennis over the past century, Jimmy Van Alen will always be a part of them—through the International Tennis Hall of Fame in Newport, Rhode Island. The Hall of Fame has charted the changes and champions of tennis over the years, reminding its

visitors (over 100,000 annually) that the sport is not the same as it once was. Visitors who enter the Casino can now, thanks to Jimmy and a generous grant from the estate of his wife, Candy Van Alen, take a walk through history, reliving and experiencing the different periods of the sport throughout the century. In the museum they can watch iconic matches like the Borg-McEnroe tie breaker,

inspect old wooden racquets and ancient looking tennis balls, and, noticing the evocative photographs, look back on the many champions who have been inducted into the Hall's ranks over the years. In the summer, visitors can also attend the Campbell's tournament on the Casino's old grass courts, or play a few games themselves. It is this mixture of change and preservation that charac-

terizes the sport of tennis during the twentieth century, and this same mixture has kept the Hall of Fame alive. Executive Director Mark Stenning is proud of the excellent condition of the handsome buildings and says he would like James Gordon Bennett to be able to enter the Casino and exclaim, "Oh! It looks just the way I left it!" Jimmy Van Alen, too, would love nothing more.

Van Alen Family Tree

James I. Van Alen 1788–1874
m. Lucy Trumbull 1788–1867

Gen. James Henry Van Alen 1819–1886
m. Mary Steward 1818–1852

James John Van Alen 1846–1923
m. Emily Astor 1854–1881

**Mary (May)
Van Alen** 1876–1959
m. Griswold Thompson
1875–1945

**James Laurens
Van Alen** 1878–1927
m. Margaret Post
1877–1969
(m. Louis Bruguiere, 1948)

**Sarah (Sally)
Van Alen** 1881–1961
m. Robert Collier
1876–1918

**James Henry
Van Alen**
1902–1991
m. Eleanor Langley
(Div. 1946)
m. Candace Alig
Vanderlip 1948

**William Laurens
Van Alen**
1907–2003
m. Elizabeth Kent
1911–

**Louise Astor
Van Alen**
1910–1997
m. Alexander
Saunderson
1917–2004

**James Langley
Van Alen**
1931–2008
m. Maris McLeod
1939–

**Samuel T.
Van Alen**
1934–1970

**William L.
Van Alen, Jr.** 1933–
m. Sidney Purviance
(Div. 1975)
m. Judith Frost Kanzler
1980–

**James Laurens
Van Alen, II.** 1935–
m. Jeanne DeBlois
Bartholomew 1943–

**Cassandra Kent
Van Alen** 1937–
m. Nicholas S.
Ludington, Jr. 1934–

Sources

NOTE: The full source listing for the James Henry and Candace Van Alen Papers at the Redwood Library and Athenaeum, Newport, Rhode Island, has been abbreviated to the Van Alen Papers.

CHAPTER ONE: THE NEWPORT BOLSHEVIK

4:    Robert H. Boyle on Jimmy: "The Deuce With Love and Advantage," *Sports Illustrated*, August 28, 1972.

4–6:   Tennis scoring history is from Caryl Phillips' *The Right Set: A Tennis Anthology.*

No one knows exactly how the original tennis scoring began but there are two stories. "The first one states that the scoring has its origins in ancient numerology. In medieval times, the number 60 was considered auspicious or 'complete' in a similar manner to which the number 100 is considered to be a 'complete' figure now. The medieval adaptation of tennis [or court tennis] thus considered 60 to be the 'game' with steps of four points like 15, 30, 45 (or 40 as it is today) and finally 60." The second story is attributed to the presence of a clock at the end of the tennis court. "A quarter move of the clock hand was made after each break with the score being referred to as 15, 30, 45 and finally 60." Information is from http://www.historyoftennis.net/history_of_tennis.html

6:    Jimmy describes tennis scoring procedures: "Essay on Tennis History" by James H. Van Alen, Van Alen Papers.

6:    Jimmy recounts the story of how he came up with the tiebreaker in James Dickenson's article, "For Those Who Don't Know the Score, a Tennis Trend," *The National Observer*, July 1965.

7:    Information on VASSS system scoring and tournaments is from *VASSS Basic Rules Sheet* and press releases, Van Alen Papers.

8:    Casino description is from Samuel G. and Elizabeth White's book, *McKim, Mead & White: The Masterworks.*

8:    Description of Wakehurst from Margaret Bruguiere is from Frank Deford's article, "Anyone Care to Play Some VASSS?" *Sports Illustrated*, July 19, 1965.

8–9:   Descriptions of VASSS tournament are from George McGann's article "A VASSSly Entertaining Weekend," *World Tennis*, September 1965, and James Dickenson's article in *The National Observer*, "For Those Who Don't Know the Score, a Tennis Trend."

9:    Tournament players comment on the change of the game: Frank Deford's article, "Anyone Care to Play Some VASSS?" *Sports Illustrated*, July 19, 1965.

9:    Bud Collins describing the VASSS tournament is from his book, *My Life with the Pros*, p. 163.

11–12:   For reactions of players to VASSS see George McGann's "A VASSSly Entertaining Weekend," p. 25 and James Dickenson's article "For Those Who Don't Know the Score, a Tennis Trend."

11–12:   Jimmy Van Alen and Barry McKay on the VASSS system as well as Jimmy's goal to promote tennis as a healthful game are from James Dickenson's article in *The National Observer* "For Those Who Don't Know the Score, a Tennis Trend."

12:    Arthur Ashe on the quiet during the tiebreaker: "Signal Flag: Sudden Death," USLTA Official Program U.S. Open, August 1972.

CHAPTER TWO: THE FAMILY

15–18:   The family background comes from *Sammy's Book: Family Memories*, the memoir of Jimmy's brother, William "Sammy" Laurens Van Alen. Some of the details come from Eleanor Dwight's interview with Sammy Van Alen in the spring of 2003, as well as from family genealogies at the New York Public Library.

15–17:   Details about Jimmy's birthday party come from newspaper clippings found in the Van Alen Papers.

17:    For Jimmy playing tennis at Tuxedo Park and teaching Sammy, see *Sammy's Book: Family Memories*, p. 57–59.

18:    General information on James Henry Van Alen is from the Van Alen Papers.

18:    James Henry Van Alen's letter to Lincoln appears in Alan Axelrod's *Lincoln's Last Night: Abraham Lincoln, John Wilkes Booth, and the Last 36 Hours Before the Assassination*, p. 23.

General Van Alen had an unfortunate death. It was reported in the *Newport Journal* on Saturday, July 31, 1886, and begins, "Word was received here Sunday night that General J.H. Van Alen…had committed suicide from the Cunard steamer *Umbria* on his return to this country. A few weeks ago General Van Alen left Newport with three of his grandchildren, of whom he is especially fond, and whom he would put in nobody's care but his own, intending to put them to school near Southampton. They had scarcely got fairly settled in England when a telegram announcing the serious illness of his only son, the father of the three little children, recalled General Van Alen to this country. He was plainly too much affected by his son's danger to make the long voyage alone, and Mr. Grinnell fearing that some accident might happen to the general in his nervous and excited condition, determined to sail with him to New York."

The Captain gave them his double cabin on the upper deck. "The general, according to a dispatch to the Boston Journal from New York, slept poorly the first two or three nights, talked excitedly at times and at other times seemed listless and depressed. He had a presentiment, he said, that he would never see his son again, and the three little children left behind in England seemed also to weigh upon his mind." A watch was put upon his movements during the day and all was well until Wednesday, July 21, 1866. The weather changed from pleasant to sultry and "there was not a breath of air stirring the whole evening," so the cabin became almost intolerable. General Van Alen "became feverish and talked incoherently…[and] even dashed his head against the walls of the narrow room." For a long time he would not sleep, but was finally quieted after midnight into an uneasy doze. After watching until nearly four o'clock, Mr. Grinnell fell asleep. "When he awoke an hour later General Van Alen was gone. Only his overcoat and luggage were left lying in disorder about the cabin. The general had evidently got up about 4 a.m., dressed himself carefully, putting on his collar, necktie, high white hat and gloves, and taking his walking stick, had passed out through the open door upon the deck. The sea was running high and the ship was pitching and tossing. The third officer is confident that he saw a passenger dressed like the general just after dawn, outside the whaleback, a part of the rail, at the very stern of the ship. Before he could look again the figure had disappeared. The Umbria rides high, and it is scarcely possible that the luckless old gentleman could have been washed overboard by the waves. He must have climbed the whale-back deliberately and then jumped or fallen into the sea." When the Umbria reached New York, there was James J. Van Alen, who had come from Newport to meet, as he supposed, his father.

18–21:   For James John Van Alen history, see Eric Homberger's *Mrs. Astor's New York: Money and Social Power in a Gilded Age*; Lady Elizabeth Decies' *Turn of the World*; Elizabeth Drexel Lehr's *The Leisure Class in America*; Jerry E. Patterson's *The First Four Hundred: Mrs. Astor's New York in the Gilded Age*; W.L. Van Alen's *Sammy's Book: Family Memories*; James L. Yarnall's *Newport Through Its Architecture: A History of Styles from Postmedieval to Postmodern*.

19–20:   On the history of the Astor family and Mrs. Caroline Astor: Eric Homberger's *Mrs. Astor's New York: Money and Social Power in a Gilded Age*; and Justin Kaplan's *When the Astors Owned New York: Blue Bloods and Grand Hotels in a Gilded Age*.

21:   Information on Wakehurst: James L. Yarnall's *Newport Through Its Architecture: A History of Styles from Postmedieval to Postmodern*, p. 124–127.

21:   Den of Wakehurst as the dining room of Lady Fitz-Herbert: W.L. Van Alen's *Sammy's Book: Family Memories*, p. 8.

21:   Descriptions of the Wakehurst housewarming and the mansion's interiors, plus comments on Wakehurst and Town Topics quotes: Donna M. Lucey, *Archie and Amelie: Love and Madness in the Gilded Age*, p. 114–115.

21:   Descriptions of other Gilded Age mansions: *A Guide to Newport's Cliff Walk* and *Newport: A Lively Experiment 1639–1969*.

21–22:   James John Van Alen appointed as ambassador to Rome and his subsequent refusal is from W.L. Van Alen's *Sammy's Book: Family Memories*, p. 10.

22:   Teddy Wharton as Secretary is from an Ogden Codman letter to his mother, Sarah Codman. Letters are located at the Historic New England, Boston, Massachusetts.

22–23:   On cruise with Edith Wharton: Edith Wharton's *The Cruise of the Vanadis*.

23:   On James John leaving America for England during Prohibition: W.L. Van Alen, *Sammy's Book: Family Memories*.

25:   J.J. Van Alen's estate of Rushton was featured in society columns when he lavishly entertained for his hunting guests. The quotes about his shooting party come from these columns: *New York Times*, January 17, 1909, "J.J. Van Alen Has Big Shooting Party; Princely Entertainment at Rushton Hall—Duke of Manchester Among the Guests. Lady Cunard Coming Here Marquess of Anglesey Also to Make an American Visit—King Dines with Sir Arthur and Lady Paget."

25–27:   Memories of James Laurens Van Alen are from W.L. Van Alen, *Sammy's Book: Family Memories*, p. 23.

27–28:   On Jimmy Van Alen's life and his early trips to Europe: James Van Alen autobiographical notes, Van Alen Papers.

29–30:   Stories about soccer games, shooting pheasants and Gowing are from W.L. Van Alen's *Sammy's Book: Family Memories*, p. 12–14.

31:   Jimmy learns tennis from Uncle Will Post and learns how to play piano: *Sammy's Book: Family Memories*, p. 58–59 and Eleanor Dwight interviews with Bill Van Alen in 2003, 2006 and 2007.

32:   Information on Tuxedo Park comes from Christian Sonne's *Tuxedo Park: The Historic Houses*.

32:   On Teddy Roosevelt and tennis: E. Digby Baltzell's *Sporting Gentlemen: Men's Tennis from the Age of Honor to the Cult of the Superstar*.

32:   Jimmy's aggressive playing style: W.L. Van Alen's *Sammy's Book: Family Memories*.

33:   Jimmy's sister Lulu's reminiscences as Jimmy's partner in the handicap mixed doubles tournament on the Riviera: W.L. Van Alen's *Sammy's Book: Family Memories*, p. 64–65; and *I Say!: Memoirs of Captain Alexander Saunderson* by Barry Head and Nick Ludington.

33:   Jimmy's penchant for pranks: Interview with Sammy Van Alen, Spring 2003.

33–34:   Sammy memories of Newport during the days he was a boy and family trips to Europe are from *Sammy Van Alen Audio Tapes* (A series of interviews conducted by James Van Alen in the 1990s).

34:   On Jimmy's schooling: W.L. Van Alen's *Sammy's Book: Family Memories*.

34:   On James Laurens Van Alen's love for cars and war years: W.L. Van Alen's *Sammy's Book: Family Memories*.

CHAPTER THREE: CAMBRIDGE

37:   Report from Newport Invitational about Jimmy and information on dance given by Jimmy's mother, Daisy Van Alen: August 1925 newspaper clipping from *New York World*, Van Alen Papers.

37:   Jimmy's attendance at Harvard University for one year is reflected in the Matriculation Book at Christ's College, Cambridge.

37:   Jimmy discusses his success in tennis at Cambridge, including his rank of "full blue" in "The Last Grand Homme" in the Van Alen Papers.

37–42: General information on Jimmy's time at Cambridge—including his grades, team memberships, and his responsibility for running the university's tennis tournaments—is taken from Jimmy's personal writings in the Van Alen papers and Eleanor Dwight interviews at Cambridge University.

39: On Jimmy staying at Cambridge for an extra year to continue playing tennis: W.L. Van Alen's *Sammy's Book: Family Memories*.

39: Jimmy objects to the piece in the April issue of *Tattler* entitled, "Portrait of the Undergraduate Life" in an essay in the Van Alen Papers.

39–46: Jimmy's poem, "Cambridge," was printed in Great Britain in 1962, and information on Jimmy's Cambridge experience is from the Van Alen Papers and from Eleanor Dwight interviews at Cambridge.

46: For Jimmy's invitation to play on the combined Oxford-Cambridge lawn tennis team against the combined Harvard-Yale team, see *The Country Gentleman's Newspaper*, August 5, 1922.

46–48: For history of the Prentice Cup, match scores, and Jimmy's responsibilities as captain see the foreword to *International Intercollegiate Tennis, 1921–1974 Inclusive*, p. 7–10 and the Van Alen Papers.

46–49: The history of Seabright is from The Seabright Lawn Tennis and Cricket Club Member's Book 2002.

49: Jimmy's quotes from *Granta* are from "The Last Grand Homme," an article written by a Long Island reporter at the end of James Van Alen's life, Van Alen Papers.

49: Descriptions of Edward Reed and his friendship with Jimmy, as well as the practice of deer-stalking, are taken from Eleanor Dwight's interview with Gavin Reed, Edward's son, in May 2008.

49–51: Descriptions of the hunting excursions are taken from Edward Reed's hunting diaries, from October 1937 and August and September 1939, Van Alen Papers.

51: The information on Jimmy's economic means while at Cambridge comes from an article entitled "The Last Grand Homme," written by a Long Island reporter at the end of James Van Alen's life, Van Alen Papers.

51–52: On the Van Alen family's holidays in Cannes, see W.L. Van Alen's *Sammy's Book: Family Memories*, p. 25–26.

52: For the Bill Tilden-Suzanne Lenglen tennis rivalry, including dates and reportage on the matches they played, see Tinling's essay, "The Old Guard," in *The Right Set*, ed. Caryl Phillips, p. 61–65.

52: Jimmy's picture appeared alongside Suzanne Lenglen's in *Le Miroir Des Sports*'s article "Le Tournoi International De Tennis De Cannes," p. 38.

53–54: On the death of Jimmy's grandfather and the Cavendish Hotel anecdote, see W.L. Van Alen's *Sammy's Book: Family Memories*, p. 27 & 91, and Eleanor Dwight's *The Letters of Pauline Palmer*, p. 17–18.

54: On Jimmy's father's death, see W.L. Van Alen's *Sammy's Book: Family Memories*, p. 29.

55: Information on the Van Alen fortune and the division of Jimmy's father's estate is from clippings and wills in the Van Alen Papers.

56: On Margaret (Daisy) Van Alen's remarriage and Lulu Van Alen's marriages, see W.L. Van Alen's *Sammy's Book: Family Memories*.

58: Jimmy's assessment of Rupert Brooke and John Milton's poetic treatments of Cambridge appears in the Van Alen Papers.

CHAPTER FOUR: THE WAR

61: Jimmy deciding to give up competitive tennis in favor of polo, hunting, and riding is from W.L. Van Alen's *Sammy's Book: Family Memories* and the Van Alen Papers.

61: The descriptions of Jimmy and Eleanor's wedding are from "Eleanor Langley and J.H. Van Alen Wed at Westbury," in the *New York Herald-Tribune* of October 12, 1929.

61: On the birth of Jimmy's first son, see "Van Alen Stork Brings Prestige Plus," in the *New York Daily News* of April 30, 1931. Information on the birth of his second son was taken from Eleanor Dwight's interview with Sammy Van Alen.

61: References to scrutiny Eleanor would receive as Jimmy's wife appear in newspaper articles in the Van Alen Papers.

63: Allison Danzig's descriptions of Jimmy's court tennis playing style appear in his article, "Van Alen Conquers Wright in 5 Sets," in the *New York Times*, March 26, 1933.

63: Allison Danzig is quoted in Robert H. Boyle's *At the Top of Their Game*, p. 21.

63–65: Jimmy's "Between the Lines" clippings are from the Van Alen Papers.

65: Jimmy's enlistment in the navy and keeping it a secret: Office of the Chief of Naval Operations, Mobilization Assignment Memo, November 27, 1939, Van Alen Papers.

65–66: On Gardnar Mulloy and other players affected by the outbreak of World War II, see Mulloy's *The Will to Win: An Inside View of the World of Tennis*, p. 35 & 77. Other details are taken from Eleanor Dwight's interview with Mulloy.

67–68: Bobby Riggs' biographer, Tom LeCompte, describes the conditions of the military tennis tournaments in *The Last Sure Thing: The Life & Times of Bobby Riggs*.

67: On the destruction of Centre Court at Wimbledon during the Second World War, see the "History" web page of the Wimbledon website, http://www.wimbledon.org/en_GB/about/history/history.html

68: Tony Trabert's memories of the war, playing tennis as a boy, and his career after the war are taken from Eleanor Dwight's interview with Tony Trabert, October 2007.

68–69: On Bill Talbert's time during the war, see William F. Talbert and John Seymour Sharnik's *Playing For Life: Billy Talbert's Story*, p. 182–183.

69–73: The details of Jimmy's tenure at Farrar, Straus were taken from Eleanor Dwight's interview with Dorothea Straus, Fall 2006.

71: Jimmy's role in publishing William L. White's *They Were Expendable* is detailed in a letter to Jimmy from Edison McIntyre, August 2, 1991, in the Van Alen Papers.

73: In memo to the Bureau of Naval Personnel dated December 12, 1942, Jimmy requests a more active role in the war effort: Van Alen Papers.

73: Jay Van Alen's memories of his father's time in the war and details of Jimmy's improvements at Naval War College in Newport were taken from Eleanor Dwight's interview with Jay Van Alen.

73–74: The sports metaphors in Jimmy's War College thesis are excerpts taken from the copies in the Van Alen Papers.

75: Jimmy's ranks and positions in the navy during the Second World War are from the Van Alen Papers.

75: The details of Jimmy's efforts to boost troop morale by cornering the lobster market and heading up the construction of a sailors' club were taken from Eleanor Dwight's interview with Sammy Van Alen, Spring 2003.

75: Jimmy writes of his rest and rehabilitation center in a letter to President Kennedy dated February 1, 1961, Van Alen Papers.

76: Jack Ormsbee describes his time together with Jimmy in a letter to Bud Collins dated July 7, 1991 in the Van Alen Papers.

77: Arthur Ormont describes Jimmy's style in the Roger Straus Papers from the New York Public Library.

77–78: For Candy Van Alen's biography, the development of Jimmy and Candy's relationship, including quotes from Candy Van Alen, see "Newport Socialite's Life was Made Richer by Love," in the *Newport Daily News*, November 8, 2001 and the Redwood Library and Athenaeum Newsletter tribute in 2002.

78: An excerpt of Candy Van Alen's interview with George Bernard Shaw is from "Newport Socialite's Life was Made Richer by Love" in the *Newport Daily News* of November 8, 2001.

78: Descriptions of Jimmy and Candy's honeymoon trip to England is from Eleanor Dwight's interview with Gavin Reed, May 2008.

78: Jimmy and Candy's letters to one another are now part of the Van Alen Papers.

79: On Jimmy and Candy's happy marriage, see George Herrick's tribute, "A Lasting Gift from a "Grand Dame" to a Grand Institution" in *Newport This Week*, October 23–29, 2002.

79: Ralph Carpenter's description of Jimmy and Candy's relationship appears in "Newport Socialite's Life was Made Richer by Love," *Newport Daily News*, November 8, 2001.

79: Candy explaining how she always lived her life in the moment is from the *Newport Daily News*, "Newport Socialite's Life was Made Richer by Love," November 8, 2001 and the Redwood Library and Athenaeum Newsletter tribute in 2002.

CHAPTER FIVE: THE CASINO

81: Candy Van Alen's *Vogue* article, "We Chartered a Baby Submarine…We Painted it Yellow so Whales Wouldn't Swallow It" is in the Van Alen Papers.

81: Jimmy on how Newport can be hard on women is from his personal writings found in the Van Alen Papers.

81: On the details of Margaret Post's life and her roots in Newport, see W.L. Van Alen's *Sammy's Book: Family Memories*, p. 42–45.

81–83: On Avalon, see *Newport Through its Architecture* by James L. Yarnall. Some of the description of the estate is compiled from photographs of the mansion courtesy of the Redwood Library and Athenaeum, Newport, R.I.

83: Information about Jimmy and Candy's purchase of the Wrentham Estate is from Eleanor Dwight's interviews with John Winslow, 2008.

83–84: For details on Jimmy's involvement in the Casino, see "Newport: Capital and Shrine of Championship Tennis" by Helen Farrell Allen written for the 1970 Yearbook, International Tennis Hall of Fame Library, p. 24.

83: On the fire at the Casino, see "General Alarm Fire Destroys North Wing of Newport Casino Block," in *Newport News* of April 18, 1953.

83: For information on Henry Phelps, president of the Casino from 1945 to 1951, and scores from the Newport tournament in 1946, see "Newport: Capital and Shrine of Championship Tennis" by Helen Farrell Allen written for the 1970 Yearbook, International Tennis Hall of Fame Library, p. 24.

84: On Jimmy's big ideas for the Casino and his meetings with the Executive Committee, see the minutes of the Executive Committee from July 3, 1952, available at the International Tennis Hall of Fame's Library.

84: Jimmy's son, Jay Van Alen, provided the details of Jimmy's attempt to establish a Tennis Hall of Fame at Newport in his interview with Eleanor Dwight.

84–85: On the architecture of the Casino and the story of Captain Henry Augustus Candy, see Robert Stern's *Pride of Place: Building the American Dream*.

85: The life of James Gordon Bennett, Jr. and the birth of the Casino is from Richard O'Connor's biography, *The Scandalous Mr. Bennett*.

85–86: The description of the Casino in its early days was taken from the "Local Matters" section of the *Newport Mercury*, May 8, 1880 and July 3, 1880.

86–87: For the history of tennis in America and the first championships at Newport, "The First American Championships" by Richard Sears, p. 22–23 in Caryl Phillips' *The Right Set*.

It should be noted that Fredrick Sears is the older half-brother of Richard Sears, America's first national champion.

87–88: For more information on Major Wingfield's Boston Story, and the New York Story, "Lawn Tennis in America" by Heiner Gillmeister, p. 16–18, in Caryl Phillips' *The Right Set*.

No one is quite sure who first played tennis in the United States or where it was first played. But most historians agree that tennis sprang up in the U.S. in 1874 in various locations.

Major Walter Clopton Wingfield also had a type of tie breaker in his rule book: if, during the 15-point game, the players reach 13 or 14 all, the players have the option to play either a 3 or 5-point tie breaker. Walter Clopton Wingfield, *The Major's Game of Lawn Tennis*, Feb 25, 1874.

88: Allison Danzig on early tennis championships: "Salute to Newport Casino: Cradle of American Tennis, Home of Hall of Fame" by Allison Danzig, International Tennis Hall of Fame Library.

90: For the Newport social milieu and its attitude towards tennis see Maude Howe Elliot's *This Was My Newport*.

90: Information on Newport's early amateur tournaments, Craig Biddle, and quote from Wilmer Allison, 1934 Newport winner are from "Newport: Capital and Shrine of Championship Tennis" by Helen Farrell Allen written for the 1970 Yearbook, International Tennis Hall of Fame Library, p. 23.

90–91: Descriptions of Eleanor Elkins Widener's Tennis Week Ball are from a newspaper clipping in the Van Alen Papers and Eleanor Dwight's interviews with John Winslow, 2008.

91–95: For more memories of early tournaments, see "Newport: Capital and Shrine of Championship Tennis" by Helen Farrell Allen written for the 1970 Yearbook, International Tennis Hall of Fame Library.

97: Organizing the Diamond Jubilee: "Gaily Newport Recalls its Tennis Past," *The Providence Daily Journal*, August 26, 1956.

97: Details on the Casino's suffering from competition come from Eleanor Dwight's interviews with John Winslow, 2008.

CHAPTER SIX: THE HALL OF FAME

99–101: Information on the erratic economic conditions of Newport in the late '40s and early '50s and the preservation of Newport buildings is from *Newport: A Lively Experiment*, p. 168–169; 418–442.

101: Rhode Island Union Bank threatened: James Yarnell's *Newport Through its Architecture*, p. 28. The bank, which was built in the early Federalist period of the United States, was razed in 1952.

102–104: Letters from Jimmy to James Bishop on Hall of Fame dated March 11, 1953 and May 1, 1953 are from the James H. Van Alen Papers at the International Hall of Fame Library.

104: On first inductees, in 1955: "Fame, Tennis: International Hall of Fame's 50th Anniversary," *The Providence Sunday Journal*, July 4, 2004, p. D10 and "Newport: Capital and Shrine of Championship Tennis" by Helen Farrell Allen written for the 1970 Yearbook, International Tennis Hall of Fame Library, p. 25.

104–105: On the first Hall of Fame exhibits: "Newport: Capital and Shrine of Championship Tennis" by Helen Farrell Allen written for the 1970 Yearbook, International Tennis Hall of Fame Library, p. 24 and Eleanor Dwight's interview with Jay Van Alen.

105: Tony Trabert's memories as an inductee are from an interview with Eleanor Dwight.

105–106: For more information about Hall of Fame inductees see "Newport: Capital and Shrine of Championship Tennis" by Helen Farrell Allen written for the 1970 Yearbook, International Tennis Hall of Fame Library and the Tennis Hall of Fame website.

106: Information on offers to buy the Casino was found in the *New York Times* article, "Members May Sell Newport's Casino," August 13, 1954.

106: Jimmy speech to stockholders is from the 1956 Van Alen Papers.

106: Jimmy's letter to stockholders dated August 5, 1959 is from the International Hall of Fame Library.

106–107: Information about the Casino shares is from Alan T. Schumacher's *The Newport Casino*.

107–108: On Jimmy using influence and persuading stockholders: Eleanor Dwight's interviews with Jay Van Alen, Fall 2006 and John Winslow, 2008.

106–109: For information on Henry Havemeyer and other stockholder holdouts see Alan Schumacher's *The Newport Casino* published by the Newport Historical Society.

109–111: On Clement Moore's "A Visit from Saint Nicholas" and Jimmy's version: Charles D. Rice, *This Week* magazine, Dec. 22, 1957; Newport Daily News, undated; and the Van Alen Papers.

CHAPTER SEVEN: JIMMY'S VASSS TOURNAMENTS

113: Owen Williams' anecdote is from Eleanor Dwight's interview with him, Spring 2007.

Frank Phelps, renowned tennis historian, also had an idea for a tie breaker in the late 1950s. In 1958, Phelps contacted Jimmy about modifying Jimmy's VASSS, which at the time called for ping-pong scoring up to 21 points for a set. Phelps had two main modifications: [1] make each game in a traditional set best of 7-points (no-ad scoring) and [2] if and when the set score reaches 7–7, play one last game, and limit the set to fifteen games. After holding many tournaments, and testing the new scoring, Jimmy mixed some of these modifications into his VASSS, which eventually hardened into the celebrated tie breaker—a 12-point "lingering death" played at the end of a traditional set score of 6–6. Frank Phelps can be credited with helping Jimmy to hone the tie breaker. In the end, it was Van Alen's connections and ability to publicize the tie breaker that allowed it to succeed. See article by Richard Hillway, "NOT SO VASSS: Did Van Alen Invent No-ad Scoring and the Tie Break?" *Colorado Tennis*, June/July 2002.

113: Butch Buchholz quote is from Eleanor Dwight's interview with Butch Buchholz.

113: VASSS scoring is from the VASSS Basic Rule Sheets in the Van Alen Papers.

114–115: Background information on roster of players at Jimmy's tournament is from Wikipedia.com.

115: Description of fans' reaction to Pancho Segura is from Jack Kramer and Frank Deford's *The Game: My 40 Years in Tennis*.

115–117: On scores of matches and reactions to the VASSS system from players: Frank Deford's article, "Anyone Care to Play Some VASSS?" in *Sports Illustrated*, July 19, 1965 and Bud Collins' book, *My Life with the Pros*, p. 165.

117: Jimmy on harnassing the power serve: Walter Bingham's article, "Suggestion: Down with Love." *Sports Illustrated*, May 26, 1958.

117: The players' confusion over the tiebreaker: Bud Collins' book, *My Life with the Pros*, p. 168.

118: Bud Collins on Jimmy's tournaments and Pancho Gonzalez: Eleanor Dwight's interview with Bud Collins, November 2006 and his book, *My Life with the Pros*.

118: Pancho Gonzalez was born Richard Gonzales, but he exchanged the "s" for a "z" at the urging of his wife. He was ranked No. 1 in the world 8 times.

118: On Laver-Rosewall match and winnings: George McGann's "A VASSSly Entertaining Week-End," *World Tennis*, September 1965.

119–120: Story of Cliff Drysdale outmaneuvering Jimmy's scoring system during the VASSS Tournament of 1968 is from Eleanor Dwight's interviews with Cliff Drysdale, Spring 2007, and Butch Buchholz.

120: Danzig quote on the exciting play is from his article, "Laver Sweeps 3 Foes to Win Pro Tennis Final at Newport," *New York Times*, July 24, 1967.

120–121: Allison Danzig's biography is from *Racquet Magazine*, September 1985.

120: George Plimpton quote is from the *Norton Anthology of Sports*, introduction, p. 13–14.

121–122: Jimmy and Danzig's correspondence is from the Van Alen Papers, Letters to Jimmy Van Alen from Danzig dated December 27, 1969 and June 1, 1975.

121: Gardnar Mulloy on how Jimmy ran tournaments and how the amateur-pro split impacted players is from his interview with Eleanor Dwight, Spring 2007.

121–122: Information about the vote to go pro is from Kramer and Deford's book *The Game: My 40 Years in Tennis*, p. 253.

122: Butch Bucholtz on the amateur system: Eleanor Dwight interview with Butch Buchholtz, Spring 2007.

121–123: Information on professional and amateur players compensation, as well as Jack Kramer's depiction of the amateur system, comes from Kramer and Deford's book *The Game: My 40 Years in Tennis*.

123: The women's championships ran from 1887 to 1920 at the Philadelphia Cricket Club, then moved to Forest Hills in 1921.

123: Donald Dell's memories of amateur days: Eleanor Dwight's interview with Donald Dell, Spring 2007.

123: Bill Talbert memories of the tennis lifestyle: Eleanor Dwight's interview with Pike Talbert, Spring 2007.

124: Jack Kramer on the eight-man trial professional event at Wimbledon and the opening up of tennis: Kramer and Deford's book *The Game: My 40 Years in Tennis*, p. 256 and 260–1 and Eleanor Dwight's interview with Butch Buchholz.

125: Allsion Danzig on developments to improve pro and amateur relationships is from his article "On Near-by Tennis Courts," *New York Times*, June 29, 1957.

125: Decision to hold another pro tournament: Minutes of the Regular Meeting of the Board of Governors of the Newport Casino, September 13, 1968.

CHAPTER EIGHT: THE OPEN USES THE TIEBREAKER

127: Bud Collins on supporting Jimmy's VASSS tournaments: Eleanor Dwight's interview with Bud Collins, November 2006 and Bud Collins, "Deuce Sets Are no Longer Wild," for the *Boston Globe*, August, 1991.

127: Bud Collins on Jimmy being "part witch doctor": Bud Collins, "Deuce Sets Are No Longer Wild," *Boston Globe*, August 1991.

127–128: Billy Talbert's biography is from his memoir *Playing for Life: Billy Talbert's Story*.

129: Billy Talbert's memories of the tiebreaker and consolation matches: Bud Collins, "Deuce Sets Are no Longer Wild," *Boston Globe*, August 1991.

129: C.M. Jones on publicity of VASSS causing a stir: Letter from Jones to Jimmy Van Alen, Feb 25, 1970 and Van Alen letter to C.M. Jones, March 9, 1970, Van Alen Papers.

129–130: Bud Collins on how Billy Talbert saw the tiebreaker and the players' reactions: Eleanor Dwight's interview with Bud Collins, November 2006.

130: Talbert on the tiebreaker at the Open and previous long matches: Neil Amdur's "U.S. Open Will Use Sudden-Death Set," *New York Times*, July 26, 1970.

130–131: Alastair Martin on open tennis: "Advantage Mr. Martin," *Sports Illustrated*, April, 1970.

131: On increasing popularity of VASSS: Allison Danzig's "Van Alen's System Gaining New Appeal Among Tennis Fans," *New York Times*, March 1, 1966.

131: VASSS used at pro tournament at Forest Hills: JHVA letter to Roone Arledge June 25, 1966, Van Alen Papers and Allison Danzig's "Laver Wins Pro Tennis Tourney Here by Topping Rosewall in Final, 31–29," *York Times*, June 13, 1966.

132: On Don Budge Masters tournament: "Laver Tops Segura to Win $25,000 Tennis Tourney," *New York Times*, August 1, 1966.

132: Approval of VASSS in consolation matches at the U.S. Open: "VASSS Event Set For Open Tennis with Cash Prizes," *New York Times*, August 6, 1969.

132: Nine-point tiebreaker used at the U.S. Open in 1970: Neil Amdur's "U.S. Open Will Use Sudden-Death Set," *New York Times*, July 26, 1970.

133: 1970 U.S. Open Ken Rosewall and Tony Roche match: "Maggie and the Little Master," *Time*, September 28, 1970.

133: Players' reactions to the tiebreaker: Eleanor Dwight's interview with Bud Collins, November 2006.

133: For more on the 2008 Match between Rafael Nadal and Roger Federer see Christopher Clarey's "In Epic Battle, A Reign Ends at Wimbledon," *New York Times*, July 7, 2008.

133: Barry Lorge comments on "sudden death" are from his article "Tie-Break or Not Tie-Break: That Is the Question," *Tennis USA*, November 1970 and "Tie-Breaking with Tradition," *U.S. Open '95*.

133: Billy Talbert's famous quote: Bud Collins, "Deuce Sets Are No Longer Wild," *Boston Globe*, August, 1991 and Eleanor Dwight's interview with Bud Collins, November 2006.

133: Jimmy Jones congratulating Jimmy on his success at the U.S. Open was found in a letter from C.M. Jones to Jimmy Van Alen, September 29, 1970, Van Alen Papers.

133–134: Bud Collins on red flag used during tiebreakers: Eleanor Dwight's interview with Bud Collins, November 2006.

134: Jimmy explaining how sudden death pumped new life into tennis: Letter from Jimmy Van Alen to C.M Jones, September 28, 1970, Van Alen Papers.

134–135: Jimmy pressing to get all of VASSS accepted: Letter from Jimmy Van Alen to C.M. Jones, August 3, 1970, Van Alen Papers.

135: 12-point versus 9-point tiebreaker debate and quote from David Gray: Steve Flink's "The 12-Point Tiebreaker," *History of Philadelphia Tennis: 1875–1995*, p. 34 & 38.

136: Jimmy's thoughts on the 9-point tiebreaker are from a letter from Jimmy Van Alen to C.M. Jones, Oct 5, 1970, Van Alen Papers. Jones' reply to Jimmy's letter is dated April 26, 1971, Van Alen Papers.

136–137: Adoption of the 12-point tiebreaker: Steve Flink's "The 12-Point Tiebreaker," *History of Philadelphia Tennis: 1875–1995*, p. 34 & 38 and Jimmy letters from the Van Alen Papers.

137: U.S. Open discontinues Sudden Death and adopts the 12-point tiebreaker: Bud Collins, "Deuce Sets Are No Longer Wild," *Boston Globe*, August, 1991, p. 62.

137: Sammy quote on "taking the teeth out of sudden death" is from Eleanor Dwight's interview with Sammy Van Alen, Spring 2003.

137: Jimmy on 12-point tiebreaker and why he didn't like it: Jimmy Van Alen letter to Lamar Hunt, October 8, 1970 and December 1970, Van Alen Papers.

137: Walter Elcock's resolution stating that after December 31, 1974 only the 12-point tiebreaker could be used was found in Jimmy's essay "From the Ridiculous to the Sublime," Van Alen Papers. Also, information on where the tiebreaker was being used and Jimmy's challenge to those who opposed him on sudden death were found in the same essay.

139: In 1975 the Hall of Fame went international and the first non-U.S. inductee was British player Fred Perry. Perry won Wimbledon three in 1930s and was the world's number one player for five years.

139–142: Information on the Davis family and the experience of John Davis at the Hall of Fame is from Eleanor Dwight's interview with John Davis, Winter 2008. Davis personal history was found in Nancy Kriplen's "Dwight Davis: The Man and the Cup," International Tennis Federation.

For trophy history see Richard Evans', "The Silver Cup," *The Davis Cup: Celebrating 100 Years of Tennis*, 1999; Bud Collins', *My Life with the Pros*, p. 298; and "The Top Trophy," International Tennis Federation.

139: The original Longwood Cricket Club was located in Boston, near Fenway Park. It was moved to Chestnut Hill after World War I.

142–143: On Joe Cullman's role at Hall of Fame: Information from "Joseph Cullman III" biography at the International Tennis Hall of Fame's List of Hall of Famers, International Tennis Hall of Fame Library.

142–143: John Winslow explains why the money to fix the Casino didn't come from Newport in his interview with Eleanor Dwight, 2008.

143: Information on refurbishing efforts of the Hall's exhibits comes from papers in the International Tennis Hall of Fame Library.

143–145: Donald Dell spoke of his career, tennis sponsorship, and Andy Roddick's endorsements in an interview with Eleanor Dwight, Spring 2007.

145: Information on Maria Sharapova's endorsements and income are from Tom Van Riper and Kurt Badenhausen's article "Sports Business: Top-Earning Female Athletes" in *Forbes*, July 22, 2008.

145: Arthur Ashe's and Stan Smith's success and Arthur Ashe endorsements of Coca-Cola were discussed in Eleanor Dwight's interview with Donald Dell, Spring 2007.

145: Television as a source of revenues for tournaments: Eleanor Dwight's interview with Donald Dell, Spring 2007.

145–146: Information on the debate on television broadcasts of tennis is from Jimmy Van Alen's letter to Roone Arledge, June 25, 1966; a reply from Roone Arledge, July 8, 1966; and Jimmy's reply to Roone's July 8th letter (undated, handwritten).

146–147: Stories from the early days tennis broadcasts: Bud Collins, *My Life with the Pros*, p. 101–123 and Eleanor Dwight's interview with Donald Dell, Spring 2007.

148–149: Donald Dell on the changes to tennis since the '60s and the introduction of the ATP ranking system is from his interview with Eleanor Dwight, Spring 2007.

149: ATP negotiating increases in prize purses and playing opportunities: Bud Collins, *My Life with the Pros*, p. 51 & 271.

149: Women's boycott of the Pacific Southwest Open and

Virginia Slims Tournament formation: Bud Collins' *Total Tennis: The Ultimate Tennis Encyclopedia* and Eleanor Dwight's interview with Bud Collins, November 2006.

149–150:Joe Cullman on the formation of the Virginia Slims tournament is from his book, *I'm a Lucky Guy.*

150–151: King/Riggs match and the "Battle of the Sexes": Mary Jo Festle's *Playing Nice: Politics and Apologies in Women's Sports;* "How Bobby Runs and Talks, Talks, Talks," *Time,* September 10, 1973; "How King Rained on Riggs Parade," *Time,* October 1, 1973; Selena Robert's "A Ray of Progress for Women as Battle of the Sexes Turns 35," *SI.com,* September 20, 2008.

151–154: On VAAGG: James Van Alen's "Untroubled Sport for Those Who Play VAAGG," *Sports Illustrated,* 1965.

154: Reponses to VAAGG article are from letters written to the Editor of *Sports Illustrated* by readers, Van Alen Papers.

155: On the Avalon fire: Clippings in the Van Alen Papers and Eleanor Dwight's interview with Eileen Slocum, 2006.

155: Jimmy's plan to convert Wrenthurst into the Moore museum was found in the *Newport Daily News,* Dec. 16, 1976.

CHAPTER TEN: LAST YEARS AND A LASTING LEGACY

157: Lee Manigault remembers a trip to Europe with her grandfather in her interview with Eleanor Dwight, Spring 2007.

157: Borg-McEnroe was the "most memorable match" in Wimbledon history: Barry Newcombe's "1980: Borg v McEnroe—The Tie-Break," Wimbledon.org.

157–158: Scores and progression of Borg-McEnroe match: The Wimbledon Video collection: *Legends of Wimbledon-Bjorn Borg DVD* produced by SRO Sports Entertainment.

158: Bjorn Borg's memories of match are from Tim Adams' article in *The Observer* (London), January 7, 2007, p. 37.

160: Lee Manigault's memories of match are from her interview with Eleanor Dwight, Spring 2007.

160: Borg's superstitions in dress and grooming are from a Wikipedia article on Björn Borg.

160–162:Borg's endorsements and income are from a biography on hickoksports.com and Allen Guttman's *Sports: The First Five Millennia,* p. 321.

162: Borg's early retirement and fans' reactions are from a Wikipedia article on Björn Borg.

162–164: Jimmy's birthday toast to Sammy and Nick Ludington and the international court tennis matches and Van Alen Challenge are from Lord Aberdare's *The J.T. Faber Book of Tennis and Rackets* and Eleanor Dwight's interviews with Bill Van Alen, Bill Wister, and Dan Gardiner, 2008.

165: Anthony Bevan recalls Jimmy's ties to England, Jimmy and Candy's England trips, and a trip to Rome with Jimmy in his interview with Eleanor Dwight, June 2007.

165–166:Jimmy's letter to Irving Berlin was written April 12, 1986, and sent May 1988, Van Alen Papers.

167–168: Poems and songs written to presidents were found in the Van Alen Papers excluding the "Campaign Song by Van Alen" found in the *Providence Evening Bulletin* dated Wednesday, November 1, 1972.

168–170:Information on Jimmy's reforms to the America's Cup is from the Van Alen Papers.

170: The story of Jimmy's death is from Eleanor Dwight's interview with Brian Stinson, Spring 2008.

171: Jimmy snoozing at the U.S. Open: Donna Doherty's "A Fond Farewell to Mr. Tennis," *Tennis Magazine,* September 1991.

171: Description of a Casino from a time long past: "The Sporting Scene," *New Yorker,* October 9, 1965, p. 196.

171: Jimmy's description of Newport in 1916 is from Bud Collins' article, "Rolls Royce Radical," *World Tennis,* May 1972, p. 29.

EPILOGUE

173: Gordon Forbes on the Borg-Natase match is from his book *A Handful of Summers,* p. 2.

173: Jimmy on pros not buying tickets to events: Bob Wagner, "Sudden Death Playoff Not Enough for Jimmy Van Alen," *Kalamazoo Gazette,* July 31, 1973.

173: E. Digby Baltzell on the rise of the celebrity player is from his book *Sporting Gentlemen: Men's Tennis from the Age of Honor to the Cult of the Superstar.*

173–174: On tennis training and Maria Sharapova and Jan Silva: "Wunderkinds," *Tennis* magazine, Jan/Feb 2008, p. 45; "Grooming Monica" in Caryl Phillips anthology; and Wikipedia entry on Maria Sharapova.

175–176:Information about the changes to racquets and grips is from Jeff Cooper's article, "An Evolutionary History of Tennis Racquets" at About.com.

177: Descriptions of the International Tennis Hall of Fame today is from Eleanor Dwight's interview with Director Mark Stenning in October 2008.

Bibliography

Books:

Aberdare, Lord. *The J.T. Faber Book of Tennis and Rackets.* London: Quiller Press, 2001.

Amory, Cleveland. *Who Killed Society?* New York: Harper & Brothers, Publishers, 1960.

Auchincloss, Louis. *Vanderbilt Era: Profiles of a Gilded Age.* New York: Macmillan Publishing Company, 1989.

Axelrod, Alan. *Lincoln's Last Night: Abraham Lincoln, John Wilkes Booth, and the Last 36 Hours Before the Assassination.* New York: Chamberlain Bros., 2005.

Baltzell, E. Digby. *Sporting Gentlemen: Men's Tennis from the Age of Honor to the Cult of the Superstar.* New York: The Free Press, 1995.

Boyle, Robert H. *At the Top of Their Game.* Piscataway, N.J.: Winchester Press, 1983.

Collins, Bud. *My Life with the Pros.* New York: Dutton, Penguin Group, 1990.

_____. *Total Tennis: The Ultimate Tennis Encyclopedia.* Toronto: SPORT Media Publishing, Inc., 2003.

Cullman, Joseph, F. *I'm a Lucky Guy.* Privately printed, 1998.

Decies, Elizabeth. *Turn of the World.* Philadelphia and New York: J.B. Lippincott Company, 1937.

Dell, Donald L. *Minding Other People's Business: Winning Big for Your Clients and Yourself.* New York: Villard Books, 1989.

Dwight, Eleanor. *The Letters of Pauline Palmer.* Milan: Scala Books, 2005.

Elliot, Maude Howe. *This Was My Newport.* Cambridge, Mass.: The Mythology Company, 1944.

Etchebaster, Pierre with George Plimpton, ed.. *Pierre's Book: The Game of Court Tennis.* Barre, Mass.: Barre Publishers, 1971.

Evans, Richard. "The Silver Cup," *The Davis Cup: Celebrating 100 Years of Tennis.* New York: Universe Publishing, 1999.

Fenno, J. Brooks and Lewis H. Gordon. *International Intercollegiate Tennis, 1921-1974 Inclusive.* Privately printed.

Festle, Mary Jo. *Playing Nice: Politics and Apologies in Women's Sports.* New York: Columbia University Press, 1996.

Flink, Steve. "The 12-Point Tiebreaker," *History of Philadelphia Tennis: 1875-1995.* Harleysville, PA: Alcom, 1995.

Forbes, Gordon. *A Handful of Summers.* New York: Mayflower Books, 1978.

Guttman, Allen. *Allen Guttman's Sports: The First Five Millennia.* Amherst: University of Massachusetts Press, 2004.

Head, Barry and Nick Ludington. *I Say! Memoirs of Captain Alexander Saunderson.* Montecito, 2005.

Homberger, Eric. *Mrs. Astor's New York: Money and Social Power in a Gilded Age.* New Haven and London: Yale University Press, 2002.

Kaplan, Justin. *When the Astors Owned New York: Blue Bloods and Grand Hotels in a Gilded Age.* New York: Viking, 2006.

Kramer, Jack and Frank Deford. *The Game: My 40 Years in Tennis.* New York: G.P. Putnam's Sons, 1979.

LeCompte, Tom. *The Last Sure Thing: The Life & Times of Bobby Riggs.* Easthampton, Mass.: Skunkworks Publishing, 2003.

Lehr, Elizabeth Drexel. *The Leisure Class in America.* New York: Arno Press, 1975.

Lucey, Donna M. *Archie and Amelie: Love and Madness in the Gilded Age.* New York: Harmony Books, 2006.

Morris, Ed. *A Guide to Newport's Cliff Walk.* Charleston: The History Press, 1999.

Mulloy, Gardnar. *The Will to Win: An Inside View of the World of Tennis.* New York: A.S. Barnes & Company, Inc., 1959.

O'Connor, Richard. *The Scandalous Mr. Bennett.* New York: Doubleday & Company, Inc., 1962.

Patterson, Jerry E. *The First Four Hundred: Mrs. Astor's New York in the Gilded Age.* New York: Rizzoli International Publications, 2000.

Pearce, Andrew. *A Cambridge Keepsake.* Great Britain: Fotogenix Publishing, 2005.

Phillips, Caryl, ed. *The Right Set: A Tennis Anthology.* New York: Vintage Books, 1999.

Schumacher, Alan T. *The Newport Casino.* Newport: Newport Historical Society, 1987.

Reynolds, David, ed. *Christ's: A Cambridge College Over Five Centuries.* London: Macmillan Publishing, 2005.

Sonne, Christian, ed. *Tuxedo Park: The Historic Houses.* Tuxedo Historical Society, 2007.

Stensrud, Rockwell. *Newport: A Lively Experiment 1639-1969.* Newport: Redwood Library & Athenaeum.

Stern, Robert. *Pride of Place: Building the American Dream.* Boston: Houghton Mifflin Company, 1986.

Talbert, William F. and John Seymour Sharnik. *Playing For Life: Billy Talbert's Story.* London: Lowe & Brydone Ltd., 1958.

United States Lawn Tennis Association, ed. *Official Encyclopedia of Tennis.* New York: Harper & Row, Publishers, 1972.

Van Alen, James (with illustrations by W.R. Dalzell). *Cambridge.* Great Britain: The Stellar Press, 1962.

Van Alen, W.L. *Sammy's Book: Family Memories.* Philadelphia: Stephenson-Brothers, Inc., 1995.

Wharton, Edith. *A Backward Glance.* New York: Appleton-Century, 1934.

_____. *The Cruise of the Vanadis.* New York: Rizzoli Publications, Inc., 2004.

Yarnall, James L. *Newport Through Its Architecture: A History of Styles from Postmedieval to Postmodern.* Newport: Salve Regina University Press, 2005.

White, Elizabeth and Samuel G. *McKim, Mead & White: The Masterworks.* New York: Rizzoli International Publications, Inc., 2003.

White, William. *They Were Expendable.* U.S. Naval Institute Press, 1998.

Interviews:

The interviews of those who kindly spoke to us are listed in the sources.

Articles:

The articles mentioned are listed in the sources.

Photo Acknowledgments

Jimmy and Candy

Image courtesy of the International Tennis Hall of Fame & Museum, Newport, R.I.

Mulloy playing Pancho Gonzalez at the Casino, August 1949

Popperfoto, Getty Images

Gardnar Mulloy, 1955, champion doubles player of the '40s and '50s

Time & Life Pictures, Getty Images

Tony Trabert during Davis Cup Match, 1955

Photos by Ernst, courtesy of the Preservation Society of Newport County

Sam and Jay Van Alen with Eleanor and Jimmy

CHAPTER FIVE: THE CASINO—CRADLE OF AMERICAN TENNIS

Images courtesy of the James H. and Candace Van Alen Papers, Redwood Library & Athenaeum, Newport, R.I.

James and Candace Van Alen, 1950s

The Van Alens bought Avalon in the early 1950s

The Casino in the 1880s

JHVA taking an overhead

Images courtesy of the International Tennis Hall of Fame & Museum, Newport, R.I.

The Championship Court at Newport on August 11th, 1929

The Newport Invitational in the 1930s

The first National Lawn Tennis Tournament, held at the Staten Island Club, September 1st, 1880

James Dwight and Richard Sears

Richard Sears, the first National Champion at the Casino

Major Walter Clopton Wingfield, creator of the Wingfield "box"

Campbell and Huntington, U.S. National Doubles Champions, 1891–1892

U.S. National Lawn Tennis Tournament, Hovey vs. Smith, August 22, 1891

A group of prominent Newport Cottagers watching the Annual National Tennis Tournament at the Casino, 1880s

Linesman watching the match, 1894

Early court roller

The Casino, 1915

Newport stars in 1892

Ladies dressed in Gay Nineties attire for Tennis Week, 1956

Courtside seats at the Casino, late 1950s

Tennis match at the Casino, 1955

Forest Hills, 1951, where the U.S. National Championships were played before being moved to Flushing Meadows in 1978

Hulton Archive, Getty Images

James Gordon Bennett, Jr., circa 1895

CHAPTER SIX: HALL OF FAME

Images courtesy of the James H. and Candace Van Alen Papers, Redwood Library & Athenaeum, Newport, R.I.

Tennis at the Hall of Fame

William Clothier and JHVA, presenting a trophy

Jimmy with Ken Rosewall and Ham Richardson

Jimmy with Bill Clothier and Joe Leandra at Newport Casino

Jimmy reading from "A Visit from Saint Nicholas"

Image courtesy of the James H. and Candace Van Alen Papers, Redwood Library & Athenaeum, Newport, R.I. and The Newport Daily News

"Net Greats Honored at Newport"

Images courtesy of the International Tennis Hall of Fame & Museum, Newport, R.I.

Clock tower entrance, circa 1910

Board of Governors, Tennis Hall of Fame, 1957

Meeting at the Hall of Fame, 1961

Jimmy presiding at the Board of Governors meeting, 1973

Board of Governors standing on the steps of the Hall of Fame Museum, 1973

Ceremony at the Tennis Hall of Fame

Jimmy with the Marquis de Rochambeau

Interior of the Tennis Hall of Fame museum, 1955

Pancho Gonzalez receiving a trophy at the Casino

Image courtesy of the Fernberger Photo Collection, International Tennis Hall of Fame & Museum, Newport, R.I.

1971 enshrinement ceremony: Vic Seixas, Althea Gibson, and Jimmy Van Alen

CHAPTER SEVEN: JIMMY'S VASSS TOURNAMENTS

Image courtesy of the International Tennis Hall of Fame & Museum, Newport, R.I.

Spectators checking the draw on the VASSS Tournament boards

Images courtesy of the James H. and Candace Van Alen Papers, Redwood Library & Athenaeum, Newport, R.I.

Van Alen pointing out special VASSS service line moved 3 ft. behind baseline

VASSS intercollegiate match, Florida State vs. Navy, 1965

Jimmy's mother, Margaret Bruguiere, at Wakehurst

Pancho Gonzalez and Jimmy exchange words at the 1965 VASSS Tournament, Life magazine photo

Images courtesy of the James H. and Candace Van Alen Papers, Redwood Library & Athenaeum, Newport, R.I and The Newport Daily News

Rod Laver and Butch Buchholz playing doubles

Tennis pros to play in the 2nd VASSS Tournament, 1966

Image courtesy of Time & Life Pictures / Getty Images

New York Times sportswriter Allison Danzig

CHAPTER EIGHT: THE OPEN USES THE TIEBREAKER

Images courtesy of the International Tennis Hall of Fame & Museum, Newport, R.I.

Jimmy and Candy at the Virginia Slims Tournament, 1972

Newport doubles match, 1967

Trophy presentation at the Casino, 1955

Candy and Jimmy with his sudden death flag

Images courtesy of the James H. and Candace Van Alen Papers, Redwood Library & Athenaeum, Newport, R.I.

VASSS sudden death scoring rules, 1970

(Jimmy with his chicken and sudden death signs)

CHAPTER NINE: THE 1970S—TENNIS AND JIMMY AFTER THE TIEBREAKER

Images courtesy of Popperfoto/Getty Images

July 30th, 1937: The victorious U.S. Davis Cup team aboard the liner *Manhattan* prior to leaving Southampton for home

Images courtesy of Michael Baz/International Tennis Hall of Fame & Museum, Newport, R.I.

Troy Gowen Hall—Hall of Fame Museum today

Ted Tinling Exhibit—Hall of Fame Museum today

WTA Gallery—Hall of Fame Museum today

Court Tennis Exhibit—Hall of Fame Museum today

Images courtesy of the International Tennis Hall of Fame & Museum, Newport, R.I.

Ken Rosewall and Joe Cullman, U.S. Open Championship, Forest Hills

Margret Smith Court, Billy Jean King, and Jimmy

Doubles match at the Virginia Slims Tournament, 1972

1984 Virginia Slims Tournament: Martina Navratilova, George Graboys, Joe Cullman, and Gigi Fernandez

Lew Hoad speaking at his Hall of Fame Induction, 1980

Image courtesy of the James H. and Candace Van Alen Papers, Redwood Library & Athenaeum, Newport, R.I.

Jimmy playing golf

Reprinted courtesy of Sports Illustrated: "Untroubled Sport For Those Who Play VAAGG" by James Van Alen, November 28, 1966 © 1966. Time Inc. All Rights Reserved.

VAAGG, or Van Alen's Answer to Grief in Golf

CHAPTER TEN: LAST YEARS AND A LASTING LEGACY

Images courtesy of Bob Thomas Sports Photography/Getty Images

"Fire and Ice": Wimbledon Final, 1980; Borg defeats McEnroe 1–6, 7–5, 6–3, 6–7, 8–6 after the famous 22-minute tiebreaker

Images courtesy of the James H. and Candace Van Alen Papers, Redwood Library & Athenaeum, Newport, R.I.

Jimmy with court tennis players from Yale, Princeton, and Harvard preparing to compete for the matches in the Van Alen Cup against Oxford and Cambridge

Jimmy at exhibition match between Nick Ludington and the British champion in Manchester, England

Jimmy with U.S. Van Alen Cup Team

Jimmy with U.S. Van Alen Cup Team and British court tennis officials and players

Jimmy and Candy

Jimmy playing his ukulele

Image courtesy of Gavin Reed

Candy with H.R.H. Prince Philip, Duke of Edinburgh, at the Hawks Club for the dedication of the Van Alen Room, 1992

Image courtesy of Michael Baz/International Tennis Hall of Fame & Museum, Newport, R.I.

Steffi Graf with her husband, Andre Agassi, at her induction into the Hall of Fame, 2004

Pete Sampras inducted into the Hall of Fame, 2007

EPILOGUE

Images courtesy of Michael Baz/International Tennis Hall of Fame & Museum, Newport, R.I.

Young Jimmy Van Alen, great-nephew of Jimmy, presenting the trophy to Mark Philipoussis and Justin Gimelstob at the Invitational Tournament, 2006

The Newport Casino today

Image courtesy of Getty Images

Maria Sharapova at 2006 U.S. Open in her Nike dress

Image courtesy of AFP/Getty Images

Serena Williams, fashionable champion

Index

Italicized page numbers indicate captions.

Acknowledgments

It was a pleasure to write *Tie Breaker* as many kind people told me their stories and Newport, with its marvelous atmosphere where I visited often, became a key presence in the book. The members of the Van Alen Family were kind in talking to me and furnishing family information. Particularly helpful were Bill Van Alen, the late Jay Van Alen, Mr. and Mrs. William L. Van Alen, Lee Manigault, Jimbo Van Alen, Nick and Cassandra Ludington, and Jimmy Van Alen, the great nephew of Jimmy Van Alen, the book's subject.

Also helpful were those at the International Tennis Hall of Fame: Mark Stenning, Mark Young, Joanie Agler, and others involved over the years like John Davis, Marilyn Fernberger and George Gowen. Many at the Redwood Library and Athenaeum were generous with their time: particularly Aimee Saunders and Lisa Long. I'm also grateful to the New York Yacht Club and the Newport Daily News who gave us images to use.

I heard wonderful anecdotes from many in the tennis world, such as Gardnar Mulloy, Tony Trabert, Donald Dell, Butch Buchholz, Cliff Drysdale, Bud Collins, and Gordon Forbes. Court tennis players helped explain to me the ins and outs of that fascinating sport: Bill Wister, Dan Gardiner, and others. Jimmy's friends both in England and at home including Gavin Reed, Anthony Bevan, Joan Bevan and John Winslow had wonderful stories. Several friends gave me hospitality in Newport over the years including Ron Fleming in his extraordinary house, Ginny and Jimmy Purviance, Angela and Gary Fischer, Cassandra and Ed Stone. My assistants were invaluable including: Yael Rebecca Lipschutz, David Thoreson, April Marks, and Michael Lipschutz, as was my editor, Ruth Greenstein. I would also like to thank my publisher Maria Teresa Train and my gifted designer Natasha Tibbott.

And finally, my husband George, added his sense of humor and irony.